The Psychology of Real Estate Sales

JASON MITCHELL

Copyright © 2021 Jason Mitchell

All rights reserved.

DEDICATION

This book is dedicated to my Grandmother Patrica Tapocik and my late Grandfather George Tapocik. I love you more than words could ever express.

CONTENTS

JASON MITCHELL 1
DAY 1: UNDERSTANDING YOUR STRENGTHS
AND WEAKNESSES 4
DAY 2: IDENTIFYING STRENGTHS 12
DAY 3: MITIGATING WEAKNESSES. 20
DAY :4 IDENTIFY YOUR FUNCTIONALITY. 31
DAY :5 SUPERMAN SYNDROME 04
DAY :6 IDENTIFY YOUR CORE CUSTOMER 65
DAY :7 PROSPECTING TO YOUR CORE 70
DAY 8: IDENTIFYING YOUR NICHE
THE NICHE WILL FIND YOU. 83
DAY 9: BE AN INFORMATION JUNKIE 92
DAY 10: CELEBRATE YOUR CLIENTS—NOT THE SALE . 101
DAY 11: STICK WITH YOUR SCHEDULE
AND BUILD A PLAN 108
DAY 12: CREATE A FUNDAMENTAL PROCESS. 119
DAY 13: WORK WITH A PURPOSE. 127
DAY 14: HAVING THE PROPER RESOURCES 134
DAY 15: BECOMING A TRUE PROFESSIONAL 141
DAY 16: MASTER THE INITIAL CALL 148
DAY 17: DISCOVERY 156
DAY :18 TOUR DAY 164
DAY :19 THE CLOSE 172
DAY :20 THE FINISH LINE 180
DAY 21: EXPECTATIONS AND FORESHADOWING. 191
DAY :22 DON'T BE SALESY. 202

DAY :23 MAKE IT THEIR IDEA 209
DAY 24: FORCING THE OCCURRENCE............. 215
DAY 25: GETTING PEOPLE OFF THE FENCE........ 221
DAY :26 CAPITAL AND MEASURABLES 622
DAY :27 TWO SIDES OF MARKETING 238
DAY :28 SELF-PROMOTION.........................246
DAY 29: MINIMUM STANDARDS OF MARKETING 255
DAY 30: OLD SCHOOL VERSUS NEW SCHOOL 264
DAY 31: PROSPECTING AND
APPOINTMENT SETTING 270
DAY 32: APPOINTMENT SETTING 279
DAY 33: CREATING A SCALABLE MODEL............286
DAY 34: EFFECTIVE TIME MANAGEMENT 295
DAY 35: WHEN TO SAY 'NO' AND
WHEN TO SAY 'YES'..............................306
DAY 36: LEVEL ONE 318
DAY 37: LEVEL TWO 325
DAY 38: LEVEL THREE 334
DAY 39: LEVEL FOUR..............................345
DAY 40: LEVEL FIVE 358

ACKNOWLEDGMENTS

I would also like to acknowledge our great real estate referral partners and the people that I have been so fortunate to build lifelong relationships with. I cannot express enough the gratitude I have for you. None of this is possible without the trust you have given us. Thank you so incredibly much.

To our amazing agents and operations team at The Jason Mitchell Group. You guys are the foundation. To my loving Marisa, thank you for giving me the ability to work as tirelessly as I do and to my Brecky boy and Asher...I love you. To the rest of my immediate family, Mom, Dad, Tommy and Danielle, and, of course, Uncle Sonny. This is for you.

To Aaron Pierson who spent countless Saturday's with my in the studio helping us put this book together. I could not have done this without you. To Mercedez Lomboy for assisting with our editing. To Sarah Weaver for your help with creative and writing.

INTRODUCTION

This book is your 40-day blueprint to building the real estate business you dream of. For a lot of you, that dream is making millions. I am here to tell you that this book will give you what you need to do precisely that. Over the next 40 days, we will go on a journey together. Some of it will be light and fun, but more importantly, I wrote this book to be impactful and add value to both you as a person, as a real estate agent, and as a business owner.

In the real estate sales industry, you will find coaches who aren't in real estate themselves. I wrote this book because I know from experience that it's hard to take advice from those that haven't been in the field for a very long time.

I built an award-winning team, the Jason Mitchell Group (JMG). Together, we have achieved more than $5 Billion in sales volume. I have been in real estate for nearly two decades. Whether you're doing $5 million in sales, $20 million in sales, $50 million in sales, $100 million in sales, $1B billion in sales, I've been there.

No matter where you are in your business, I have been in your shoes. I wrote this book to give you what you need in your business. This book will walk you through the steps you need to take to take your business from wherever you are today to $50 million in sales or more.

I built my business from nothing to the number one team in the country. In ten years, I went from having no clients to being the number one real estate broker in the state of Arizona. I have been ranked the number one real estate agent in the state of Arizona for several years. I was also named Real Estate Agent of the Decade in 2020.

This book is a peek into how I made that happen and how you can, too.

At the end of this book, you will understand the true critical path to real estate sales. Allow the book to walk you through each step, so you don't have to figure this out on your own like I did or like many other agents before you. Each chapter is dialed in and detailed. Prepare yourself to write and rewrite your business plan over the next 40 days.

I write in detail about structure and mindset because they are indeed the foundation of a great real estate business. That, paired with systems and protocols, will be what you need to grow a real estate business better than your wildest dreams.

The book is 40 days across eight weeks. Each week has five days or five topics. Of course, you can choose to binge it if you want, or you can choose to do it day-by-day, it's totally up to you. I encourage you to take the time needed to get through each week and put in the work.

Do the assignments. Go at your own speed, but it is best to complete the book in eight weeks.

This book will show you precisely what it takes to get to the next Level. In Week Eight, you will find I define what I call "Levels Coaching" and guide you through each Level. I can show you how to go from Level One to Level Five because I have helped countless other agents do the same thing. I know what you're struggling with and what you need to do to get to your business's next Level

Let's get you where you want to go.

Lastly, I want to say thank you so much for purchasing the book. For more interaction, be sure to follow me on Instagram, Jason Mitchell, @jasonmitchell_jmg. I hope you not only enjoy this 40-day blueprint but also see results. Here's to your success.

Week 1 Day 1

DAY 1: UNDERSTANDING YOUR STRENGTHS AND WEAKNESSES

Today, you will identify your strengths and weaknesses. Our strengths and some of our shortcomings change over time. You picked up this book to improve as a real estate sales professional. You want to be a better agent, right? That's why you bought this book in the first place. Now, I am here to tell you that you will have to work on your strengths and weaknesses if you are serious about being the best agent. Now, let's begin.

Understanding your strengths and weaknesses is a critical step towards the path of success. You must identify both. People will tell you to only focus on your strengths and hire out your weaknesses. Sure. I'm not here to tell you that it is not sound advice, but I am here to tell you that you are doing yourself a massive disservice if you ignore your weaknesses. We will identify your weaknesses tomorrow. Let's focus on your strengths today.

For me, my strength has always been sales. Selling came so naturally, even at the beginning. I could sell better than anyone. There weren't hundreds of webinars I needed to attend before I felt ready to sell. I felt ready before others believed I was. I believed because I knew sales was my talent, an innate skill. I don't have to think twice about negotiating or persuasion. Maybe you feel this way, too? Perhaps you don't.

I will talk later on about work ethic and how waking up and diving into work has never been a struggle for me. But you know what I struggled with more than anything? Organization. If you asked me to slow down and organize my calendar or heck, even my day. No way.

My weakness has always been organization. It wasn't always easy to put together a contract perfectly. It was tough for me to continually remind myself to make sure you put that on your calendar.

You must understand your strengths and weaknesses.

Focusing on weaknesses is crucial to your success. This is what we really need to improve on. Today, we will better understand what your struggles and challenges may be.

Our strengths will typically always be our strengths. That's kind of you on autopilot, right? Recognizing what our strengths are is the easy part. We know what we do well. And if you do not know, today's exercise will help.

The problem most of us have is that we do not take the time to identify what our weaknesses genuinely are. We don't take the time to believe our own BS. Slow down and look at what we're not that good at right.

This was really tough for me.

I felt as though I was Mr. Make it Rain. I was picking up the phone again and again without losing sight of my goals. I wasn't just working in the chaos that is real estate sales; I was thriving in it. I'd get off the phone with a potential listing, and the sales part of me would be saying, "right on! You got the listing appointment. Pick up the phone and do it again."

Instead, wait and alow down, add this on your calendar, send a follow-up email confirming the time and date. Then start putting together a listing packet or ping someone on my team to complete these tasks for me.

My strengths are cold calling, building trust, negotiating—all things sales. My weaknesses are organization, consistency, structure, and patience.

But what happens if I only focus on my strengths? I pick up the phone and get the next listing appointment, sure. But then, I am stuck cleaning up the mess down the road. I can't locate the correct address, or I am scrambling to put together listing packets. I misplaced my notes on the conversation I had with the seller. I could potentially jeopardize and screw up both appointments. Or, at least, I am making things harder for myself. Instead, if I slow down and focus on what I am bad at, the organizational piece, I am creating structure.

Working in chaos will kill you.

Today, you will identify your weaknesses, so you can create structure in your day. This will allow you to recognize what you need to focus on. By structuring your day, you start to overcome those things you call weaknesses, then of course, you become better as entrepreneurs and as sales professionals.

We become better at our own business structure because we're understanding the weakness that we identified. You realize something and admit to yourself that: I need to improve on that.

You first have to identify your weaknesses in order to get to this place in your business. Set up a step-by-step process to improve on areas where you are lacking.

Identify the things that you do excel in. Whether it be the details, communications, negotiations or marketing, every real estate agent excels at something. This week, I want you to discover what that is.

Some of you may excel in communication. That's why you chose sales.

Do you call people back quickly? Do you communicate with your clients quickly and thoroughly? Or do you wait and do it on your own terms? Communication in real estate is everything, but are you good at it? Are you willing to pick up the phone every time? Are you willing to deliver good news and or bad news? Or when it's bad news, do you delay and drag your feet? Or hope the phone goes straight to voicemail?

Some of you may excel when it comes to structure and organization. Whereas, some of you may wake up every day and allow your email inbox to dictate your day. You simply start your day, and however the day ends is the way the day ends. That is what you have to avoid. You must wake up every day with a set structure in place to ensure you complete 100% of your daily tasks.

By the end of this week, you will start to better structure your day to set you up for success. The first step is to identify your strengths and weaknesses.

DAY 1 WORKSHEET

Ask yourself: What am I really good at? **Sales, orginization, Retaining informa** **Thinking outside the box.**

You need to be honest with yourself here. If you're not honest with yourself, how will you be honest with your clients?

What is the number one thing you hear from your peers, your past clients and those closest to say about you?
Majority of people are blown away / star struck from what I created & How I did it,

Phil *(your name)*, you are just so good at **Thinking**.

I don't feel like it's anything special but people also tell me I am good at **Sales**.

People are often telling me that I am really good at **Thinking outside the box**

My favorite thing about myself is my ability to: **Think**

I have also always thought I was really good at **Sales**, but no one seems to mention it or I have never seen this come up in my reviews or client testimonials.

Reviews and testimonials do not lie. They are a great indicator of what we excel in.

Did they mention constant and clear communication? Did they mention seamless transactions with little confusion? Did the buyer mention your thoughtfulness or closing gift delivered with a handwritten note?

(Not a realtor)

Identify three things your client testimonials have included:

1

2

3

Three things you should always be doing:

1. Asking for a Client Testimonial. Every. Single. Time.

2. Save your client compliments into a folder in your email or copy them into a living document like a GoogleDoc.

3. Refer back to this list every time you're feeling discouraged or like you want to quit. Or when that asshole of an agent on the other side of the deal is making your life hard. This will happen in your career if it hasn't already, brace yourself. When it does, and it will, refer back to your Client Compliment folder.

WEEK 1 DAY 2
DAY 2: IDENTIFYING STRENGTHS

Yesterday, you identified some strengths. Today, we will look at these strengths a little bit closer.

As I mentioned earlier, our reviews are a good indicator of what we're doing well. Hopefully, you took some time yesterday to dig in your email to find compliments past or current clients have paid you. Or better yet, you already have a growing list of reviews online or on your website. If you don't, we'll talk more on that later.

When you start to see the same phrases mentioned in reviews, listen. When I get a five-star review, what is that person saying?

Pay attention when you start to see redundancies. You will likely know, intuitively, what your strengths are, but this feedback and outside opinion should reinforce what you already believe to be your strengths.

What are the common themes you see in what others say about you? Are agents on the other side of the transaction telling you how easy it is to work with you? Are your sellers impressed by your timeliness?

Are your buyers grateful for the thoughtful touches you included in their home buying experience?

Lean into awareness here. Never shrug off a compliment. Do not become defensive or humble here, either. Do not let imposter syndrome seep in. Accept it with grace and humility. Be aware of the truth, and don't hide from it. Like in most parts of our lives and our business, the truth comes out whether we like it or not.

Let's take showing feedback, for example. When you show a home and later, the listing agent asks you, "what did your buyer clients think of the listing?"

A lot of times, we don't hit them with the truth, right?

We want to let them down easy. We don't respond with, "that is the worst house I've ever seen."

We hide that. We respond with things like, "they just weren't interested." or "That didn't quite work for my client."

Reviews, on the other hand. This is where the truth comes out; it doesn't have to be hidden. Pay attention to what people are saying about you in reviews. When you ask for feedback from your clients, what are they saying about you and the service you provide?

PRO TIP: Throughout the process, say to a client, "remember this moment when I ask for a review." Say this with genuine kindness when something good happens for your buyer. When they get their offer accepted, you find the perfect off-market deal, or you negotiate repairs like a pro. And, for your seller, when their listing photos look incredible or when they have six showings confirmed within an hour of listing. Remind them kindly again when they get an offer for $30,000 over asking and a quick close. Again, telling them, "remember this moment when I ask for a review," is a way to mentally prepare them that you will be asking for a review. That way, when you do ask for a testimonial or review, they aren't surprised you asked. And you will ask for a review.

Once you've identified those strengths, let's take it to the next level.

Aside from sales, my work ethic has always been my strength. Nobody has to get me out of bed. For me, work ethic is ingrained.

We weren't middle-class Michigan. We were poor. I had my first job when I was eight years old. In Michigan, you can return cans and receive ten cents. There, I was eight years old counting cans for people and giving them their money. I was making something like $2.50 per hour, under the table, of course. If you have children, imagine looking at your eight-year-old and telling them, "today you're going to work."

This childhood taught me the value of work ethic and hustle. From the way I was raised in Detroit, working hard and giving my all is something that I do not need to think about. It just happens.

Other real estate agents in town may consider a full day of work to be three showings, returning emails, and having coffee with a Title rep. For me, that's not a full day. I am not ending my day until I have hit all my sales metrics, including listing appointments set and calls completed.

For five years, I was doing 30 hours a week of open houses. Even when I hit $46M in sales in 2012, I was sitting open houses. If I missed a day, I would make up the hours the next day. I would work my showings around open houses. So, no. For me, a full-day as a real estate agent is not a few showings, emails, and a coffee date.

Are you one of those real estate agents doing the bare minimum and patting yourself on the back? Or are you grinding all day with little notice of what others are doing or not doing? Is that one of your strengths? If it is? Excellent, you've identified that strength. Play on that strength. Let that become your mantra.

Identifying these three core strengths of mine are things that I intuitively do. The best thing about a strength is that if you're crystal clear on what you're good at, and you know you are, you can go out there with confidence in the field.

When you're talking to clients and intuitively know with confidence that this is what you excel in, you will be the best real estate agent they have ever worked with. If you know that no one creates a more streamlined contract-to-close process, dive into that and make it known to your clients. If no one analyzes a deal better than you, tell—or better yet, show—your investor client with confidence. If securing offers over asking is what you excel at, show your sales stats at your next listing presentation.

It takes time identifying what you're good at, and mastering it step-by-step.

That's how great businesses are formed.

Once you have identified your strengths, you can become confident in your strengths. Then, you can master the world.

But you must first acknowledge your strengths and identify them so that you can later harness them.

Once you do, you can walk into your business with more confidence. You will sell more once you clearly identify your strengths. Do not skip this step.

Below, identify the three core strengths that you will later use to build a million-dollar real estate business.

Tomorrow, we are going to look at what you're not-so-great at, and we are going to improve that, too.

DAY 2 WORKSHEET

Identify at least seven things you excel in:

1

2

3

4

5

6

7

Include more if you'd like. Don't be shy.

Of those seven items, identify three core strengths.

1

2

3

Include more here if you'd like:

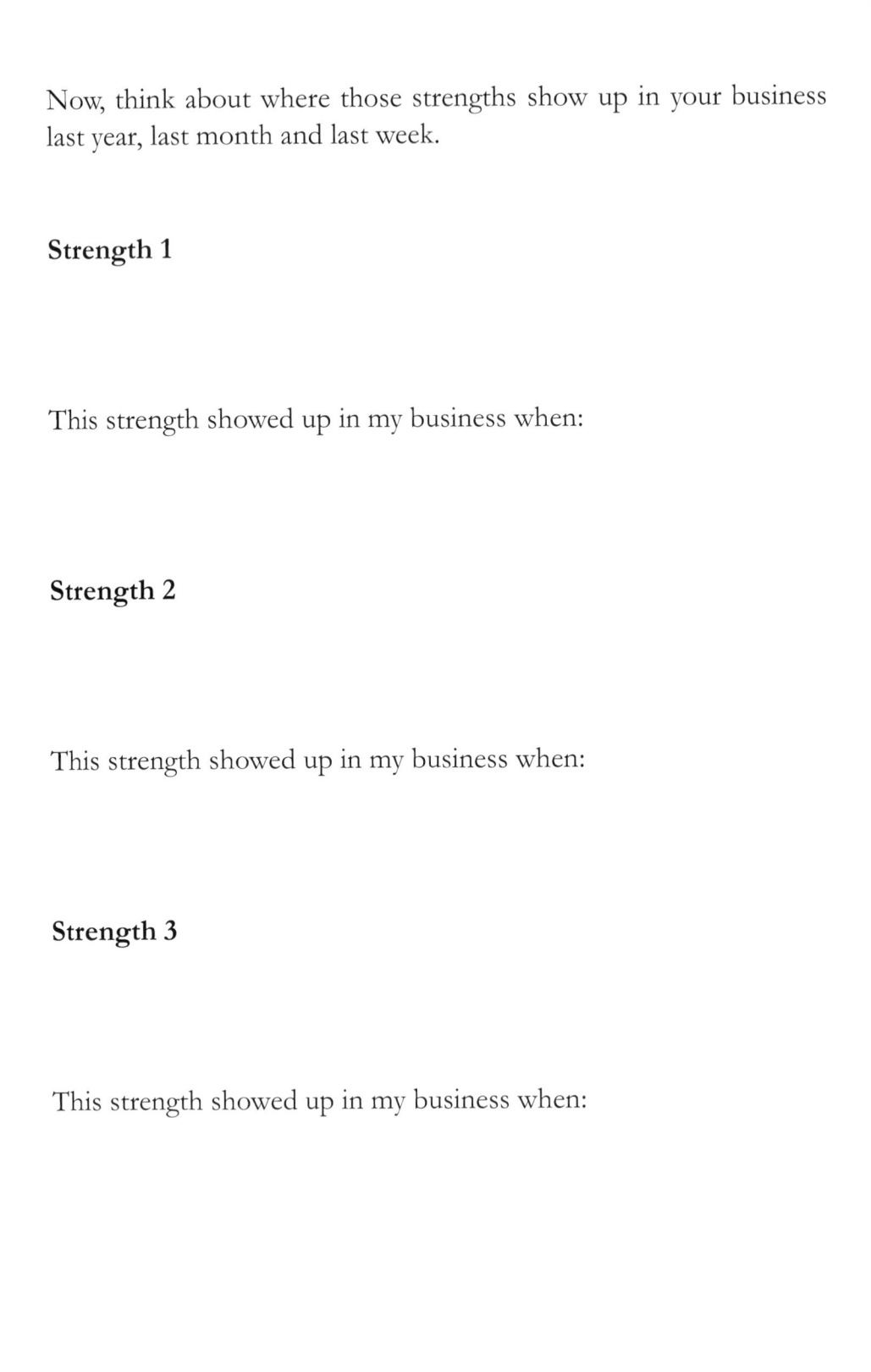

Now, think about where those strengths show up in your business last year, last month and last week.

Strength 1

This strength showed up in my business when:

Strength 2

This strength showed up in my business when:

Strength 3

This strength showed up in my business when:

What is one way your strengths came into play today?

How did your strengths that you identified help you today?

For me, I did not hit snooze on my alarm this morning. I hit the gym, and afterward, I was in the office before everyone else to begin prospecting before the competition. They may still be at the gym or, worse yet, in their pajamas at home or even in bed.

Week 1 Day 3
DAY 3: MITIGATING WEAKNESSES

Yesterday, we took a closer look at your strengths. Take a moment now to revisit the three core strengths you wrote down in yesterday's workbook. Now, we are looking at your weaknesses. Do not skip this step thinking that you do not have any weak points. You do. I certainly have more flaws than I do strengths.

As you did yesterday in the workbook, look at your day and ask yourself: what are some of the weaknesses that got in the way of today truly being a ten-out-of-ten day?

Ask yourself: what could I have gotten better at? What could I have done more of? What could have helped me to succeed?

If you identify your weaknesses, call out your own bullshit, and then set aside time to improve these weaknesses, you get better and better over time. Believe it or not, they actually then become our strengths. But first, we must identify them. We must know what we can improve before we can take action.

I admit this is the hardest part. We don't want to even think about what we are not good at, let alone dwell on those shortcomings, or, worse yet, try to improve them. That will take work as well as admitting you are not good at something. If you want to get better as a real estate agent, as an entrepreneur, business owner, and even as a person, examining your flaws is a requirement. You must have a willingness to improve your weaknesses, not just your strengths. This will take practice. Even Allen Iverson hated practice. Why? Because no one likes to do things that they are not that great at.

You may not play basketball like Iverson, but you played sports as a kid, right? Remember what it felt like to be on the blacktop as the captains picked teams. It felt terrible to be picked ninth, tenth, or even last. Didn't it? But you didn't get picked first because you were not the best at the sport. You were picked last because it was the sport you practiced the least or, at least, not enough. If you spent hours upon hours practicing, you would not have been picked last.

PRO TIP: Listen to what others say is your weakness, show up to practice, and be open to coaching. Only then will not only you improve but also your business.

"We're talking about practice. Not a game. Not the game that I go out there and die for and play every game like it's my last. Not the game. We're talking about practice, man. I mean how silly is that. And we're talking about practice. I know I'm supposed to be there…. We're talking about practice. We ain't talking about the game. We're talking about practice, man." Allen Iverson said to Comcast SportsNet's Neil Hartman in an interview, "But we're talking about practice, man. We're not even talking about the game. The actual game. When it matters. We're talking about practice." - Allen Iverson

"Iverson still doesn't understand the difference between coaching and criticism," Sports journalist Stan Hochman once wrote.

It is the same thing in business. Identify what you're not good at so you can practice at it. If you dedicate time to practice, you get better. How do I mitigate your weaknesses? It's easy. You identify them. Then you work on them.

You have to work on improving your weakness in your day-to-day life. I am going a hundred miles an hour because that is what is required of me. Or so I think. I must go from this appointment to the next at warp speed. I don't have time to slow down and look at what I am not good at.

But that just isn't true. It's a lie.

This is what you tell yourself because it's hard. It's easy for me to run from appointment to appointment, to use my speed dialer to cold call another expired listing because I am good at these things. This is where I excel. It is hard for me to slow down and practice organizing my notes. It is damn right near impossible for me to stop what I am doing and double-check my contract before sending it over to the listing agent or my client via Docusign. But I have to. This is what I must do in order to be the best real estate agent my client has ever worked with. This is what I must do to close $1M more in sales this week.

Slow down. Identify your weakness. Then set up a structure so you can practice what you're not good at so you, too, can improve.

On day one, I talked about how it was easier for me to go from cold call to cold call. Using the speed dialer calling expired listings became second nature to me. Taking two minutes to slow down and enter the appointment into my calendar did not. I am not intuitively good at scheduling and calendaring or frankly, any administrative tasks related to this. But you know what happened? I missed appointments. I knew I couldn't operate at my highest and best if I continued to work like this. I needed to be on point. I couldn't miss a meeting or, worse yet, a listing appointment. That behavior would never mean I would be the best agent in my brokerage, the agent in my state, or the best broker in the country. I needed to mitigate this weakness, and I needed to do it now—no time to wait. I cannot continue to allow this weakness to affect me, my clients, and my business negatively.

So, I changed, and I challenged myself. No matter what happens, you must always put it in your calendar. As my business grew, the need to be structured and organized grew with it. If I didn't make a choice right then in my personal and business to mitigate this weakness, I would never reach my full potential. Never.

Did I want to slow down and put this in my calendar? Hell no! All I wanted to do was go sell, sell, sell.

But the more I sold, the busier my life became, and the more apparent it became that organization and structure were going to be key to my success as the state's top agent.

So, I worked at it and you know what happened? It became a part of my day. I trained my brain to stop, pause, log that, and put that in your calendar. I recognized what I wasn't good at that. Now, I don't even think about it.

I trained my brain like an athlete trains their body. I had to train my brain to do it. Now, scheduling now intuitively a strength of mine, and I don't miss any meetings. Imagine what that did for my business.

Now, imagine how structured my day was back then. If I couldn't slow down enough to enter a meeting into my calendar, do you think I had structure in my day? Of course not! I was chasing shiny objects and doing the things I was good at—the fun stuff. By zeroing in my weakness of organization, it was natural that I had also to face my second weakness: structure. Identifying organization as a weakness of mine allowed me to create another strength, structure. Because you see, weaknesses bump into other weaknesses. It is a domino effect. If you're not good at organization, you're likely not good at creating and maintaining structure in your day, managing your time or even creating consistency for your clients.

The Psychology of Real Estate Sales | 23

If you are new to this career, you will have a pile of weaknesses.

If you are not great at public speaking, you may not be great at coming up with things to say on the spot. Your sales pitch may be lacking. You may not be as smooth as you want to be when you first initially speak to a lead. This may mean you aren't the best at handling objections at your listing presentations if it wasn't already rehearsed. This something you can practice. Yes, there's that word again, Iverson. Practice.

If you want to get better at something, there is only one thing to do: practice.

PRO TIP: Something to practice: role-playing.

You know many times I've role played? Thousands. Thousands of times I've roleplayed with another agent, with my mentor, friends, and colleagues. and I have even with my significant other. I've made people roleplay in front of me time and time again. You know why? Because I wanted to get better. I knew I needed to practice in order to improve.

Role-playing is something you should be doing even if you think one of the core strengths is sales and persuading others. You are never too good to role play. Never.

Practice. Period.

We will talk more about this on Day 16.

If you want to improve, look at who in your brokerage is consistently making the Top 10. Who is consistently number one in your brokerage?

What do they do? What do they do well? Why is that board always pretty much the same people? It is because they've practiced their craft. Those top agents have identified their weaknesses and they have gotten better at them.

If you are new to this career, you will have a pile of weaknesses, and you should because you're new. You have never done this before. The first time you picked up a basketball, you weren't making three-pointers, nothing but net. No, you looked like a fool as you learned how to dribble, then walk and dribble. Then finally you learned how to make a layup. Next, you learned how to make a free throw. Then after hours and hours maybe even after a year of practice, you made your first three-pointers consistently.

Real estate is no different. You may not nail your first listing appointment, or, heck, even your first open house. You may stumble and look like a fool. But if you practice, you will be making threes all day. Securing listing after listing, writing contract after contract. But it will take practice.

You must identify your weaknesses.

It may be a long list. Heck, it may be a laundry list of 10-20+ items. That's okay! You are going to start working on improving one or two this week and over time you will shrink that list. But if you're waking up and continuing to fail due to your weaknesses without identifying that as a weakness, you cannot see what it's going to take to fix that weakness because you haven't identified it.

Now, let's begin.

Day 3 WORKSHEET
Part 1

Write down at least seven weaknesses.

1

2

3

4

5

6

7

Include more here and remember it is okay to have 20+ items.

If coming up with more than three is a struggle, ask someone closest to you what your weaknesses are. This may be a partner, a parent, a teammate, or even the agent on the other side of the listing. Leave your ego at the door and know that identifying these weaknesses will bring you one step closer to structuring your day, which is a key step in building a successful real estate business.

Day 3 WORKSHEET
Part 2

_____ got in the way of today being a ten out of ten day.

Maybe you can identify more than one thing here. Maybe the way you structure your day is not setting you up for success. Are you waking up too late? Are you spending too much time scrolling on social media? Are you focusing on tasks that are not income producing?

Now, let's look beyond today or yesterday. Let's look at the last six months of business.

Identify three things you could have done more of in the last six months.

1

2

3

Include more here if you'd like:

Identify five things that could have helped you succeed in the last six months.

1

2

3

4

5

Now, you may be wondering, "how long do I need to work on these?"

You will work on them until you don't have to have them on the list anymore. Until it becomes a part of your intuition. That's how long you work on them. It may take a few months for some of these. Sometimes it takes years just to make something so instinctive that it is simply a part of your regiment. I will admit, some are easier than others. But focus on the ones that you feel like if "I get better at this one thing, then my career will get better. Then I become better as a person."

From the same list above, choose two things that would have the biggest impact on your business financially.

1

2

From the list of five above, choose two things that would have the biggest impact on your happiness or personal satisfaction.

1

2

Do not try to do them all.

You will fail.

If you try to do them all at once, you will not master any of them. Knock them out one at a time.

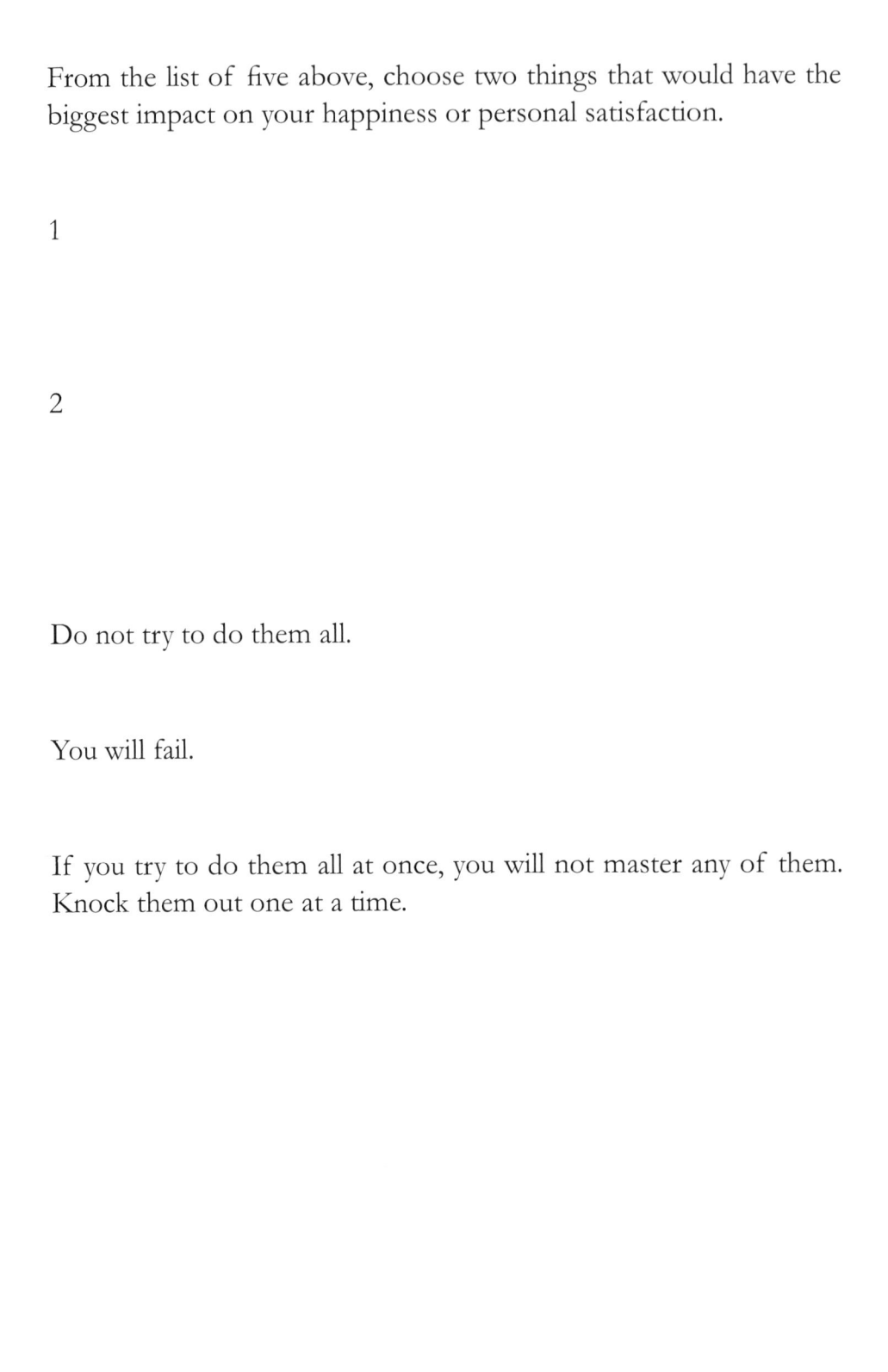

Week 1 Day 4

DAY 4: IDENTIFY YOUR FUNCTIONALITY

Yesterday, I spoke about structure and how creating systems and structure in my day was my weakness. I knew to become the best real estate agent in my state, I would need to structure my day, so I improved. I slowed down even when I didn't want to and I made scheduling my day a priority. I cannot explain to you how much this positively affected not only my business but also my life. I want you to take a moment and think about how you structure your days.

Today, we are going to talk about when you function at your best. Personal functionality affects business functionality. This is so important, yet real estate agents of all ages do not master this. How are you fifty-five years old and you don't know what time of the day you function at your best?

How can you want to close $100M in sales, yet you don't know if you have more energy at 9 a.m. or noon? It is time to structure your day to fit best you and your needs, not the needs of your buyers' agent or your transaction coordinator (if you don't have those, I will talk to you later). If you are always structuring your days around what time works best for your clients and never what times work best for you, are you really serving your clients to the best of your ability?

Let's take my day, for example. My mornings are the time of the day where I allow myself to sit with my own thoughts. That time is sacred to me, and client appointments or team members' needs are not scheduled during that time. Period.

Do you do that enough? When was the last time you closed your eyes to just think? Never underestimate the power of being able to sit there in your own thoughts.

Let's practice now. Read through the following six questions and then close your eyes to think through these. Yes. Think.

What does today bring? What's my day look like? Did I put it together the right way? What did I prioritize today? Does today look like it's going to be a great day? Am I ready for today?

In order to answer all of the questions, you are going to need to find out what time of the day you are at peak performance. Today's exercise is identifying your functionality.

Personal functionality affects business functionality.

Are you best after working out in the morning, or can you head straight to an offer after a quick, healthy breakfast? You know yourself. You know your body. Now, if you listen, that's a different story. I will touch on that later.

Let's take a moment to make a list of the times of the day you feel you're best, you feel the most energized, feel the most motivated, feel the most clarity, and when do you feel the sharpest?

Stop reading and skip to today's workbook and fill in Part 1.

When do you have your best ideas? For me, I have the most incredible ideas when I get up in the middle of the night, sometimes at two o'clock in the morning. This is the reason I have a pen and paper on my nightstand next to my bed. Its times like those when it's pitch black in my room, and the house is silent. I am lying in bed, and I come up with these ideas.

It is really bizarre. I actually look forward to waking up in the middle of the night, and I do it a lot. I come up with some excellent ideas. The clarity I have in the middle of the night, for some reason, is truly something I look forward to and value. The next day, I take a picture of the pad of paper and upload it to the cloud to revisit it when I get into work. That way, I can execute on those ideas.

A clear mind will catapult your business.

Maybe your clarity comes later in the morning after a cup of coffee (or two). Perhaps you're like Mike in my office who likes to get straight to the office before everyone else. This allows him time to dive straight into the work that needs to get done for the day. He'd prefer to exercise later in the day or, heck, mid-day. Then he does showings and listing appointments in the evenings before his mid-day workout restores his energy levels. There is nothing wrong with going to the gym at 1:00 p.m.

I know someone who complains when he sees people at the gym or the store or the cafe in the middle of the day.

"Don't these people have jobs to be at?" he mutters.

I never understand that. I always think, "Sweet! These people have structured their workdays, careers or businesses, so that they can be at the gym at 1:00 p.m. on a Tuesday. Good for them."

Are you a gym person in the morning? Are you a gym person in the evening? Are you a gym person in the middle of the day to take a break from work? Fine, great. If that's what makes you function the best, then do it. Don't be afraid to go to the gym in the middle of the day.

Never be afraid to take a break in the middle of the day. If you function best after a long walk or heck even a quick walk around the parking lot, do it. Take a break. If that gives you clarity and gives you energy to finish out the day, then make that part of your routine.

Whatever you identify that helps you function at your peak performance, structure it into your day.

Maybe you are like Leslie. Leslie's routine is waking up, making a healthy breakfast, and going to the gym to start her day. She makes that a part of her daily routine, and it ensures that she is more energized with more clarity mid-morning. Leslie knows she is sharper in the morning, so she schedules to show homes in the morning.

Maybe your routine is like more Craig's. Craig loves to get into the office early, so he does not get distracted. He starts his workday before nearly everyone in his entire brokerage. Then Craig goes to the gym after his workday. He gets his mental relaxation after the workday.

Maybe you are like Tom. Tom does not make any appointments before 10:30 a.m. He does not function well in the mornings, and he knows this about himself. Whereas Tom is full of energy and clarity by 4:30 p.m. or even six o'clock when most others are wrapping up their day or heading home. He packs his schedule in the evenings. A majority of Tom's clients are busy professionals, and they love being able to do a seven or even eight o'clock showing and are impressed by Tom's ability to never miss a beat even after a long day.

There's no right or wrong answer. It comes down to what works for you.

Self identify what best fits the person that you are. You know who you are, you know, if you'd like getting up in the mornings early or you don't. You know, if you are better off, getting your mental relaxation at night like Craig. Maybe it is quiet at home. Perhaps your evenings are your time to breathe. Take a breath. Or perhaps you can actually plug away at night like Tom.

If you like to work at night and you like getting things done at night, great. Then you're probably a go-to-the-gym-in-the-morning type person. Take care of your mental health in the morning and physical health in the morning if that's the case. Then you can work the later part of the day into the evening.

A healthy mind drives a healthy business.

When you identify your functionality and understand where to best fit tasks into your day, you will achieve peak performance.

Let's revisit those same six questions.

1. What does today bring?
2. What's my day look like?
3. Did I put it together the right way?
4. What did I prioritize today?
5. Does today look like it's going to be a great day?
6. Am I ready for today?

You know when you can perform at your best. Now, use that information and make better decisions as you structure and plan your day and week.

Then, there are the things that, quite frankly, we all know do not help us function so well—the eating like crap, the drinking, and the going out.

Listen, you don't need me to tell you that everyone's entitled to have a good time. But I promise you those who go out without thinking of that early morning meeting or the lead generation that they should be doing at 8 a.m. are not consistently making the top ten in their brokerage. Those people are not reaching their wealth goals again and again, or maybe even at all. Here's the thing, if you are going out thinking, "I have tomorrow to think about." you are going to close more deals and better serve your clients than the ones who just always choose to live with no consequences.

Your personal life affects your business life greater than anything else.

In real estate, I have seen the ones that repeatedly over party. They're the ones that are drinking too much, and they're the ones that are staying out too late. I know where their real estate careers are going even before they do.

That's why those of us who understand and make decisions knowing that I have responsibility in the morning will always surpass those who don't understand the value of the next day. That's functionality.

Everyone should have a good time, but there must be limits to it. If having a successful real estate business and living a full life is a priority of yours then you must start with high functionality.

Day 4 WORKSHEET
Part 1

What part of the day do you feel the most motivated?

What part of the day do you feel the most clarity? When do you think the sharpest?

When do you have the most energy?

Day 4 WORKSHEET
Part 2

When do you have your best ideas?

What activities do you notice positively affect your mood?

What activities do you notice positively affect your mood?

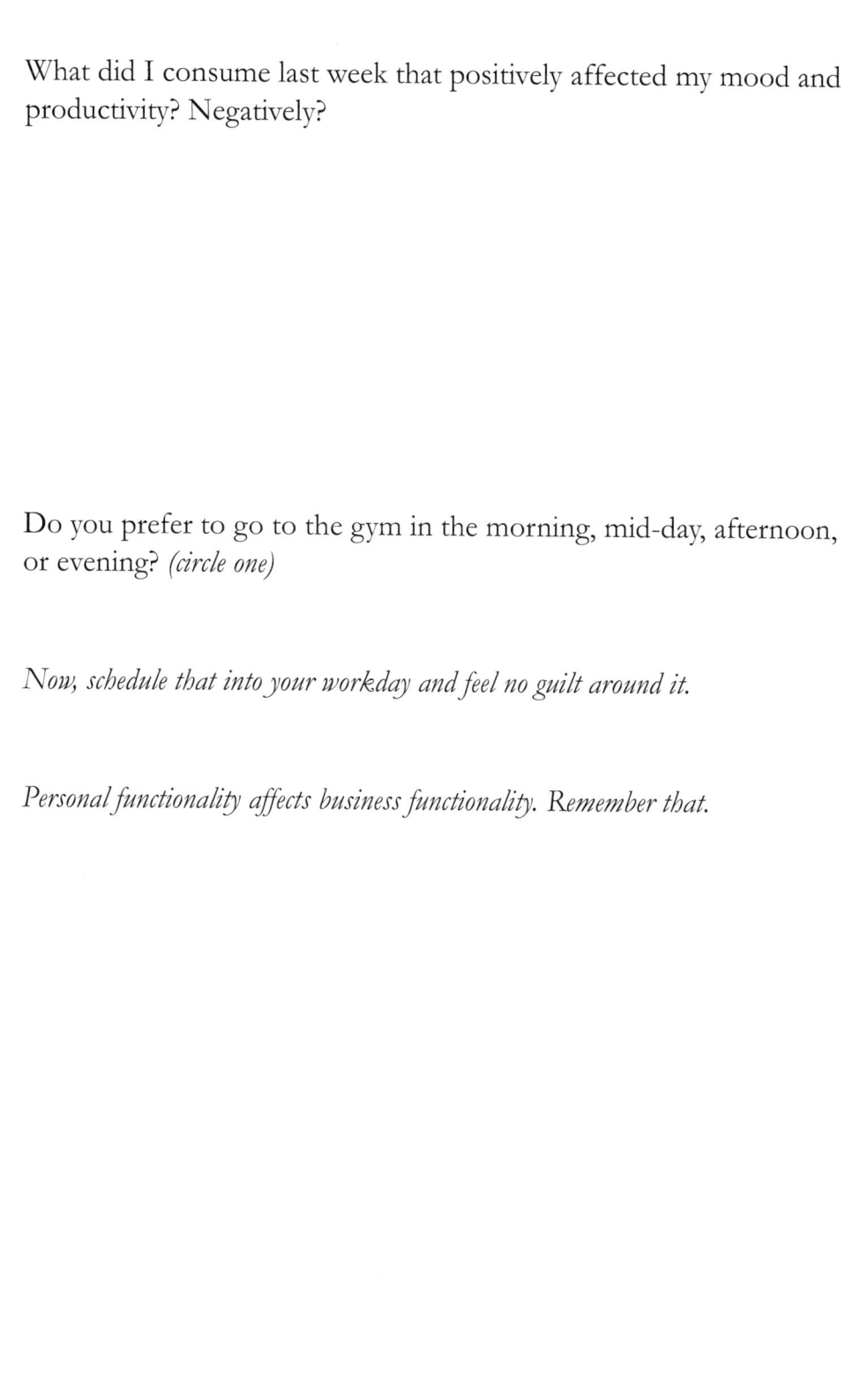

What did I consume last week that positively affected my mood and productivity? Negatively?

Do you prefer to go to the gym in the morning, mid-day, afternoon, or evening? *(circle one)*

Now, schedule that into your workday and feel no guilt around it.

Personal functionality affects business functionality. Remember that.

Week 1 Day 5
DAY 5: SUPERMAN SYNDROME

"Are you ready to give up some control to make more money?"

"More money, heck, yes! But less control? I don't know about that."

"Are you ready to tell yourself that you're not Superman?"

"Wait, what?"

"You can't do it all."

"Yes, I can. Plus, I have to. It's only me."

You are going to be your greatest obstacle in your journey to being a successful agent if you cannot give up control and let go of greed. Period. End of the story. It is that simple.

Today, I am going to give you the golden ticket to all that is real estate sales.

But first, you need to know that you can't do it all.

Once you understand that, you will start building a successful and scalable business. I am telling you right now that if your business isn't scalable, it isn't successful. I don't care if you closed $10M last year. Good for you. Were you showing buyers properties 80%, 90%, or 100% of the time? Did you put a lockbox out on more than two homes? If you are and continue to do so, you are not going to be a rainmaker. Your business isn't scalable—end of story.

New agents fail because they try to be the master of everything. They want to be the master marketer, the master of social media, the master salesperson, the master processor, the master of showing homes, the master of walkthroughs, the master of closing day, the master of everything. Those agents fail. I am here to remind you, you can't, nor should you do it all. Now, when I speak on stages to real estate agents, 90% of the audience is on their own. They don't have an assistant, an in-house transaction coordinator, a marketing coordinator, a buyers agent, an inside sales agent. These real estate agents are solo agents, so they say to me, "I have to do everything. It's just me."

Wrong.

Just because you haven't hired an assistant yet does not mean you cannot hire a transaction coordinator or a marketing manager as an independent contractor. Notice the word "yet." You will hire people if you want to be successful in real estate sales. Period. If that scares you to the point of paralysis, find another business. Real estate sales is not for you.

Let me tell you that it's never just you. You may think it's just you, but it's never only you. Support is available to you. And I will be the first to tell you. If you want to become really successful in this industry, help has to be on its way. Because at some point, you just get too busy and available. That's the goal, right? The goal is to have so many listings and so many buyers that you are making the money you want. It's awesome. There's nothing like it.

I will not be the first person to tell you that a majority of real estate agents fail. You know this. You heard it when you were getting your license. You heard it when you joined your brokerage or at new agent orientation.

Do you know why new agents fail? Agents fail because they don't have the hustle. Some real estate agents simply lack that drive. When I first became an agent, you would not outwork me—my drive, my spirit. I'm from Southgate, Detroit, Michigan.

I just had that hustle.

I did not come from much; I had to work for it.

I had to have drive and determination. That's why in my first several years in this business, I crushed it. Agents alongside me who were newer to the business, I just kicked their ass because they didn't have the drive and the hustle like I did. I knew I could not take a day off. I had to stay sharp because I didn't have a blanket to fall on.

The goal is to get so busy to where you need help.

As an agent, you have to have that hustle and drive especially in your first few years because it is pretty much just you. You are right that it is just you, but there's always support. There's somebody that can help with processing paperwork; there's somebody that can help with transaction coordinating; there's somebody that can help hold open houses; there's somebody that can post on social media for you. You know just as much I do that no one works for free. But if paying $300 to process an entire file means that I get to prospect more, of course, I spent the $300. And you guys, you pay the fees after you close. How no brainer is that?

I see agents hunched over their laptops, worried looks on their faces as they act as their own transaction coordinator. I see agents that will go out and actually hang lockboxes instead of paying someone fifty bucks. For those two hours of the day—you know, the most critical hours of the day—you're going to spend two hours driving to a house to put a lockbox on it. That's crazy.

If you're not going to pay a transaction coordinator a few hundred dollars to do all your paperwork on your file, you need to reevaluate how much your time is worth. And by the way, you don't even have to pay them upfront, you guys; you pay them when it closes. That's not worth $300 to you.

Are you insane? No, you're not crazy. You're not insane. You're greedy. Yes, you are so greedy that you cannot let go of $50-300 so that someone better equipped for that task can take that task off your plate so that you can do your job: bring in more business. And then people get greedy, instead of paying someone far more capable of that task, they say, "I'll do it. I'll take care of it." At what cost do you want to take care of that?

See, we're never really alone. We think we are, but we're not. There is always support there for us in real estate. You don't want to pay for the support because you think they need to hold onto that $300. You're wrong. Your time is better spent creating new business.

Even as a new agent, if it allowed me to do more business, I paid a Transaction Coordinator $300 bucks to process a file. If that meant I did not have to pay attention to the paperwork, no problem.

There comes a point where you can't do it all. This is one of the most significant struggles agents have. It's honestly one of the top questions I get asked by agents: "When should I hire an assistant? What does that look like?"

My answer is as soon as possible.

Because you need that time. The time it takes you to work on marketing, the time it takes you to put together a listing packet, the time it takes you to even think about social media, let alone post on it. That is all time you should be spending bringing in more business.

Your job is straightforward. Your job is to be the Rainmaker. Bring in more business and more closings out. It's a circle. No one is going to be the Rainmaker. That's your job. You want to be great at real estate sales? You want to sell 40, 50, or 100 million dollars a year? You have got to be the Rainmaker. It is crystal clear to me, and it should be clear to you that you can't be the Rainmaker if you're out hanging lockboxes. You can't be the Rainmaker when you're sitting there trying to organize your paperwork.

If your day looks like this:

8:00 a.m. coffee with Title rep

9:15 a.m. showing with buyers A

10:00 a.m. walkthrough for buyers B

12:45 p.m. closing at the Title company for buyers C. Hopefully, swing by my listing to ensure everything is ready for the 3:00 p.m. showing. Then, I'll likely be eating lunch in the car.

2:30 p.m. another walkthrough for buyers D

4:00 p.m. close and lock up my listing after its 3:00 p.m. showing

5:30 p.m. showing #2 with buyers A

What part of that day were you making it rain?

What are you doing attending every closing and every walkthrough? Your job, as the Rainmaker, is done here. You already made it rain. Why isn't somebody else taking it to the finish line so you can do your job: make it rain.

"Well, I can't afford somebody else."

You need to hire now for where you want to be one, two, three years down the road. You need to set aside your greed and pay someone to do the work you should not be doing. If you are spending three days a week with the schedule above, those are 156 days a year that you are not doing your job. Do you know the missed opportunity cost here? Agents who are prospecting five or even three days a week are getting listings that you're not.

And if you aren't having someone do your walkthrough for you or attending your closings because you think no one can do as good of a job as you, you have an ego problem. Let it go.

You are not Superman. You cannot do it all. If you cannot lose some of your power and control, get over that.

Especially when it comes to hiring your first buyer's agent.

I hear it all the time, "I have too many buyers. I am too busy because I have too many buyers."

If you cannot prospect or attend listing presentations because you are continually showing buyers' houses, you need to stop what you're doing and find a buyer's agent today. Not tomorrow. Today.

Your number two priority is to find a buyer's agent. Your number one priority is to make it rain, in case that wasn't clear.

If you have told your spouse, partner, broker, or even your grandmother that you're just so busy, then you need to hire a buyer's agent today.

"I don't want someone else driving around my buyers!"

Again, let go of your ego.

"No, it's not that. I want 100% of my commission. I don't want to give my leads to another agent even if I get 60% of the commission split."

Now, we're back to the same reason why you do not want to pay a Transaction Coordinator $300. So, it is about greed. It's about the fact that you don't want to give something up. Wake up.

In this business, when you give some things up, you get a lot more back. The most crucial thing you get back is your time. You now have the time to make it rain.

Now, your day looks like this:

    8:00 a.m. coffee with Title rep only if you want to
    9:00 a.m. prospecting
    10:00 a.m. negotiating contracts and back to prospecting
    12:00 p.m. lunch away from your desk
    12:45 p.m. listing appointment #1
    2:30 p.m. listing appointment #2
    4:00 p.m. showing with your luxury buyer
    5:30 p.m. listing appointment #3

If you're still not convinced that someone else can serve your clients better than you can, let's talk about your level of customer service. If you're that busy, guess what, you're not really providing your clients with excellent service. They're better off with somebody else, the team down the hall from you. Or an agent at another brokerage because you clearly cannot serve them well if you are too busy and refuse to get help.

"What if I bring on a buyers' agent and they bring me leads? And I still serve my clients?"

What buyers' agent is going to join your team if you are not offering them warm leads? What buyers' agents will join your team if you have no time to mentor them or even allow them to shadow you? If you are too busy and too greedy to share anything with them? Why would they join you?

If you are reading this and honestly thinking that buyers agents will line up to join your team to be a part of your great teachings and philosophies of real estate. Then maybe you're even more insane than the agent not willing to pay $50 to have someone place a lockbox for them.

People don't want to join your team to just learn from training. Better said: quality people don't want to join your team to just learn from you.

They want to grow their business. You have all these buyers, yet you're not willing to give any of them up. That's greed.

"I don't want to give up 50% of my commissions to my buyers' agent."

Why did you bring them on?

"Well, that's why I'm not bringing one on."

Oh, I see. I see. So, you're gonna always be stuck at capacity? Because at some point, capacity plays a role, right? You can only have so many clients at one given time. You can not work with 30 buyers. What does that mean? That means you have an unscalable business model. Wonderful. Congratulations, you'll be capped at $10 million, maybe $30 million a year in real estate. Congratulations. Just great. Your greed is keeping from meeting your max potential as a real estate agent and Rainmaker.

I want to work that buyer because I want to make the full $6,000 commission.

Control freak.

Picture this: you arrive at a showing at 7:00 a.m. on a Saturday because their daughter has a soccer game in this part of town at 8:30, so they want to see the house before the game, right? You eagerly agree even though you know you do not function well in the mornings.

We went over identifying your functionally yesterday, remember?

You agree to the 7 a.m. showing anyway because you think you need the money. The family of four, including their little soccer player, walk into the family room, shin guards and all, and immediately turn to you and say, "Oh, I hate the kitchen."

You begin to explain that can be changed... The husband cuts you off with, "This color is hideous. I could never live here."

The daughter chimes in and says, "this house feels haunted!"

You start to turn off the lights and wave them goodbye, "good luck at your game!"

Defeated, you rush to get a second cup of coffee before meeting your other buyer clients, a lovely couple from the other side of town. They come to you with a list of six houses they want to see in addition to the three you sent them. You spend the next seven hours showing them homes you know they either will not buy or will not qualify for. You spent your entire Saturday showing around buyers who will not buy.

Talk about a catastrophic waste of time.

Let me paint a terrific picture for you. You have a buyer client looking for a single-family home ranging from $200,000 to $275,000. You meet with them and get them to sign an exclusive buyers agreement because you build rapport quickly, you have an excellent reputation in town, and maybe they were a referral. They see you as an expert in the market, and you agree that you're the best in town.

Now, you walk her through the contract-to-close process, you have a full buyer's consultation with her to find out exactly her needs according to her lifestyle and desired location. In the end, you explain to her that she will now meet your trusted buyer's agent. He will be the one showing her the properties and meeting her at the properties. After all, you want her to feel comfortable. You tell her that your job is to negotiate the contracts. Your job is to get her the house she wants at the best value. Plus, it's a competitive time in the market. You need to best position her if she wants to get under contract in the timeframe she laid out for you. You explain to her that the moment she and your buyers' agent tour a house that she wants to make an offer on, the first phone call your buyers' agents will make is to you. It is your job to negotiate the offer. That's your expertise. Plus, you will also now be looking for on- and off-market properties that meet her criteria.

Guess what, you guys? She is thrilled with you. She sees you as a professional in your field, a master in your craft. She doesn't pout and say, "Oh, I wish it was you sitting in traffic and showing me eleven homes this Saturday." No! She wants you to scour the market for her dream house. She wants you armed and ready to negotiate the heck out of the contract once she walks that dream house.

To be clear, if you do not set the expectation that someone else is going to be showing them properties and then last-minute, someone else shows up at a property with them. That's where people get upset. No one gets upset if you say, "Hey, look, we got these five great properties. My showing assistant is going to help you take a look at those today. If and when you find the right one today, we're going to discuss it, and we're going to see where we can purchase that home at the best value. Does that sound okay to you? Sounds great to me. Great."

This is called Foreshadowing. With all your clients, you should be setting up expectations for how you will best serve them and what that service will look like.

I highly recommend you do this with every single client, even the buyers you will serve personally.

There are some buyers that you should personally show properties to. Your high-end clients and your grandmother should have you showing them their properties. Depending on your market, maybe sub $500,000 goes to your buyers' agents, whereas you handle anything over $500,000. Maybe in your market, a better metric is $1,000,000. You know your market, and you know your buyer clientele. Do not be greedy. Give your buyers' agents buyers to show properties to so you can close more deals.

The Psychology of Real Estate Sales | 49

Wake up, people. Your buyers want a great house at a great price. They also hope to experience exceptional service along the way. Do you honestly believe having a buyers' agent won't help you accomplish this more often and with more clients?

You still will have to show homes. That's going to happen, but the point is, it doesn't happen with every client. It can't. You need to spread yourself out.

> *The best part about real estate is closing a deal. If you're looking at every dollar you make you will not make it. Do not be greedy because it will bite you in the butt.*

You're not going to go let the million-dollar buyer go with your buyer's agent, at least not right away. But if you have a ready and willing buyers' agent that says, "Look, give me what you got. I'm hungry. Give me your $150,000-350,000 buyers, and I'll go out and do the work. I'll go bust my hump out there. I want to build my business."

This is the type of person you find.

When that happens, that's when you become a real Rainmaker. When that hungry buyers' agent joins your team and does what they say they're going to do. And you, as the Rainmaker, set the expectations that I just told you, "my showing assistant is going to get you into the home, I'm going to negotiate, and we're going to do whatever it takes." You're still involved but guess what, you're not spending your days showing multiple properties, attending walkthroughs and closings. You are not attending twice as many, if not four times as many listing appointments. That's worth a 50/50 commission split. Can't you see that having a buyers agent to better serve your clients is worth a 60/40 commission split?

Oh, and by the way, when you do that, guess what you've created?

A scalable business model.

You created a scalable business model that allows you to make it rain, and bring it in. Now, everybody else on your team can go out there and make money, including yourself. Like most things, this is a shift in your mindset.

When you start accepting that your job is to be the Rainmaker, you bring more business. Then you can begin to do even more business, and guess what? You make more money than you did when you were showing buyers from 7 a.m. to 3:00 p.m. on a Saturday.

Once you produce enough business as a rainmaker, you can hire more buyer brokers. Now all of a sudden, you are making money in your sleep. That's the power of a scalable business. You have people on your team working around the clock providing top-notch customer service to your clients—a level of service that would have been impossible for you to replicate when you were doing it alone.

How cool is that? The only thing you have to do is to bring in a ton of business. Yeah, isn't that amazing? I just gave you the golden ticket to all things real estate sales. Go make it rain, and the rest will take care of itself.

But you're gonna get in your own way. You're gonna get in your own way because of greed. And because you're a control freak. I see it happen all the time.

Here is a list of things you get to do when you are a real Rainmaker:

Pick and choose who you work with

Say no to 7 a.m. showings

Say yes to lunch with a significant other

Attend 10x as many listing appointments

Work on your business (and not just in it)

Hire the best marketing person you can afford

Improve your systems

Make money in your sleep

Go on vacation

Hire more people as you can because now the sky's the limit for you and your business

All of this is possible for you because you're not greedy. You're not a control freak. Because of that, you have now created this unbelievably great real estate team. Wow. There's that breaking point, guys. That breaking point is when you realize you're not Superman. You let go of some control so you can have more control of your life and your time. You can welcome freedom back into your days because you have built a scalable business, one that you can grow to heights that you've never thought possible. Now, you know how the true rainmakers of real estate think about their business.

Day 5 WORKSHEET

Take a blank piece of paper and keep it with you for the next three days. Write down every thing you do every day for three days.

This may be the worst assignment I will give you, but it is also one of the most powerful.

If you commit to doing this, a few things will happen. *You will likely stay more on task and more laser-focused for the next three days.*

You will quickly see repetitive tasks that can be either grouped together or changed altogether. For example, I sent the same emails every Monday to my sellers after holding their houses open over the weekend. I quickly learned I could automate this system by creating a templated email and using a system like Open Home Pro. Another example that came from doing this exercise for a week was that I was buying one-off gifts. Instead, I could buy the same gifts in bulk, use my office postage scale, and print labels right there in the office—this saved time and money.

You start to notice what tasks take a lot of time but produce no income.

After you fill it out, circle everything that is reactive in red. Everything proactive can be circled green. Do you notice a trend?

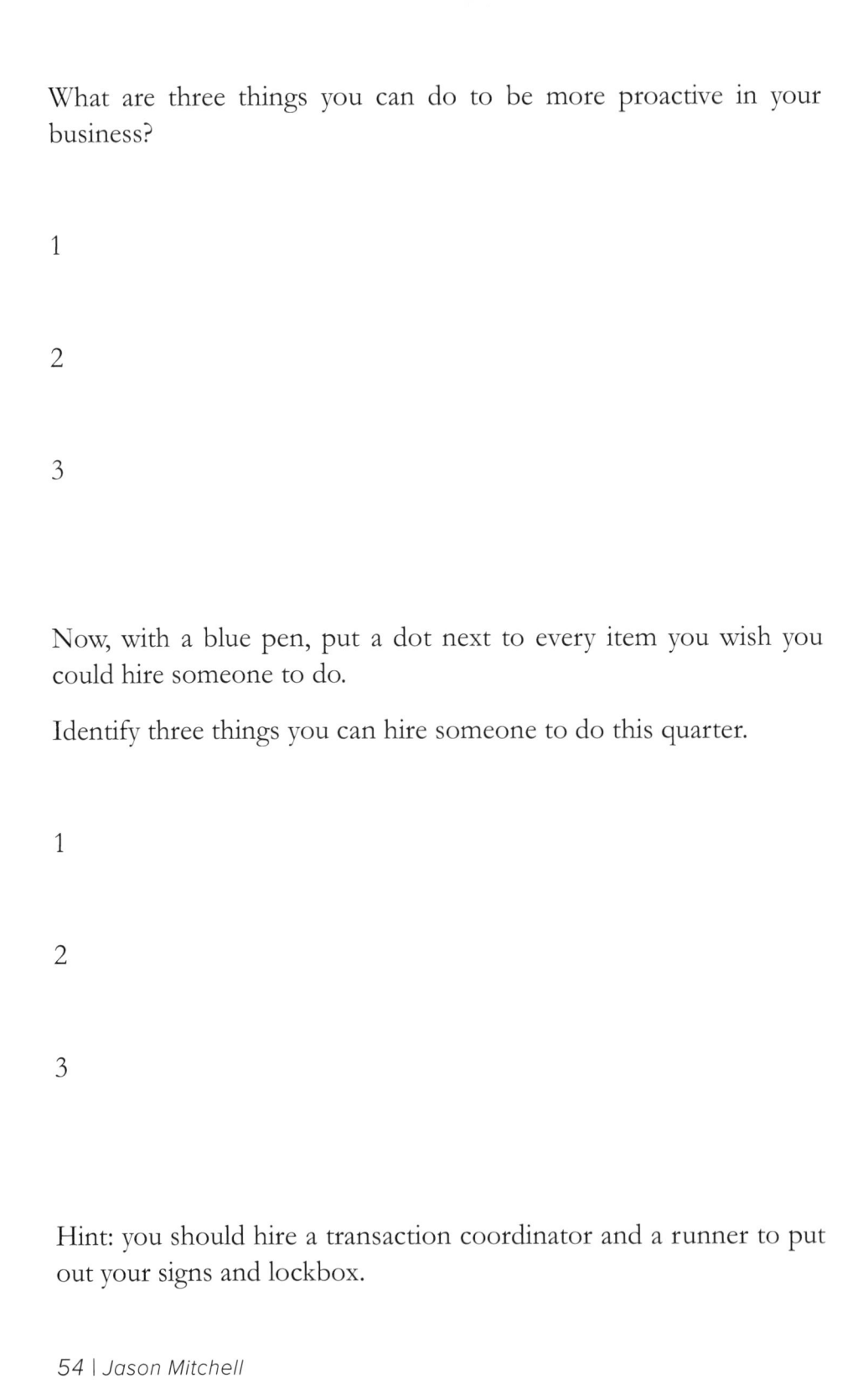

What are three things you can do to be more proactive in your business?

1

2

3

Now, with a blue pen, put a dot next to every item you wish you could hire someone to do.

Identify three things you can hire someone to do this quarter.

1

2

3

Hint: you should hire a transaction coordinator and a runner to put out your signs and lockbox.

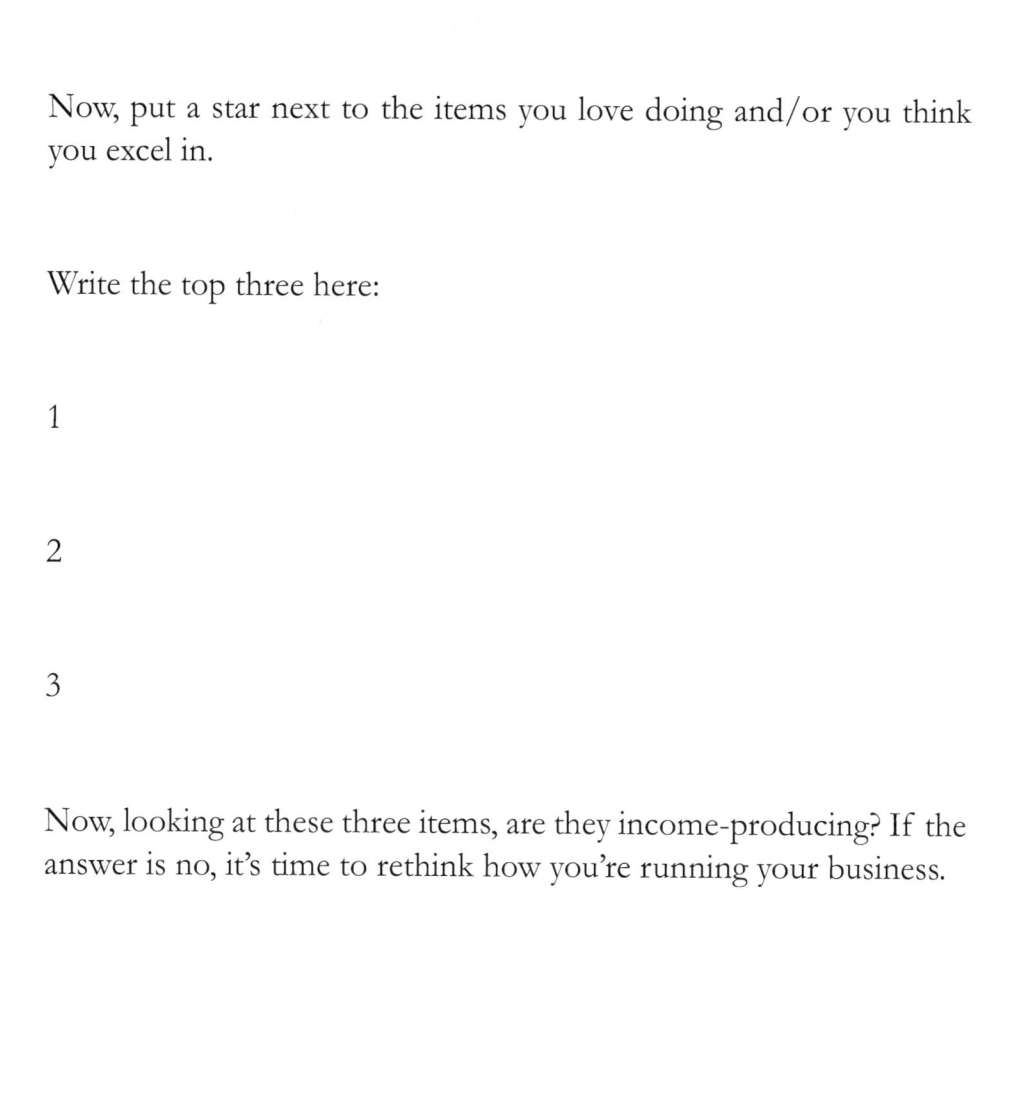

Now, put a star next to the items you love doing and/or you think you excel in.

Write the top three here:

1

2

3

Now, looking at these three items, are they income-producing? If the answer is no, it's time to rethink how you're running your business.

Week 2 Day 1
DAY 6: IDENTIFY YOUR CORE CUSTOMER

Today, we are identifying your ideal customer. We will call this your core client base and your inner core. It is so important you know exactly who you want to work with and why. Your ego may get in the way here if you're thinking, "I can work with anyone, Jason."

I am here to tell you that this will get in the way of maximizing your potential as a real estate agent.

You cannot work with everyone, and you will not work with everyone. Eventually, you may get to a level where your team may work with nearly everyone. But chances are you're not there yet. You, as an individual agent, will not work with everyone. It is impossible.

What is possible? It is possible for you to become a wildly successful real estate agent if you identify who you want to work with. It is possible to do this faster than you thought possible. Let me show you how.

Last week, we spoke about how you will be your most significant obstacle to success. You also committed to working on that last week. You identified what you're good at as we looked more in-depth at your innate talents and strengths. We learned how to start mitigating weaknesses by first identifying them.

Then you came to terms with the fact that you cannot do everything. You now understand that you cannot do it all. You are not superman.

Today, we will identify your ideal customer so that you can market to your core client base.

When you strategically market to your core client base, they'll bring more clients to you. Then your core client base begins to expand. As it grows, you will sell more houses and make more money.

First things first, identify your core client base. Identifying your core clients will help you deliver concierge-level service to them. When you truly know your clients including their wants and needs, it is easier to best serve them.

Once you identify it, you can exploit it. When you do that, your inner core will grow larger and larger. As it grows, that is what we call your outer core. When you develop your outer core, your sales will increase. In addition to increased revenue, your happiness will increase. You will get to a point where you can pick and choose who you work with. When you can say, "this is my ideal client," and you start working with only your ideal client, you begin to find your stroke of genius. It's a step-by-step process.

First, let's have a three-second lesson on marketing. Step one to fundamental marketing and prospecting is knowing who you are marketing to. I am not talking about choosing your target audience for Facebook ads or looking at Google Analytics. I am talking about you understanding who you are marketing yourself to. It is crucial to your success as an agent that you clearly identify your ideal client. Then, once you know who, you can start to have influence over them. We will talk more about marketing in Week Six, but for now, this client identification is incredibly crucial to your growth as an agent. It will single-handedly make getting clients easier. By the end of this week, you will understand who you can influence the most and how to do it. Let's begin.

Once you identify who you have the most influence over, you will sell more homes. Deena, an agent on my team, knows her core client base better than anyone I know. Her client base is military families and veterans. Deena works almost solely with veterans. Deena is a veteran herself, and her spouse if active duty. She and her family live near an army base. As you can imagine, Deena understands the family dynamics of military families. Her core group of friends are also in the military. Her kids go to school with a majority of kids who also come from military families. Years ago, when Deena was just starting out as a real estate agent, she noticed her clients worked with the same Lender. The Lender's name came up again and again. Eventually, Deena built a solid relationship with this Lender. This VA loan specialist now feeds Deena leads and vice versa.

Deena teaches a seminar every third Thursday on buying a home with the VA loan. The Lender sponsors the event, providing food and beverage—nothing fancy. From each workshop, both Deena and the Lender get warm leads that turn into loyal clients for them both.

When Deena holds an open house, it is in a neighborhood near the base. It is a desirable neighborhood because of its proximity to the military base and because it feeds into the best school district in her town. She holds open houses 2-3 days a week, and the Lender sponsors those open houses as well. Open houses and the monthly VA-buyer workshops feed Deena enough leads that she never has to cold call or even send direct mailers, but she does that, too. Deena's military experience taught her to be incredibly disciplined. Her time serving her country also taught her that she doesn't want to spend months away from her family. She builds her real estate empire because she doesn't ever want to miss a football game again. She wants to be there when her daughter takes a limo to Prom. Deena doesn't have to think about missing important family events because her business is built around her life—not the other way around.

Deena can provide concierge-level service to her clients, because she knows what they need. She will walk a property on video with them if they can't fly in to view a home because they are stationed overseas or at another base across the country. Deena sends care packages when a clients' spouse is deploying. No realtor in her market serves military families better than Deena because she knows first-hand what her clients need and want.

Deena was closing $25M on her own. This year, Deena is on track to hit $58M in sales because she has ironed out a process to capture these core clients. Her expertise helps her retain them and create loyal fans out of them. If you ask any military family in her market who the best agent in town is, Deena's name comes up repeatedly.

Admittedly, it wasn't always like this for Deena. Deena started out just like you: thinking she could serve everyone. She is disciplined and determined. Her military career taught her that. Deena is also focused and fun to be around. She could work with anyone, or so she thought. In the beginning, Deena was holding open houses in dozens of neighborhoods all over town. It wasn't until she started working with officers in her husband's squadron that she began to recognize her strength. They were impressed by her knowledge of the transaction when it came to using the VA loan. A newer soldier in her husband's unit didn't realize you could put 0% down using the VA. She started teaching military families how to use the VA loan. That's how the idea of the monthly workshops was born.

When you do a great job, your core will pay you back.

It became clear Deena had found her niche. She stopped holding open houses that were an hour drive from the base. Deena zeroed in on her farm and started farming. We will talk more about that in the next chapter. She identified her core client base: military families and veterans.

Deena set the expectation that she was a military-friendly agent and an expert in her field. Military families perceived this to be true even before it was true. That's the power of perception, folks. If you set your clients up to think you are an expert at this one thing and do everything in your ability to make them believe that, they will. And for Deena, they did. When you do a great job, your core will pay you back.

Military families told their friends, families, and entire units about Deena. It got to the point where Deena's phone was ringing constantly because clients were calling her to list their home.

You know what the most beautiful thing was? When military families trust you, they are loyal. Most happy clients are faithful to you. Deena was not only assisting them with one purchase. When they moved, which they did, that's the nature of the military, Deena was there to list their house. She was getting a referral fee when they purchased their next home. They trusted Deena to refer them to the agent in their next place of duty. Deena would collect commission when they bought, collect commission when they sold four to eight years later, and collect a referral fee when they bought in their next station. Military families move a lot; that is part of their jobs. Deena was creating repeat business for life and loyal referral machines.

Had Deena believed that she could best serve everyone, she would be showing houses two hours north, one hour east and helping a family here and a family there. Now, Deena is crystal clear on who her core customer base is and how she reaches them.

Your assignment today is to discover who is your core client base.

Think about your social life. When you go out and about, who are the people that you're going out with?

When I am socializing, most of the time, I find myself surrounded by people in our industry (i.e., Mortgage Brokers, Title Representatives, Luxury Builders). These are people that have influence over our industry, and you know what? They become incredible referral partners. I am referred to more business from my Lender than any other referral source. That's because I add value to his business and continue to offer concierge-level customer service to their clients. Their clients are my clients because they are satisfied with my level of service.

Plus, I am always top of mind for these guys because I spend time in front of them. Later this week, I will share how to stay on the top of mind for your clients even when you're not spending a lot of time in front of them.

I spend a lot of time with these industry professionals, and I make it clear that they should send me business. That's right. I ask for their business. I never assume they will just send me the business. I ask for it.

When they give it to me, which they do, I say thank you by referring them to more clients. No money is exchanged between us, but a level of respect is built. That is priceless.

Stop reading and skip to Part 1 of Week 2 Day 1 Worksheet

An agent, Payton, was brand new to the business. His broker told him to start by emailing ten people a day, letting them know he had left finance to do real estate sales full-time.

Payton did as he was told. He sent dozens of emails and Facebook messages to old colleagues and friends. On day five, Payton received the following Facebook message:

"Hey, Payton! Talk about good timing. I am wanting to sell my rental property in Mesa. Can you help?"

Payton didn't even know this friend owned rental properties, let alone that he was looking to list a house. And why would he? His friend didn't realize Payton was a real estate agent now. His friend also didn't know Payton had his license for less than 30 days, but they didn't need to know that. Payton had the support of his broker and would offer exceptional service to his friend.

A year later, Payton helped this same friend buy a rental portfolio of fifteen multi-family properties all across town. Before he knew it, Payton was serving real estate investors full-time.

Payton's finance background made it easy to learn how to analyze investment properties. It also made it easy for his clients to believe he was an expert. Wouldn't you want your investment-savvy real estate agent to have a degree in finance? It doesn't hurt, does it?

Payton learned how to analyze deals and calculate cash-on-cash. He also taught himself how to find off-market properties better than anyone else.

PRO TIP: Are you a secret agent?

If you are not telling everyone you know that you help people buy and sell real estate, you are leaving hundreds of thousands of dollars on the table. Stop what you are doing right now and tell ten people you know that you are here to help them when they want to buy and sell real estate.

Do people closest to you know that you are an expert in real estate sales?

Maybe you don't feel like an expert yet? You will get there.

When Deena first started working with active-duty military and veterans, she didn't know the VA loan's ins and outs. And why would she? But her clients did not care because they didn't even know. Deena gracefully referred those loan-specific questions to her Lender. That's what she should have done even if she knew the answers by heart.

Payton now knows his core client base. Before he started messaging friends and colleagues, Payton had no idea that he would end up being an agent who worked with investors. He didn't even know what cash flow meant, let alone how to calculate it. But he learned, and he learned it well.

It is okay if you don't know who your ideal customer is after today's lesson. It may not be clear to you now, but look how much easier it becomes to attract them once you find out. Once you identify your core client base, find ways to become more ingrained with that culture. Put yourself in front of the people that can give you the most opportunity.

Deena attended more events on the military base targeted towards families. Payton started attending every investor meetup he could. He asked investors where they network. Once Payton found out where they frequented, he started showing up. Next thing Payton knew, he was receiving referrals from other investors he hadn't even worked with yet. That's because investors saw Payton at every investor-focused event in town. They didn't know Payton hadn't been an investor-focused agent for years. That was their perception, though.

When that investor was asked, "What agent should I work with?" They quickly said, "Payton works with tons of investors." And now, Payton does.

Identify a group of people who want to work with you. If you're going to work with Chinese investors, but don't speak Mandarin, that might not be the best group. Identify a group of individuals who will easily say yes to you.

Identify a group of people that they will readily accept the fact that you're their go-to agent. If you're going after groups that most likely wouldn't say yes to you, you're wasting your time.

Now, you may be thinking, "I am going to be a luxury agent. I am only going to work with high-net-worth individuals."

If you have not sold a million-dollar home, or if you are newer to the business, there is no reason you should hold luxury open houses. The people that walk into that home are reasonably not going to work with you.

Even if you get lucky enough to go on a listing appointment for a $2 Million home, don't you think the seller will do their homework?

Anyone who identifies themselves as a luxury agent but hasn't sold luxury is making a massive mistake.

Yes, you have to start somewhere. Start with your core client base. Identify them and start building a business around them. Plain and simple, people. Start with your influences.

As you sell more to your core, your core will introduce you to more people. Look at Deena and Payton.

As you get to know more people and sell more homes, the opportunity will come to sell the higher-priced homes. Luxury agents start by selling $300,000 and $400,000 homes. After that, you may be selling homes for a half a million. Maybe you are specializing in serving the aging population. Perhaps they are downsizing, and you help them buy their $300,000 house. You do such an outstanding job that you turn around and snag the listing for the $650,000 home. You then hold open houses in that neighborhood every weekend for three months, and you start listing more houses on that street. Do not say no to the low-hanging fruit because you never know where it will lead. Plus, you're new. Check your ego at the door.

PRO TIP: Become the face of the community. If you are in an organization, become that organization's go-to real estate agent.

You're the real estate agent of that church; you're the real estate agent of that baseball team. You're their go-to agent.

As you start closing a couple of people within that organization or community, they will talk to the other people in that group. They will begin to tell people outside that community. Then people in that community are going to introduce you to more people outside of that community. That's the exponential power of this. And guess what, now you've got your core clientele, and it grows.

Week 2 Day 1 WORKSHEET
Part 1

Your assignment today is to discover who is your core client base.

Did you come from the tech industry? Do engineers trust you because you're great with numbers and an analytical thinker? Are you active in your church? Are you spending a lot of time on the sidelines at little league?

Ask yourself: who do you see once a week consistently? Who do you see multiple times a week? What kinds of people do you surround yourself with? What types of people do you wish to surround yourself with?

Think about your social life. When you go out and about, who are the people that you're going out with?

Identify the five people you spend the most time with?

1

2

3

4

5

Week 2 Day 1 WORKSHEET
Part 2

Think about the past month. What organizations or associations did you attend? Where did you spend most of your time?

Identify at least three organizations these three people are an active member of:

1

2

3

Now, write a list of ten people you wish you spent the most time with:

1

2

3

4

5

6

7

8

9

10

What are two action steps you can take this week to get in front of at least three of those people?

1

2

Who is someone that you believe knows more people than you?

Identify three ways you can build trust with this person.

1

2

3

Week 2 Day 2
DAY 7: PROSPECTING TO YOUR CORE

Yesterday, you identified your core client base, your inner core. Today, we will talk about prospecting to your inner core. If you are reading today's lesson, but you have not yet identified your core audience, return to yesterday's lesson. You need first to determine who you are going to market to before you can begin marketing.

We can spend unlimited marketing dollars. Listen, I spent so much money on marketing. Often on stuff that just never came back to serve me or my business. At first, I did not understand the philosophy of prospecting to my inner core. Thus, I wasted thousands of dollars.

I sent postcards here; I posted ads there. I wanted to market everywhere because I wanted to work with everyone. My ego got in the way.

I found myself getting leads here and there. So, here I was with an ego thinking, "it's working!"

I was selling houses, sure. I was getting buyers under contract, right on! I thought that my prospecting and marketing must be working. I was getting leads; I was closing leads. Here I was thinking, "This is it, guys. I have made it!"

But, here's the thing. The leads would come from all over the place. I wasn't tracking where my leads were coming from or who came from where. I was not reporting on what was yielding results because I didn't even know. I was simply moving a million miles a minute, patting myself on the back as I went.

This lead came from an open house in this neighborhood, this one came from an open house in this New Build community, this lead heard me speak at an event, and this lead heard me on the radio. This one saw an ad in a magazine but didn't even remember its name, so I never found out.

I wasn't focusing on prospecting to my inner core, so there was nothing to replicate. I continued to put money into marketing but had no idea what was working and what wasn't.

If you are just aimlessly throwing things out there, that is not prospecting. Throwing things out there to see what sticks is not smart. Prospecting is smart, yet it takes time.

Once I identified a community, my inner core, my audience, it became easier to bring in business. You will start by prospecting to your inner core and once you find what works, you can prospect to your outer core. When you prospect to your outer core, they become your inner core. This is an ongoing cycle.

Prospecting is not this crazy algorithm. Great prospecting is answering this one question: What is the best way to get in front of my inner core, one in which I don't have to spend a ton of money?

Yesterday, we talked about identifying your core client base. This is what we call the inner core. Then as they refer you to their friends and family, you start to meet their inner core. Eventually, your inner core grows and grows. Those people who were once in your outer core are brought to you from your inner core. Today, we will talk about strategically prospecting to your inner core so that your inner core hears about you consistently. Once they hear about you consistently and they understand the narrative that is written about you, that's when they comfortably and confidently start telling their inner core about you.

What is the narrative you want them to hear about you? That you are the expert real estate professional in their market!

Prospecting is about writing a story for the people to read. We will dive into this more today.

First, let me tell you about Matthew. Matt was a new agent. Personable and charming, Matt was what he calls a recovering attorney. Matt was not excited to door knock, but his mentor told him that was the best way to hit his big goals. As a long-time academic, Matt did as he was told. He memorized scripts and objection handles and door-knocked until his knuckles were blue.

But here's the thing, Matt was picking a random area to door knock. He's not a quitter, so he was doorknocking four days a week for months. There was little rhyme or reason to the neighborhood he was choosing. Do you know what happened? Matt was exhausted and only had three buyer clients and zero listings. He then picked up a part-time job at Trader Joe's, and you know what happened next.

> *Prospecting is about writing a story for the people to read.*

In that same summer, Caitlin started doorknocking because she was given the same advice as Matt. Caitlin's dream house was in a neighborhood twenty-five minutes from where she lives. Admittedly, she couldn't afford to live in this neighborhood, but if she could, this is where she would buy a house. It had easy access to the highway and conveniently located close to the best restaurants and her favorite grocery stores, likely the Trader Joe's Matt now works at. Caitlin would drive to this neighborhood, park her car and run in this neighborhood because she likes passing the nicely manicured lawns more than those in her own neighborhood.

When her mentor advised her to go door knock, she knew she would be doorknocking this neighborhood. That's what she did. In the morning, she would doorknock street after street. In the evenings, she memorized stats on the area. On the weekends, she'd hold open houses. The neighbors even started to recognize her. They would wave when they drove by as she put open house signs in the yard. One day, a grumpy old man approached her as she walked up a neighbor's long driveway.

"Excuse me. Are you the lady that knocked on my door a few weeks ago?" Mr. Martin asked with a scowl.

"Yes, sir. How can I help you?" she answered with a smile.

"Well, I thought about what you said, and I'm ready to sell my house."

Caitlin followed the man to his house. She was walking slowly beside him as he talked about how his home was the best in the neighborhood. He wanted to show her all the updates he had done on the house in the last twenty-seven years. She gracefully followed him room-by-room with her notepad in hand, taking notes as they went.

When it came time to list the house, Caitlin knocked on all the neighbors' doors, letting them know that she would be holding Mr. Martin's house open on Sunday. She had built a relationship with a few of them, so they were not surprised when they saw Caitlin's face at their door. However, they were surprised by the news of Mr. Martin listed his home with her. It turns out Mr. Martin's very own son is an agent.

When Caitlin later asked Mr. Martin why he chose to list his house with her and not his son, Mr. Martin replied saying, "My son never told me my house was worth $675,000."

He looked Caitlin straight in the eyes and said, "And he sure as hell would never walk in this heat knocking on doors."

That was the closest Caitlin would get to a compliment from Mr. Martin even when she sold his house in less than ten days for $39,000 over the asking price.

Then do you know what Caitlin did? She knocked on every door in the neighborhood to let them know: "I just listed a house in your neighborhood for $39,000 over asking price. It sold in less than ten days. If you or someone you know is looking to sell, here's my number."

Within the year, Caitlin had listed four homes in that neighborhood. She sent postcards with her face on them, saying, "No agent has sold more houses in this neighborhood than Caitlin." On the back, it said: "I'd love to sell your home. When you're ready, here's my number."

> *Do not go out there trying to be everything to everyone. Identify the groups that you work well with.*

One of the oldest terms in real estate is farming. It's incredible how it still works. Farming a community works. Look at Caitlin's story. Eventually, she was able to say, "I have sold more homes in this neighborhood in the last thirty days than anyone else." That postcard got some attention. Her phone started to ring.

The postcard didn't say, "I have sold more homes in this neighborhood in the last year than any other real estate agent."

Do you know why? Because that wasn't true yet.

Caitlin was just starting out. She was hungry and knew the power of farming. She was harnessing the power of writing her story.

"I am going to be the best real estate agent in this neighborhood," she told herself. Then she started telling her broker, her friends, and her peers. Next thing she knew, she was able to tell the homeowners in that very neighborhood, "I am the best real estate agent in this neighborhood. I just sold Mr. Martin's home next door and the large Tudor one street over."

Farming works. Writing your story works. People started to see Caitlin as the neighborhood expert because she began to see herself as one.

That's the story she wrote for others. She reverse-engineered farming by knowing her core client base. She didn't waste her time like Matt with neighborhoods on the other side of town or a community she didn't personally love.

People listed and bought with Caitlin because she sold the neighborhood and the community with ease. You could genuinely tell that she wanted to live there because she did. And eventually, she did. Within three years of selling Mr. Martin's home, Caitlin bought the house next door.

Write the story you want others to hear. Caitlin not only wrote her story, but also she had proof. Look, I sold this house two days ago. Listen to this: I sold four homes in this very neighborhood this year alone.

Eventually, Caitlin's inner core brought her initial sales. Then, those people brought her more sales. She no longer needed to doorknock three days a week; neighbors started telling neighbors to use their real estate agent, Caitlin. Caitlin's name and face were recognizable in the

The Psychology of Real Estate Sales | 75

neighborhood because they saw her 'For Sale' signs every month and her open house signs nearly every week.

Now, those sales can bring you more sales because they're now in your inner core. Tell a story.

But it had to start from somewhere. Maybe you can't say that you have sold more homes in this particular neighborhood. That's alright. Can you say that "my listings, on average, sell in seven days, typically above asking price?" There is always a story to tell. It is your job to find out what that story is.

Over time you will start to see a story emerge. Once it does, tell these stories. It will never work unless you tell the story. When you start telling your own story, you sell yourself. But you have to identify that core, you must identify the audience for your story.

The next step, very simple. You're going to sell more homes, because people are going to hear your story. They're going to want to be a part of your story. That's what happened to Caitlin. Don't you see that?

She began to add people to her inner core, her prospecting core. Then, as she sold more homes, she had more stories to tell.

No one wants to work with somebody that doesn't have a story.

You must first identify the core audience. Next, discover what you can say. When you can put your story in writing, that's when you can start to use it. Instead of just hoping that the prospects come to you, bring the story to them.

Then after time, the story tells itself. That story is then your credibility, you guys. Prospecting is exploiting your credibility. No one wants to work with somebody that doesn't have a story. They want to work with someone great; they want to work with a professional. So, now prospect to that core and begin to tell your story.

Do not go out there, trying to be everything to everyone. Identify your inner core. For Caitlin, it was personal. She loved that neighborhood. For you, it may be more client based than the area. Maybe you bode well with younger clients, so you doorknock in the up-and-coming neighborhood close to downtown or you network at events targeted at young professionals.

People want a reason to work with you. It would be best if you told them the story. Give them the motivation to do so. That is prospecting to your inner core.

Who do you want to be? Matt or Caitlin?

Week 2 Day 2 WORKSHEET

If you look deep into your sales, there's always a story to tell. Write out all the transactions you have closed in the last six months.

Note: If this isn't a living document somewhere, this is a problem. You do not need to have this information memorized, although it's ideal if you do. You must have this information readily available. It should be the statistics you use when you go to a listing appointment. It should be on your social media profiles and your website. If you aren't tracking your sales, are you even running a business?

Now take five to ten minutes to connect common themes in your sales. Take a moment to think about your sales and clients right now. Can you tell a story about them? I bet you can.

There's always a story to tell.

What is that story?

Next, you will take that story and put it in the prospecting. Identify three ways you will tell your story.

1

2

3

Whether you're door knocking, sending flyers or postcards, you will use this story in a way to market yourself to your core client base. Whether you're targeting a certain area in town or a particular audience on social media, you will take the audience you identified yesterday and begin to market to them. Maybe you are cold calling? No one uses a phone anymore. Now, identify two ways you will prospect for new leads.

1

2

Week 2 Day 3

DAY 8: IDENTIFYING YOUR NICHE. THE NICHE WILL FIND YOU.

Last week, you identified your strengths, your weaknesses, and your functionality. This week, you have identified your inner core. Then we zeroed in on the story you will tell your clients and potential clients to better prospect. Today, we are identifying your niche.

The riches are in the niches.

Your niche will find you. I love this topic because it's so relatable to everybody. I don't care if you're in real estate or retail; if you're an engineer, a doctor, a dentist, or an educator. It doesn't matter what profession you're in. At some point in your career, your niche will find you. Often you don't find your niche; it finds you.

When you think about your career right now—where you are today, what have you just kind of fallen into? I didn't expect to be here two years ago. But yet, here I am. I'm servicing all of these clients because this niche found me.

Today, you will identify your niche, so we can turn around and exploit the niche. We will continue to market you better, and in turn, you will be prospecting better.

Jono lives in California. He grew up in Redondo Beach. As a realtor, he has sold a lot of beach homes. Guess what? Jono's niche is that he is the California beach real estate expert. It's that simple.

Admittedly, that wasn't what Jono set out to do as an agent. Over time, he examined his sales and exclaimed, "Wow. Thirteen of the last thirty homes I sold have been beachfront property."

And guess what, guys? Beachfront properties aren't cheap. So, it became pretty clear to Jono that he would write his story to be the California beach real estate expert, and he did. Now, fast forward two years, and thirty of his last forty listings were beachfront properties. He hired a marketing expert who used Google Ads to target his core client base: people looking to buy on the beach in these six zip codes. He also used that same marketing expert to send postcards in those same six zip codes.

You may be sitting in Indianapolis, thinking, "what on earth is my niche?"

Pay attention to your numbers and your sales. Then, you may start saying, "for whatever reason, I'm selling a lot of homes in this zip code."

First, the numbers show you the story. Next, you tell your story.

For example, I am the number one agent in the zip code 85255. I've sold more homes in the last six months than any other real estate agent.

Maybe another agent has sold more houses in that particular zip code in the last year, so we don't tell that story. But we tell the story about the six months.

Find the numbers in your sales. This community, this area, or this organization. I'm the guy; I'm the go-to guy to sell your house.

If you start to see a trend in your sales, exploit that. Bridget, in my office, noticed a lot of her clients were divorced. She brought this up in her coaching call with her coach. You know what he said to her?

"Great! Why don't you immediately schedule lunches with Divorce Attorneys in your town? Tell your clients' stories and the top-notch service you provide them—the win-win scenarios you have created as their top agent. Then, tell the success stories you will create with them by working with their clients. Ask how you can work together because you want to send him more business."

Bridget found her core client base. She had a story to tell. Now that she has identified this niche, she is using it to grow her book of business.

If you notice that for some reason, you're doing a lot of business within this realm, ask yourself: What can I do to get more of it? What can I do to be the go-to real estate agent for people in this area, this zip code, this organization, or this community?

If you're reading this, then you already have a niche. You simply haven't worked on it.

Maybe you don't have a niche yet. Don't worry, it'll come. But you must pay attention and look for it. Once you see a pattern, do not ignore it. Bridget admittedly didn't seek out working with divorcees, it merely happened that way. And for Laura, too.

Laura's husband, Brandan, is a doctor. Their core friend group are friends he met in medical school. Laura hangs out with spouses of doctors, other doctors and nurses, and those who work at the hospital. Because of this, Laura sells condos and houses to lots of doctors.

Meanwhile, she is trying to sell houses to all the moms in her book club. Wake up, Laura. Don't you see that 70% of your clients are doctors?

Once she notices this, what should she do? Exploit it as best she can.

How? Since they're all probably following you on social media, how about you post about selling another great home to another great doctor.

Laura should be posting about it continuously. "Doctors in the house! Sold this gorgeous Victorian to Mr. and Dr. Bowles."

Are you exploiting it? Are you doing it the right way? The only way you can exploit your niche is if you identify it.

When you post that you are so happy to help a client of an organization and love working with this organization, don't you think people in the organization will see that?

Laura's clients start telling their colleagues, and the next thing she knows, she has sold a house to nearly every doctor and nurse in Brandan's unit.

Whatever your niche is. Start talking about it. I'm the king of 85255. I'm the master of this Boulevard. I'm the king of beach sales. I'm the queen of starting your next chapter. Talk about it.

I talked about being a secret agent. Don't. Share what your niche is. Tell everyone you can.

Your niches ultimately find you.

You will quickly become known as the expert in your niche. Then, people start coming to you for their real estate needs. But something else happens. Maybe another niche opens up. Because you did such a great job here, people over there want to work with you, too. Laura started out serving the other doctor's in Brandan's unit. Now, it's the nurses. Next thing, she is helping the paramedics.

Now, you found yourself in this place where your inner core is growing organically. You are gaining credibility quickly inside your community because you are sharing it with everyone. They see that you have been listing a lot of new construction homes later. You have sold more than 100 New Build Homes for this Builder and guess what? Because you did an excellent job for that Builder, now this other Builder is knocking on your door. Well, guess who the new construction King is?

PRO TIP: You don't have to be a VA loan specialist or even know one like Deena. You don't have to be selling beach homes like Jono.

You don't need to go to church or have kids in school to find your core client base. Think creatively.

I know an agent, Mikaela, who is a dog-friendly real estate agent. That's right. Dog-friendly agent is her niche. Mikaela has a large dog crate in the back of her Jeep wrangler, which is also well equipped with dog treats. Mikaela offers a downloadable PDF with a map of the best dog parks in town. She has also partnered with a trustworthy dog walker in the city to provide his dog walking services to her clients when they have a schedule showing.

You can host a meetup on a topic you feel closely tied to, like helping divorced families sell their homes. You partner with a divorce attorney to feed you leads. Maybe you help single twenty-something buy condos downtown. Perhaps, you help dog lovers find dog-friendly homes for their furry friends. Whatever you end up doing, do it well.

I have always enjoyed selling New Construction. For me, I always knew it would be my niche.

When I was in college, I had an internship with one of the country's largest New Home Builders. Sean was the best boss I have ever had. I also had an incredible mentor, Mike. He was the top Sales Director at the time. I built great relationships with both Mike and Sean. I would shadow them as much I could. I learned more about selling homes in that summer than I could have ever guessed.

I had been an intern with them all summer and was getting ready to go back to college for my last year at Central Michigan University. Jeff, the Division President at the time, called me into his office. Jeff sat there with Mike and Sean. They told me about a neighborhood of new builds on the Eastside of Detroit. They told me that if I could sell out the community before I went back to school in two months, I would have a full-time position with the company when I graduated. If I could do that, I wouldn't even have to interview. The job was mine.

I sold six houses in nine days.

I am so thankful for my time at that company. From the training to the relationships, the time I spent at the company is how I got to where I am today. Mike, Sean, and Jeff, along with my friend Lance, were instrumental in getting me to where I am today.

Your niche may not be selling new construction, working with doctors, divorcees, or listing beachfront properties. You need to find out your niche if you want to be wildly successful in this business.

A few days ago, we identified your core customer base. These are the people you're going to go after to build your inner core. If you do that successfully, your niche will inevitably come.

Are you Laura marketing to her mom group when she is already selling to the doctor community? You may be marketing here, but selling there. That's okay! Pivot.

Don't ever be afraid to turn your focus. If it's successful and working, look at how you can build on that success. Exploit that niche.

Week Day 2 (Day 8) WORKSHEET

What is your niche?

If it is still not clear to you, skip to question five. And do not worry. You can come back to this exercise as it becomes more clear.

Now, you have identified your niche, are you exploiting that? Circle yes or no.

If yes, list three ways you feel you are exploiting your niche.

If not, write three possible ways you can start exploiting your niche.

1

2

3

Identify four ways you are marketing to your niche?

1

2

3

4

Lastly, identify four ways your niche could encompass or develop into another niche.

1

2

3

4

Identify five areas or niches that you would enjoy if they were your niche.

1

2

3

4

5

Week 2 Day 4
DAY 9: BE AN INFORMATION JUNKIE

Do you have a friend who is always up-to-date on the latest technology or a friend who hears about current events before anyone else? Some calls these people information junkies. Now, you may be wondering how on earth could being an information junkie relate to being a great real estate agent and excelling at real estate sales? Today, I will tell you how becoming an information junkie will bring you more sales than you can ever imagine.

Information gathering is so unbelievably critical to growing your sales business. The information I am talking about is information related to your clients. The more you know about your clients, the more you can suddenly get back in front of them.

Remember, I told you that I spend a lot of time in front of industry leaders. My social circle is full of mortgage brokers, lenders, title representation, and home builders. I am in front of them, so they send me referrals because I am top of their minds.

Today, I will show you what it means to be in front of your clients, even when they aren't your immediate social circle. But first, I want to talk about random acts of kindness.

We have all heard of random acts of kindness. It is something we learn about in school. Hopefully, it is something that we practice in our day-to-day lives, too. I am here to tell you that random acts of kindness will transform your business. It may even change you as a person.

Random acts of kindness tend to mold you into being an exceptional person, both professionally and personally. Let me tell you something, being better at the latter is more important. Being an extraordinary person is not only good for you and the people around you. It is good for business. When people like you as a person, they're going to trust you. When someone trusts you, they will allow you to sell their $1M home; they will refer you to their parents and their first-graders teacher. People do not do business with people they do not trust.

When people trust you and like you, they're going to continue to come back to you. The goal in real estate is to get them to like you, so they buy and list with you.

What do random acts of kindness have to do with being an information junkie?

Performing random acts of kindness gets easier as you gather more information on your clients.

Pay attention and gather information.

Imagine that you're sitting at lunch with your friends celebrating your birthday, and your phone buzzes. You assume it's your brother or your mom or maybe your best friend that lives across the country.

You stop what you're doing, and to your surprise, you read a text from your real estate agent—me, Jason. You bought your house three years ago. You haven't talked to me in months, yet here I am, sending you a personalized text from my personal cell phone number.

"Happy Birthday, buddy. It's been a while. I hope you're doing well and celebrating with a bottle of your favorite whiskey."

First, how did Jason 1) know it was my birthday? And 2) how did he remember that I love whiskey? A bit of a whiskey connoisseur, if I say so myself.

My client is going to remember me and how thoughtful I was. Then, the next time someone is talking about real estate, they will be sure to mention me and recommend me. If their buddies or coworkers ever start talking about real estate, my name is top of mind. "Jason is the best."

A survey in 2017 found that more than 65% of clients do not remember their real estate agent's name just one year after using them to buy or sell a house. Want your clients to remember you? It's not as easy to just do a better job than those agents. Nope. Another survey found that more than 60% of people surveyed would use their real estate agent. The problem isn't the level of service you did or didn't provide to them during the sale. The problem is that you have not stayed in front of them ever since.

That's where you make a difference. You not only remember to text your past client on his birthday. You have to remember to text people you haven't even worked with yet. That's right. You should be staying in front of people you want to work with and those you are prospecting. Remember that listing you didn't get a few months back? You left the listing appointment and immediately wrote down that the husband's home office was decked out in Boston Red Socks memorabilia. So, when the Red Socks won Game 2 in 2018. You sent him a quick text, "Hey, that was incredible. It's Jason. Anyway, I just wanted to say congrats. Hoping they pull it off. Talk soon."

Keep it nice and short. A reminder that: hey, I'm here, and I'm paying attention.

In order to do this well, I am regularly paying attention to my clients. The more information we know about our clients and our prospects, the more we can do these random reach outs.

Make these reach outs a part of your weekly routine. If routine, organization, and structure are a struggle for you, put this on your calendar.

I told you on day one that organization was my biggest weakness. There was little structure to my day when I first got into real estate. Now? I not only thrive on structure, but also I am incredibly organized.

Currently, my days are structured. These client reach outs are a part of my weekly schedule. At first, they were on my calendar because, I admit, I would forget. Now, I do it naturally. I don't need to be reminded. I trained my mind to be looking for things that I could later reach out to a client and bring up. Now, it comes easily. The prospect's home office tells me that he's a Red Socks fan, I write it down. That client is always posting on social media about expensive whiskeys and posting from his favorite whiskey bar in town. I write it down.

You know what this did? This made me a better listener. I now don't sit there thinking of what I am going to say next. I am intentionally listening to my clients. I am looking for things to capture. I am deliberately looking for tidbits of information that I can use later to reach out to them randomly.

Not every agent does this. Heck, very little do. Whether it is a text, an email, a comment on social media, or a handwritten message, these random messages are more powerful than sending somebody a gift.

"I just randomly reached out and wanted to tell you, I hope you're doing well."

Well, guess what? That person likes you now. Maybe they liked you before. But now, they like you even more. It is important to note that now they also remember you; you're currently at the top of their mind. So, when they are at a dinner party with their wife's friends, someone mentions moving. Guess who's name gets mentioned?

Being top of mind is crucial in real estate, when more than half of clients will forget your name. You have to fight to stay remembered.

There is nothing monumental about sending a birthday text; I get that. I'm not saying that telling a past client happy birthday is earth-shattering. But guess what happens when you do it, and none of the other agents do?

Or better yet, watch what can happen when you continue to be an information junkie.

Kendra adds all of her clients on social media. Kendra isn't the best at posting or social media marketing, but she is a whizz at information gathering. Kendra follows an old coworker on Instagram and sends them a direct message congratulating them on having a baby.

Don't you think that goes a long way? Because I'll bet you their agent didn't send that text or Instagram direct message. No, 90% of the time, agents do not send that message. Well, guess who their new agent is? Kendra.

I cannot tell you how many hours and hours and hours of random acts of kindness I have thrown out there. I wouldn't even be able to begin to describe how much it has paid back.

Pay attention and gather information. Stay in front of both your clients and prospective clients. Make it clear that you see what's happening in their lives and that you care. When we know the information, we can easily reach out to them. Look at what Kendra was easily able to do. It's because she had the information readily available to her. She set herself up for success by following her clients and potential clients on social media, and taking the time to gather information.

Then she reaches out. Kendra could not reach out if she didn't have this system in place.

If you do this correctly, when people think of real estate, they think of you. But if you don't have the information and you're not paying attention, they can't think of you because they have forgotten about you.

Even if you had a flawless transaction, it almost doesn't even matter that you found them their dream home or that you got them $20,000 over asking or a quick close. If you don't stay in front of them, they will forget you.

Also, this is key: stop talking about the home and start talking about them. I don't want you to talk about real estate. I want you to talk about them. The real estate will follow.

At this stage, they should already know you're a real estate agent because you're not a secret agent, right? So, there's no need to be talking about real estate. Instead, talk about them. People love talking about themselves. Everyone loves feeling seen and being heard. Send them a quick text: "Hey, did your son win the championship last week? … Yeah, I saw that Mikey was playing in a soccer championship on Sunday. Did they win? They did win? Great! That's awesome. Tell them, Congratulations."

They like you. Check. (possible image of checkmark)

You're now top of mind. Check. (possible image of checkmark)

You didn't even talk about real estate, a home, or the market. Instead, you showed them that you are paying attention to them.

You mean to tell me that I can be crazy successful in this business by paying attention to people and randomly reaching out to them to talk about anything other than real estate?

Yes, basically. There you go. From there, you are going to offer concierge-level customer service and handle their transaction like a professional. But first and foremost, you're going to gather information, pay attention and reach out to them.

Frankly, you will not even get the chance to handle their transaction if you're not doing these things. People want to work with people they like and people they trust. Build trust and get them to like you by becoming an information gatherer.

Week 2 Day 4 WORKSHEET

Identify eight people you can reach out to in the next eight days.

1

2

3

4

5

6

7

8

I don't expect you to do this every day for the rest of the year. However, do this for the next eight days to practice. It will train you to gather information. You will begin to look for things in conversations or on their social media profiles. Then from there, schedule it in once a week.

Identify one or two people in your life that are already good at this. They always seem to reach out randomly or remember important events in your life. What are their names?

1

2

How do they make you feel?

Week 2 Day 5

DAY 10: CELEBRATE YOUR CLIENTS—NOT THE SALE

This week has been all about identifying your inner core and outer core. I shared how prospecting to your outer core will start to bring those clients into your inner core. We identified your niche and how you would bring in more clients from your outer core into your inner core.

Yesterday, we talked about the power of random acts of kindness and how being an information junkie would make those kind acts easier. You now understand the importance of knowing who your ideal client is and your niche. You will now be looking for information to gather based on your inner core. When you have the information handy, it becomes easier to reach out to our clients and stay top of mind.

Today, I want to talk about celebrating your clients.

People notice when you put your clients first. They see that you are talking about them and their wins, instead of your own.

Everyone sees if you are continually puffing up your chest, talking about being #1. Suppose your marketing is continuously saying: I am the best in my market, #1 in my city, selling 43 homes this year, and closing $3M this month.

We've talked about prospecting and what we need to do to get more people into our inner core. Later on in our journey together, I will share how to become your best promoter. But, let me be clear here: becoming your best promoter is not bragging about yourself and your accomplishments. It is quite the opposite. It is about bragging about your clients and their successes—not yours.

I had a client a few years ago who got a promotion at work. I was lucky enough to be one of the many phone calls he made that week. He was alerting me of the promotion. Why? Because he could now afford to move his family of five into the neighborhood of his liking.

> *"I discovered a long time ago that if I helped enough people get what they wanted, I would always get what I wanted and I would never have to worry."*
>
> *– Tony Robbins*

I was so excited for him and I told the world about it, too. "I'm so proud of my client he got a great promotion. And because he got his great promotion, he was able to move his family into this extraordinary property that I was fortunate enough to be a part of."

Don't you see? It is not about bragging about yourself. Ever. It is always about your clients. Always focus on them and celebrate them. It is not about you.

You will begin to build momentum around this, and that will lead you to sell more. When you are selling more homes, you will naturally start to work with more people. In turn, more people are paying attention to you.

As more people start to tune into you and pay attention to what you're doing and saying, you must remember not to get in your own way. Do not let your ego get in the way of your success. You're only successful because people have allowed you to be successful. You would have never hit $20M in sales if your clients did not allow you to act as their agent. You would have never sold seventeen homes this quarter if your clients did not allow you to list their homes.

I shared yesterday that when people like you, they will work with you. The likability factor in this business is so critical. Thus, one of the most remarkable traits out there is humility. We spoke about your ego getting in your way in week one. As you grow your real estate business, it will become harder to set your ego aside.

"Look at me."

Look how many houses I sold. Look how many listings I won. Stop that. Stop making this all about you. It is never about you.

> *One of the most remarkable traits out there is humility.*

If humility does not come naturally to you, find someone to hold you accountable. Your family, your closest friend, or a teammate can hold you accountable. If you have started to hire out your marketing, make sure your marketing coordinator knows to check you. Your message is so important, especially as you grow because more people are watching. As you become more successful, more people are looking for ways not to like you. As I've said, when people like you, they will trust you, and they will choose to work with you. One easy way to screw this is up is by letting your ego get in the way.

I admire those who praise others before they praise themselves. They effortlessly make it about other people; they don't make it about them.

As you add more and more clients to your book of business, they have to see that you're celebrating them and their successes over yours.

Focus on celebrating your clients. Allow your social media feed, marketing materials, and website to share their wins. When you do this well, and you do this often, it is okay to share something about yourself every once in a while. It won't come off as self-absorbent because every other post is about your clients.

> *As you add more and more clients to your book of business, they have to see that you're celebrating them and their successes over yours.*

Now, each month, I can post about a small win that I had. When I close $3 million this month, I can post about that on our company Facebook page without anyone questioning my intentions and my humility. Every other post is about my clients and their wins. Today, I can post about my win without getting any slack from anyone.

Instead, people likely think, "Wow, Jason is the go-to guy for real estate. His team is crushing it."

For me, it is never, "Hey, look at my cars! Check out my planes."

No. Stop that.

My successes come from my clients' successes. Plain and simple. I never forget that no matter how big I get, how big the team grows, and how many sales we close.

When we hit $1.5 Billion in annual sales, you better believe I was celebrating our clients. Everyone on my team was celebrating how grateful we are that you got a chance to help that many clients. Whether it was a client buying their first home, or a client selling their family home, we celebrated them as if they were our only client. For that day, and for always, it is about them.

Later in the book, we will talk more about building your brand. Today, I want to focus on building habits that promote humility. First, you know it is not about you, right? It's always about them. Put your clients first; without your clients, you're out of business.

I have built an exceptional business. My business makes more than a billion dollars a year. You know what, I would have none of this without my clients. Yes, other things have made this business possible, like systems and processes. But without the clients, I'm out of business.

And your business is not different.

Week 2 Day 5 WORKSHEET

Identify five past clients you can celebrate.

1

2

3

4

5

Make your marketing about them. What are five ways you can celebrate the five clients above?

1

2

3

4

5

Now, review your marketing from the past three months.

Identify three to five times when your marketing language could be changed to focus more on your clients.

1

2

3

4

5

Identify three to five times when your marketing language did a great job of celebrating your clients.

1

2

3

4

5

Week 3 Day 1

DAY 11: STICK WITH YOUR SCHEDULE AND BUILD A PLAN

This week is our preparation series. As a real estate professional, you need to prepare for the transaction and the questions your clients will have. Plus, you must also plan for the year ahead and the business you want.

Today, I am talking about your schedule because your schedule and how much you keep to that schedule are a crucial metric of your success. If you are not disciplined enough to stick to your own schedule, then you'll never be disciplined enough to build a scalable business. You certainly won't become a multi-millionaire; I promise you that.

As a real estate agent, you must stick to a schedule; your business cannot grow if your schedule is scattered. You will never make it to Level Five. I will tell you what Level Five means in Week Eight.

Sticking to your schedule is crucial to the success of your business. Now, this does not mean you cannot pivot, because, of course, your schedule will change. As a real estate agent, flexibility is critical. However, your schedule and your plans should not haphazardly change because you are not disciplined. If your schedule is thrown off every time a buyer calls you, you have a problem. A scalable business cannot operate in this manner.

Sticking to your schedule sounds simple, yet few people do it. It's crazy to me that real estate agents lay out a plan, but then abandon it when something shiny comes along. Clients will call you. Your phone will ring. Showings will change and transactions will fall through. How you react when it happens will be the difference between a scalable business and a dead-end job.

Once a quarter, Devin lays out a fundamental process; this is his plan of attack. He starts to pat himself on the back as he follows the plan for two to three weeks. Then, by week four, Devin is back to golfing whenever his friends invite him. He skipped prospecting last week because he had three listing appointments. He didn't think he had time for more. Devin did not cold call expired listings this week, even though it is in his plan, because instead he was posting on social media.

Devin is not the only one. I have heard agents say so many times, "Yeah, but I got busy," and "I was doing this, but then this happened."

> *Your phone will ring. How you react when it happens will be the difference between a scalable business and a dead-end job.*

It's okay if schedules shift, but the fundamental basics of the schedule cannot change. If you truly are "too busy" to prospect, that's a sign it is time to hire.

As you grow, it will become apparent that it doesn't have to be you doing all the tasks that need to get done to make each translation a smooth and flawless experience for the client. Someone else can handle these tasks.

Before we talk about the schedule of the team, let's talk about you. In Week One, you discovered what you excel at by identifying your strengths. Think about your strengths as you divide tasks. If you are terrible at writing marketing emails, that task should not continue to belong to you once you hire someone.

"But Jason, how can that person write an email if it comes from me."

Listen up, take your ego and step aside.

> *The fundamental basics of the schedule cannot change.*

If you want to grow a scalable business, you need to offload tasks onto other people you trust. Realize that you didn't know how to do half the things you now know how to do. Someone on your team can write your emails for you. Someone on your team can schedule inspections for you. Someone on your team can design and print listing packets for you. Believe it or not, someone can do all of these tasks better than you.

In Week One, you also identified your functionality. By now, you are planning your day around the times that you are at your best. If you are not sharp before 9:00 a.m., do not schedule listing appointments before 9:00 a.m. It is that simple.

"But, Jason, they asked if I could come at 9:00 a.m."

Tell them no. Schedule tasks on your calendar that you excel in and schedule those tasks when you function your best. In Week Two, we identified your inner core and your niche. You now know who you are going after and why. Lay down the plan of attack. Whether you are door knocking, cold calling, holding open houses, whatever it is, put it in the calendar. Stick to your schedule, and you—and your business—will grow. Skip it and see what happens.

Skip to Part 1 in the workbook.

You should have the ultimate goal of being on autopilot when it comes to your business. Your schedule dictates what you do, and before you know it, you are on autopilot. You can look at your business and think, "Wow. Things are getting easier. I have more closings pending this month than last month. I have more closed volume year to date than I did last year."

Yes. That's the point. If you're disciplined enough with your own schedule, your business will grow. Plus, everyone on your team does this, too.

When your team is growing, you can serve more clients, sell more houses and make more money.

Your assistant, buyers' agents, marketing person, listing coordinator, and processor all stick to their schedule. They do it at the same time. If you talk to anybody in my company, in any department, they do the same thing. Every day, every week, every month like clockwork, it's static, it does not move.

Every Tuesday, my marketing coordinator does 'x'. Every Wednesday, my transaction coordinator does 'y'. Every Thursday, my buyers' agents do 'z'. On Fridays, they wrap the week up with these tasks. It's the same process for each person on my team. It must be the same for you as a real estate professional.

Your job as the Team Lead is to make a plan. The plan revolves around the following things:

Marketing

Process

System

Execution

Sales

Think through each aspect of your business. It is often easier to create a plan by looking at each step of the transaction.

As you add more people within your organization, the attack plan can grow because you can add more responsibility to others' plates. Until then, you will handle each step. Do not overload yourself. Stick to the basics.

Before you dish out responsibilities, create a clear, strategic plan for your employees. Your employees want to know what your expectations are so they can meet them. No one starts day one thinking, "I can't wait to disappoint my boss today." Set them up for success by having a plan laid out for them. Remember that your new assistant will not be able to input listings into the MLS on day one, even if they have done it for another agent before. They have never done it for you before, so show them how you want it done every time.

Show your employees the plan and how to execute it. No matter who you're hiring within your organization, this needs to happen every time. Tell them that this is your roadmap to success and how you need them to be successful.

Don't let your employees come to work and just work on things. That won't work. It won't work for you; it won't work for your employees. It sure as hell won't work for your clients as you grow and scale your business.

Once they master that process, you can then start adding things. This works so well when you build a plan that somebody can literally look at and say, 'Oh, that's how I do that, I got it."

Then your employee does it three or four times. Eventually, they won't have to look at the plan each time, but they will have to reference it when they get started. And that's on you.

This is an excellent problem to have. If you're crafting roadmaps for other people's successes, you're growing. When your team is growing, you can serve more clients, sell more houses, and make more money.

But you can't create scalability and efficiencies in the mindset of, "am I doing this, right? I don't really know what to do."

If you have a team and you're getting upset that they didn't do it right, but you didn't train them, the problem starts with you.

When you stick to something, it becomes a habit. Once the method feels manageable, and transactions are running smoothly, you can add a few more things.

I challenge you this week to consider everything going on in your world. Take a breath. If you are going about your week with little notice of your schedule, you're going to burnout or allow things to fall through the cracks. If serving your clients is your number one priority, start by sticking to a schedule.

Week 3 Day 1 WORKSHEET
Part 1

Identify at least two tasks you are going to put on the calendar to expose your brand further.

1

2

Identify at least two tasks you are going to put on the calendar to ensure you stay relevant.

1

2

Identify at least two tasks you will put on the calendar to ensure you become more efficient.

1

2

Identify at least two tasks you will put on the calendar to ensure that you train your team members better. Skip this if you have not yet hired someone.

1

2

Week 3 Day 1 WORKSHEET
Part 2

Think about your current business and where you want to be. What do you need to do on a daily, weekly, and monthly basis?

Identify three tasks that need to happen every month to be successful.

1

2

3

Identify three tasks that need to happen every week to be successful.

1

2

3

Identify three tasks that need to happen every day to be successful.

1

2

3

Now, get out your calendar and plug-in those tasks. When are you going to complete the tasks listed above?

Week 3 Day 2
DAY 12: CREATE A FUNDAMENTAL PROCESS

Yesterday, you looked at your schedule. Some of you may have realized that you don't have a clear plan or schedule. You may be an agent who is waking up each morning and begins checking off a To-Do List but quickly abandons it as you bring on more listings.

If this is how you conduct your business, what happens if you have four listings this month? Do you notice that you are prospecting less? more? or the same amount?

If you are putting prospecting on hold to cater to your current listings, what happens two months from now? Will you have four listings in three months if you press pause on prospecting this month?

No, you won't.

Real estate sales seem to be like this for a lot of agents. I call it 'Peaks and Valleys.' One month you're feeling highly motivated. You are cold calling For Sale By Owners (FSBOs) and regularly attending listings presentations, and the next month, you're feeling great because you have more listings than you've ever had before. The month after that, you're celebrating because you closed those listings, and you're getting paid. It feels good when the checks start to come in.

Then, you hit a valley. You have no listing appointments scheduled; you have no clients in the pipeline. That's because the moment you got a few listing appointments, you stopped cold calling. This is a classic case of Peaks and Valleys.

Do not do this to yourself. Do not do this to your business. If you are experiencing this, your business is not scalable.

Today, we're going to get into creating a fundamental process tailored around preparation.

Once we have the roadmap, everything gets better.

An agent, who had been in the business for two years, walks into my office. He was the classic example of Peaks and Valleys. He was closing $5-7M a year and feeling pretty proud of himself. Here I was, not impressed.

He came into my office to ask me a question about a somewhat tricky seller. I shocked him by asking this: If you were to get nine listings today, could you manage that?

He was caught off guard and said, "Well, I think so?"

He was not quite sure what to make of my question. He took a moment to regroup, and then sheepishly responded, "Well, probably not."

"You have been in the business for two years now. Why have you not been preparing to take on more business?" I asked him. "If the goal is always to bring in business, why are you not prepared for it?"

His silence told me everything I needed to know, so I continued, "Well, I'll tell you what happens, you get busy. You find ways to make excuses for not building a fundamental process and a plan."

He began to defend himself, "Jason, I am so busy as it…"

"Everyone's busy," I interrupted.

I told him what I am about to say to you: If you're not creating a fundamental process, you will never make it in this business.

Isn't the goal to get as many listings as you can? First, you need to set up your business in a way that you can handle that many listings and more.

If you are not functioning at a high level, you're only running around selling homes here and there.

I witness agents experiencing these peaks and valleys far too often. They're scatterbrained. Until you set up your business in a fundamental way, you will, also.

You know in the back of your mind that you are not doing this the right way. "Why do I always feel like I am doing everything?" and "Why is every transaction different?"

In reality, every transaction is the same. It feels that every transaction is different only because you haven't built a process. Once we have the roadmap, everything gets better.

At this point, you now know:

Your strengths

The weaknesses you are working on improving

Your functionality—when you work at your best

Who your ideal customer is—your inner core

Your niche

How to gather information on your clients

How to prospect

Your schedule and how to stick to it

Today, you are going to begin creating a fundamental process for your transactions. Yes, in real estate, not every listing is the same, and not every buyer transaction is the same. However, the stages of the transactions are the same. As the lead agent, your job is to ensure a fundamental process—the roadmap is built and followed.

> *Once the foundation of success is laid out, we have to make sure that the process works.*

From inquiry to close, there is a path a buyer follows each time. If you haven't already, you will recognize through this exercise that the real estate transaction stays the same nearly every time. While every client is different, the stages of the transaction remain the same. Ultimately, the steps don't change. I believe we're in the most fantastic industry you can be in because it is so scalable. Real estate agents are so lucky because we can duplicate and create scalability so easily. Whether it's a $100,000 contract, or a $10 Million contract, they all follow the same process.

Every time you order an inspection, you write the same email:

"Hey, Mr. Inspector, I just got a new deal. The address is _____. The clients' names are _____. The square footage is _____ square feet, and we are looking to get into the property by _____."

Then you write another email:

"Oh, hey, escrow, we just opened escrow. And these are the details of the transaction."

> *If you're not creating a fundamental process, you will never make it in this business.*

Suppose you do not already have a templated email for this. Stop what you're doing and create one now. Why are you recreating an email that's the same information? Create a system around this, including templated emails and a process. Better yet, create a checklist. I want everything in your life and your business to be more straightforward. An email should be a few clicks of a button and sent. Every time we start a new transaction, we have the same people we have to reach out to. Make this process simple, and next time you ask yourself, "If I were to get nine listings today, could I manage that?" It will always be a resounding, yes!

The goal is to get to a place where deals are just coming in, and other people are managing them for you. Your job is only to be there in case something goes haywire. You're the Rainmaker. You're bringing the deals in, and then your team is handling the transaction from there.

When you take the time to build this fundamental process, you'll realize it's actually not that hard. It's just a bunch of checklist items, right?

Then you can look at your team and say, "Here are my checklist items, and here are your checklist items."

Once the foundation of success is laid out, we have to make sure that the process works. As a new agent or a solo agent, you can create an internal process for everything. Your process is everything.

Every transaction is the same. It feels that every transaction is different only because you haven't built a process.

Create your process now because eventually, you are handing a checklist to a transaction coordinator and, ultimately, a buyers agent. You read in Week One that you're not Superman. You cannot, nor should you, do everything. If you are still running lockboxes to every listing, you have a problem. No real estate agent can work with every moving piece of the puzzle. You are a Rainmaker, building a scalable business. You are creating a machine. Now, you can scale.

You cannot scale if there's no fundamental process to your business. In today's worksheet, you will begin to create a fundamental process so you and your business can become a machine. If you have an opportunity to take on nine listings tomorrow and you are too scared to do that? You don't have a process. Now, let's build your process.

Week 3 Day 2 WORKSHEET

Could you manage nine listings today right now? Yes or No.

What are you busy with? List ten things that you feel make you busy.

1

2

3

4

5

6

7

8

9

10

During a transaction, how many people do you have to communicate with? Think about repair items, the lender, the other agent, escrow, title, etc. Identify every person you speak to during a transaction.

Hint: you don't need to talk to those people; somebody else can do that for you.

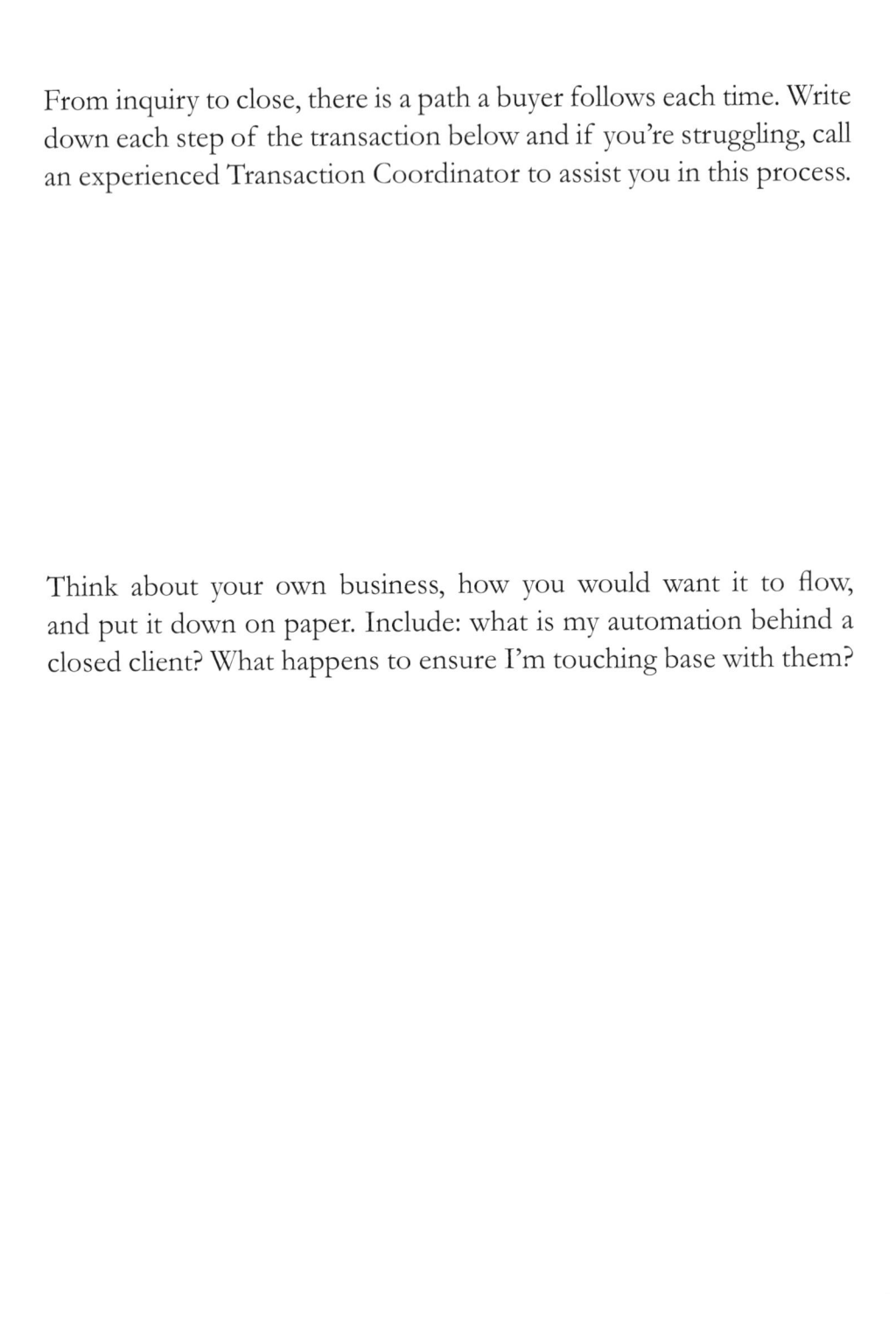

From inquiry to close, there is a path a buyer follows each time. Write down each step of the transaction below and if you're struggling, call an experienced Transaction Coordinator to assist you in this process.

Think about your own business, how you would want it to flow, and put it down on paper. Include: what is my automation behind a closed client? What happens to ensure I'm touching base with them?

Week 3 Day 3
DAY 13: WORK WITH A PURPOSE

Today, we're going to talk about working with a purpose. We keep hearing this question all the time, "What is your why?"

Today's exercise will help you answer the question: Why are you doing what you do every day?

You will also be able to answer a few fundamental questions on building your business with purpose. This week, we talked about sticking to your schedule and creating a fundamental process. You are beginning to get all of that down on paper. But now, what's the reason behind it? Why are we doing all this work? What's the purpose behind it?

Are you wanting to build this successful sales business to create financial freedom for your family? Or for yourself? Is there ego there? It's okay if so. I don't believe people should have an ego, but I do think we should have confidence. As you get more successful in your career, you gain confidence and become prideful in your work. That's okay. Heck, that's downright awesome.

Are you building this business because you want to win? I am obsessed with winning; I want to be the best. You're not going to outsell me; you're not going to win. Because I'm going to work harder than you. I can control how hard I work because I choose to do so. Nothing can stop me from working harder than you.

And guess what, the craziest thing, I never thought that I would build a billion-dollar company. I was just working toward that goal, yes. Then all that hard work and all that planning starting to take shape. I was clear when I was setting goals. Then I was taking care of the day-to-day. Over the course of a decade, we got there. I am living proof that it can be done because I started with nothing.

You can achieve more than you think is imaginable, and I will show you how. If you put your mind to it, you will achieve your goals. The power of the mind is more than you can fathom.

> *"One reason so few of us achieve what we truly want is because we never direct our focus; we never concentrate our power. Most people dabble their way through life, never deciding to master anything in particular."*
>
> *– Tony Robbins*

I started telling myself that I'm going to reach my goal at all costs. When you become so dedicated to that goal and that project, you will be amazed where that will get you.

To me, there are two purposes.

The purpose of today.

The purpose of the goal. What are we striving to achieve? And why?

Once I know those two things. I can ask myself: what do I need to do in my day-to-day to get there? Internally, we call them tasks and projects.

Tasks are the day-to-day and projects are what you work on.

It should be easy to know why you are doing the tasks you are doing today. If not, you have some work to do. Ask yourself: how do these tasks contribute to this project? How does this project help me achieve my immediate goal?

Once you have a clear answer to these questions, ask yourself: how does that goal help me achieve my ultimate goal?

A lot of people focus on their 'Why'. The phrase "What's your 'Why?'" has become popular in many industries, including real estate. And while your 'Why' is necessary, the day-to-day tasks also have to have a purpose. This allows us to prioritize. As you look at that ultimate goal, you can build the tasks around that ultimate goal.

What do I have to do today to get to the next step? What's the purpose behind these tasks? The purpose becomes even more critical as you delegate tasks to your assistants, your transaction coordinator, your marketing coordinator, and your buyers' agents. If they know why they need to use this checklist, they are more likely to do it. If your buyers' agents understand why she needs to slow down and fill out this form, she will do it every time. If you don't explain the purpose behind the task, she's likely to skip it.

Everyone on your team should know how many new accounts you are looking to bring on in this timeframe. Next, it is your job as the Rainmaker to tell them how you will get there.

By the end of the 40 days, you will be a well-oiled machine, one powered by efficiency and purpose. You will go out there and make it rain by focusing on the day-to-day.

You're building a machine. That's the best part of building efficient internal processes and systems. You begin to create a well-oiled machine that masters tasks allowing you to plow through projects like a professional and reach your sales goals faster.

Today, you will determine your reason, your why, and your purpose. You are going to write a clear vision so you can answer: Why am I doing this? Once you do this, you can determine your projects and tasks. This is what it's going to take to get you to the next level. Once you have gotten there, you may decide that it isn't where you want to stay. Maybe from there, you choose to take your business to the next level. That's what I did. Find your purpose, make it clear to yourself what you are working for, and go get it!

Week 3 Day 3 WORKSHEET

I want you to take time today to go on a walk. Even if you can only afford to step away for five minutes or to do a lap around the parking lot. Stop what you're doing and step outside. No, really, I want you to step outside, go on a walk and think about what moves you?

What are your long-term goals? Close your eyes and paint a clear picture of what your life looks like ten years from now. What do you look like, what does your life look like, what do your relationships look like, what does your day look like?

Now, where are you three years from today? Take a moment and repeat the exercise above but think about where you are three years from today.

Now, what are your goals for this year? What needs to happen in the next 12 months to get you from today to where you want to be in ten years and three years from today?

What is your purpose? Why do you do what you do?

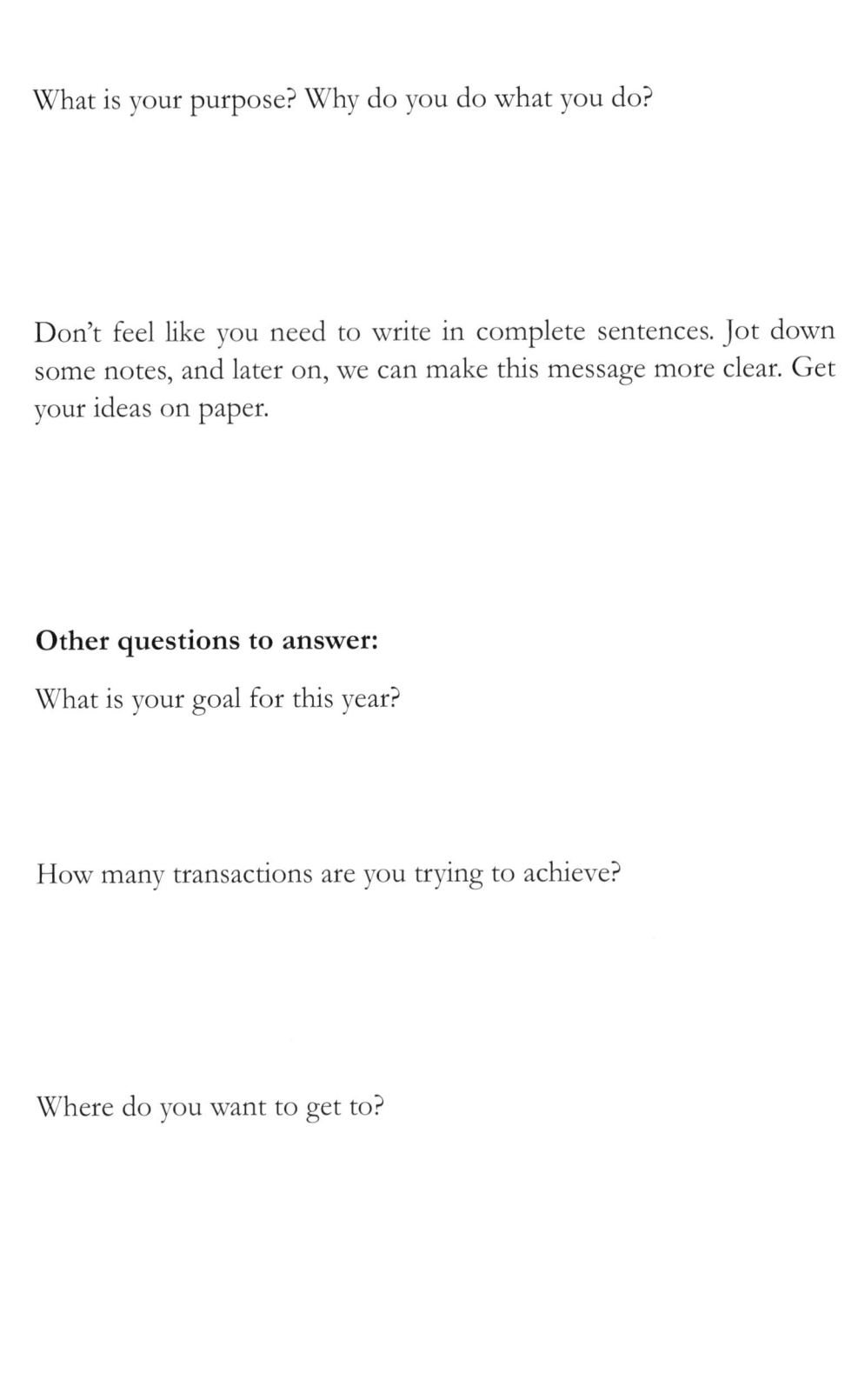

Don't feel like you need to write in complete sentences. Jot down some notes, and later on, we can make this message more clear. Get your ideas on paper.

Other questions to answer:

What is your goal for this year?

How many transactions are you trying to achieve?

Where do you want to get to?

How many clients are you looking to help this year? Next year? Five years from now?

What is my ultimate goal?

Week 3 Day 4
DAY 14: HAVING THE PROPER RESOURCES

As part of our preparation series, you have now developed a schedule. You should also have a plan set in place on how you are going to stick to your new schedule. You created a fundamental process for your transactions because you should not be reinventing the wheel with each transaction. I eventually want you to operate on autopilot, so you can focus on being a Rainmaker. Yesterday, I drove home the importance of having a purpose and understanding the intentions of your daily tasks.

Today, I want to talk about being prepared to be a go-to resource for your clients. As a real estate professional, your clients will ask you a lot of questions. As a top real estate professional, you must be resourceful because your clients trust you to have the right contacts. Clients will ask you if you have a good lender, inspector, and contractor. Clients moving in from out of town want to know what school districts are best. Potential clients will ask you if you have a packet they can look at before choosing to work with you. If it hasn't been made clear to you already, clients are going to ask a lot from you. Today, we are going to set up a plan to get you prepared.

Week 3 Day 4 WORKSHEET

Think about who you who you're sending business to. Identify the five people you refer the most business to.

1

2

3

4

5

Now, circle the names of the people above who show you appreciation. Underline the name if they send you referrals.

For those you did not underline, are you asking them specifically to refer you business? Yes or no?

Now, let's review your marketing materials.

When you go to the listing appointment, is your marketing package appealing, crisp, and easy to follow?

When someone goes to your website, what is the story you are telling them?

When you look at your marketing materials (social media, postcards, business cards, website, and listing packet), are you someone you'd want to work with? Yes or No?

Do your marketing materials tell the story you want to tell to your clients? Yes or No?

Does your email content include up-to-date information about you and who you serve? Yes or no?

If no, what are five things you can do over the next five weeks to improve this?

1

2

3

4

5

Week 3 Day 5

DAY 15: BECOMING A TRUE PROFESSIONAL

Throughout our preparation series, we've been talking about working with a purpose, creating a fund, and having some proper resources. Today, we're going to talk about being a true professional.

When you hear the word, 'Pro,' you may think of professional athletes. They have become masters in their craft through hours of privileged access to the best facilities and years of practice. They're practicing their craft. You, too, need to be practicing your craft in order to become a pro.

In our business, we have professionals, too. Think of the real estate agent or team always on the leaderboard in your office. Who in your market is consistently the top sales agent or broker? They are not piecing things together and running a mismanaged business day-to-day. They show professionalism in every aspect of their business, from their personal presentation to their marketing materials, which we spoke about yesterday. A professional in real estate treats their business like a business. Being a professional has everything to do with preparation. It's the one thing you can control.

You cannot control if that house has termites. You cannot control when funding falls through for your buyer or if something falls out of escrow for your seller. That's the fault of the home or financing. Things happen that are out of your control. What you can control is you the way you look. You can manage your appearance, your communication, and the habits you practice.

An unprofessional agent works in the day-to-day, not on the day-to-day. In case you don't already know, these are two different things. Today, let's talk about how to prepare to be a professional.

First, let me take you back to an open house I attended last year. I had an out-of-town buyer who flew in for the weekend to view properties and, hopefully, find their next home before flying back to Chicago, where he was graduating from Northwestern. He was a referral, the son of a loyal client, so I was the one showing him properties that day.

We parked on the street, at the end of the driveway of this house. It was listed at $497,000 and likely to sell quickly. As the buyer and I walked up the driveway, I noticed a car parked there.

It's worth noting that, if you are holding a house open, you should park the seller's and seller agent cars away from the home to leave the driveway empty for ascetic purposes but also if a buyer wants to park there.

You need to be practicing your craft in order to become a pro.

The car parked in the driveway had open house signs piled high in the backseat with the listing agents' name on them. I immediately knew this had to be the agent's car. It was filthy. The outside of the vehicle was in dire need of a wash, and the inside was a mess. In addition to the open house signs, the car had food wrappers on the floor, papers stacked in the front seat, and what looked like a change of clothes on the front seat passenger's floor.

If you are listing a half a million-dollar house, you can afford to take your car to the carwash. To the agent's credit, he was impeccably dressed when we walked in. However, I had already cast my judgment on the agent and his ability to run a professional business. If he couldn't keep his car clean, how would keep a smooth transaction should my buyer make an offer on this house?

First impressions matter, and this is ever so true in the business of real estate. Both you and your car need to be presentable at all times. You never know when your next ample opportunity will call. Be prepared. It is essential to dress the part of a professional. This doesn't mean expensive designer clothes if you can't afford them yet. Start where you can. Wake up and show up to work looking good and smelling great.

If you are looking to become a luxury agent, you will need to dedicate time to looking the part when it comes to your wardrobe.

PRO TIP: Open houses done right.

No matter the price point, if you are holding an open house, you need to present the house in the best light. This includes turning on every single light in the place. You should have water, beverages, and snacks available when people arrive at your open house. It would help if you had music playing to create a welcoming environment. Bonus: try pre-made cookie dough in the oven minutes before the open house starts to add an extra welcoming aroma to the house. Be careful to set the alarm and not burn the cookies!

Professionalism goes beyond looking the part. You also need to act the part.

If you have unfortunate news to deliver to your client, do you wait for them to call you? Or do you pick up the phone and approach the problem head-on?

When someone calls you, you call them back that day. I cannot tell you how many times I'll send an email. I won't get an email back for a day from an agent. Do you mean to tell me that you cannot respond to me the same day? If you are guilty of this, you need to fix this right away. If you have spread yourself so thin that you are not responding to emails within 24 hours, you need to reprioritize your day, or maybe it is time to hire someone.

If you're not going to take your business seriously, no one is taking you seriously.

I love going to work every day. For me, every day is the next step closer to the next best thing. But if you're waking up every day and you're only showing up to see what happens, you're not a pro. You're not prepared. You do not have a plan. Let's evaluate you and your business today to ensure you are prepared to be a professional. On a scale from 1-10, how professional is your vehicle? 1 being unprofessional, and 10 being utmost professional.

Week 3 Day 5 WORKSHEET

On a scale from 1-10, how professional is your personal appearance? 1 being unprofessional, and 10 being utmost professional.

On a scale from 1-10, how professional is your communication with your clients? 1 being unprofessional, and 10 being utmost professional.

On a scale from 1-10, how professional is your communication with other agents? 1 being unprofessional, and 10 being utmost professional.

On a scale from 1-10, how professional are your marketing materials? 1 being unprofessional, and 10 being utmost professional.

On a scale from 1-10, how professional is your contract to close processes? 1 being unprofessional, and 10 being utmost professional.

If any of the previous answers were less than a 7, then you need to take time to shape up your business. If any answers were below a 9, what can you do to improve your professionalism in that aspect of your business?

Take a moment to think about that in your day-to-day right now. Write down Prepared or Not Prepared as you reflect on the previous week.

Monday

Tuesday

Wednesday

Thursday

Friday

Saturday

Sunday

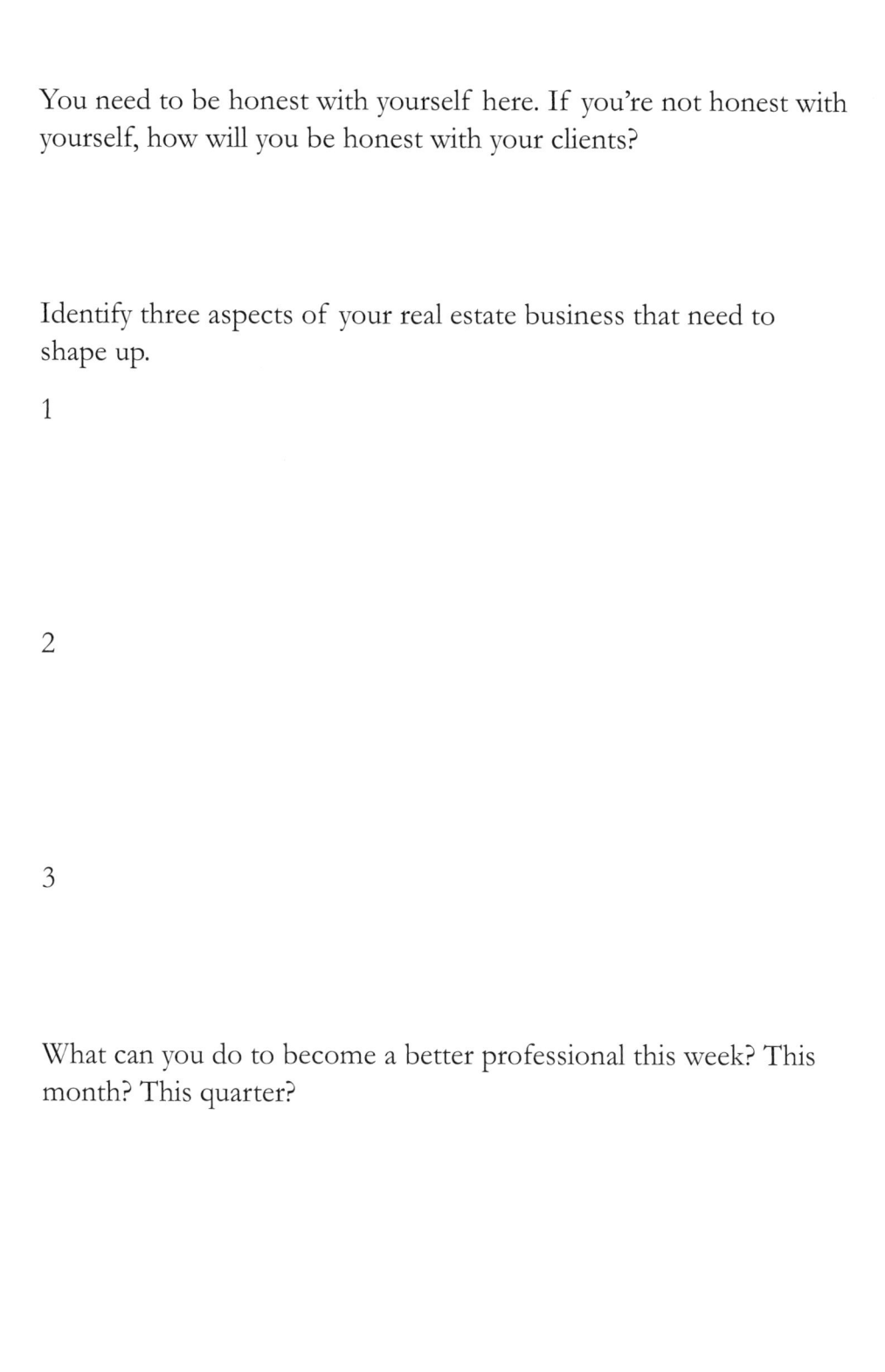

You need to be honest with yourself here. If you're not honest with yourself, how will you be honest with your clients?

Identify three aspects of your real estate business that need to shape up.

1

2

3

What can you do to become a better professional this week? This month? This quarter?

Week 4 Day 1

DAY 16: MASTER THE INITIAL CALL

This week is where the rubber meets the road. We will deep dive into sales techniques and talk about one of the most critical aspects of what we do every day. And that is mastering the critical path of sales. We're into it, we've prepared ourselves, and we're ready.

Together, we have identified who we are, and who our target customers are.. Last week, during our preparation series, we prepared for this. As I mentioned, it's as if we are going to battle,

We're ready to go to war. We're here. Now, let's talk about it, we're going to get detailed here.

Your journey to being great at sales has officially begun. If you're already great at selling, you're going to get even better. Your job is to prepare the client for every step of the journey. First, you must understand this critical path. And what is the critical path? The critical path is how we take a client from a new client to the closing table.

This week, you will master the initial call, what we call 'buyer consults.' We will cover what to do when we finally get to show homes. When the buyer starts to think, "I like this home," I am going to show you how to close. The final step is, of course, the finish line at the closing table. It's one thing to get your client under contract. It's another thing to get that contract to close.

What's the old saying, "Never count your money until it's in your bank account?" That's the finish line, folks. This week, we will cover each of the five critical aspects of the sale; the crucial path to mastering real estate sales.

…

Mastering the critical path of sales starts with mastering that initial call. An initial call could be with a potential client that you've never spoken to before. It can also be with a new client who was a referral from a past client, friend, or family member.

There are a variety of ways that people get introduced to you in our business.

You must tailor the initial call around that specific person. We spoke in Week Two that it is never about you, and it's always about your client. Refer back to Day Nine if you need to.

This initial call is not all about them. It is all about them liking you. I tell my team that likability and being liked is the number one trait to selling more houses. You need to build rapport like your life depends on it—because your business does. If a potential client or prospect hangs up the phone, and they like you, they're going to buy—or list—with you.

But remember, that's their choice. If you're beating around the bush, or worse yet, you're not really paying attention to what the person is saying, you will not win the client.

If you're not prepared, and some of the things that you're saying aren't making sense, the prospect has thousands of other real estate agents to choose from that will be prepared for them. They will not work with you. So, let's get prepared. Let's master the initial call so that you can win the client every time.

Remember that every part of the initial call should help you build rapport. You want the prospect to like you and trust you by the end of the first call. Focus on keeping the client talking about themselves. Every question you ask should lead to the next question.

First, ask the client to tell you about their lifestyle. Next, ask them what they are looking for in a home. Be sure to use "home" instead of "house" to get them to answer with emotion.

I want to repeat this because it is so important: every question you ask on that initial call leads to the next set of questions. What you're doing is building ammunition so you know precisely what is on their mind. The more you know, the more you can close.

It is your job to figure out their needs.

Lifestyle questions include: what do you like to do? Do you like to go out? Tell me about what you and your wife like to do for fun? What do you like to do to relax? Tell me about work; where is it located? Where did you grow up? Are you local, or are you moving here? Do you have children? If the answer is "Yes," then schools are probably important to them. If they say "no, I'm single." or "This is my first home, " then remember, a first-time homebuyer wants to make a good investment.

If they say, "I'm nervous, I have never bought a home before." it is your job to make them feel comfortable. "Great, let's talk about it." You are the expert. If you have helped 300 first-time homebuyers, you need to mention that on the call. Build rapport and trust quickly. But again, this is not about you. This is about them. What can I do to make you feel more comfortable? Would you like to come in and walk through the contract together before we go and look at homes? Would you like me to connect you with the best lender in town to familiarize you with the home lending process? What can I do to make this a great experience for you?

"Let's talk about how I can set you up in a home that will yield you a great return."

As their real estate agent, you should be adding value. Give them the tools they need to make this a successful transaction, and a happy one. You want them to feel good about their purchase when you hand them their keys at closing.

During the call, make them feel good about you. By the end of the call, they need to be comfortable working with you. If you do that well, you're going to get your clients. However, if you're not educating and building rapport, you will not win them over.

In this call, it is your job to figure out their needs.

If you're nervous, they can hear that. If you're calm and confident, the client can feel that. Awkward silence will kill a deal. If you prepare for this to happen, then you will immediately know how to pivot and save the call. How do you become more confident in your ability? You practice.

We talked about role-playing and practicing on Day 3. Refer back to the Pro Tip on Day 3. I tell you that I role-play all the time. Even when I was closing $100M a year, I was role-playing. You are never too good to role-play.

> *As their real estate agent, you should be adding value. Give them the tools they need to make this a successful transaction, and a happy one.*

On this initial call, it is your job to guide them through the path. That's called foreshadowing. "Okay, Elizabeth, here is what is going to happen next, and after that, this happens. Along the way, we are going to have some fun. How does that sound?"

If you exclude urgency on an initial call, you are shooting yourself in the foot. You must create urgency on every initial call.

"Mr. Bowles. I'm not saying you need to buy a home tomorrow, by the way, but if we go out this weekend and you find something that you like, you should be ready to write an offer.

"Rates are so low right now—what an incredible time to buy."

"John, a lot of folks are looking for good homes like the one you described. The good news is that houses like that come on the market that meet your criteria. But know that they go quick, so let's make sure that you're not afraid to pull the trigger. I am here to prepare you so that you're ready because I am ready. My job is to make sure that the first tour we have is the best tour. You know what, most of my clients actually do buy on their first tour."

Have this conversation with every client as they get in your car. Create comfortability in writing an offer and buying a house.

Creating that urgency on that initial call is critical. If you get off the phone and you did not create a sense of urgency with that client, guess what? You are going to become a tour guide. It's either going to be hard to get them in the car, or almost worse; it's going to be hard to close them. They're going to look at every home in the city—all over town.

Master the initial call. Build rapport, create urgency, and set both you and the client up for success.

Week 4 Day 1 WORKSHEET

Create an intake form for your initial call. No matter how many clients you have or how many times you have done this, you must have a system set in place, so nothing falls through the cracks. Ever.

List five questions you will ask every initial client. Hint: you should gather information on their lifestyle, wants, needs, and critical information.

1

2

3

4

5

List three ways you will create urgency with your clients.

1

2

3

How will you end each call?

Week 4 Day 2
DAY 17: DISCOVERY

This week, we are mastering the critical path of sales. Yesterday, we spoke about the initial call and how to make that call a success. After the initial call, the next step is discovery. Today we're going to talk about the discovery component of our critical path. In this step, you will learn your clients' needs.

You may be thinking, "Well, Jason, you, you mentioned this on the initial call."

Yes. That's true. You may have started the discovery portion during that first initial call. However, not every initial call goes the same way. That's why we practice, prepare, and roleplay.

Some initial calls lead to meeting for coffee whereas others lead to scheduling a showing or tour day.

Oftentimes, the initial calls do not get into the discovery stage, so I want to make sure that we separate those two—initial call and discovery stage.

Your ability to be a good listener is crucial to your success both in the initial call and in the discovery stage. On Day 9, we talked about being an information junkie. As a real estate professional, your job is to gather as much information on your clients as possible. This allows you to not only close them but also make this transaction the best experience for both you and them.

Being a good listener is crucial. If on day 3, mitigating weaknesses, you discovered that listening is not a strength, you must work on this. Your clients need to feel heard and you need to discover their wants, needs, and motivation.

As I said yesterday, every question we ask should lead to the next question. This is both true in the initial call and the discovery call. Let me show you an example.

I happen to live in Phoenix. Like Las Vegas, like Los Angeles, and like a few other parts of the country, Phoenix is a very transient town. Thus, one of the first things that I discuss on an initial call is: are you coming from out of town? Then I get to ask: "How long have you lived in Phoenix?"

Then I get to ask, "well, where do you live in Phoenix? ... Great. Where are you looking to purchase? Why are you moving from here to there? What's the basis of that? Oh, I see."

Every question just naturally leads to the next one.

If it's a past client, or a friend of yours, we may already know a little bit of information about that client.

If they were referred to you, you must talk about the person that referred them, and how you helped them along the way.

Your client will tell you everything you need to know, so long as you listen.

Tell them what a great experience you had working with the past client. That way, you are telling the referral that you not only remember their friends, but you also created a positive experience for their friends. You will do the same thing for them. How long have you known them? Oh, you went to college together? What school? Oh, you went there? Great. What did you get your degree in? Oh, great. Step by step. Right? Every question in the discovery leads to the next question. So listen to what they're saying.

Also, it's psychological. They're thinking, "Jason said all of these nice things about my friends. He is going to say good things about me, too. I like this person."

Your client will tell you everything you need to know, so long as you listen.

They will tell you how to win with them, so long as you're listening. Everything that they answer will lead to another question, and before you know it, after seven or eight questions, you will have all the information you need to put this person in the best position.

Comment on what they are saying. If they say something generic like, "I am not looking for a really big house," you must ask: "what is a really big house to you?"

If they say that they do not want to live downtown, ask them why. If you know that this client cannot afford an area or neighborhood that they're interested in, you're not going to come right out and say, "Well, you can't afford that area."

That would be crazy! They don't know you. They're gonna look at you like you're a jerk. Instead, tactfully tiptoe around that.

"I've got to tell you. You know, it's getting expensive over there, I'm seeing the homes sell for quite a bit more than I thought they would." Then show them the numbers and the facts.

"Can I send you the last three houses sold in that neighborhood to give you a good idea of the price tags we're seeing in that neighborhood?"

"Can you show a house in this neighborhood? I am seeing a lot of value increase in this neighborhood. Plus, I am seeing houses appreciate in this area. Plus, it's beautiful. Here, let me show you."

Turn the discussion around from what they can't get into into something that they can.

Our goal is to set expectations. Yesterday, we talked briefly about foreshadowing. You prepared them so they have the ability to write an offer on the first day of looking at houses with you. Prepare your client for what you're going to accomplish together.

For example, you should tell them, "When we find the house that you could see yourself living in, we're going to submit an offer."

Remember when I talked about urgency yesterday? It is your job to steer the ship and set expectations. You want them to have a fear of loss that encourages them to make decisions quickly.

End the call by thanking them for their time. Repeat back to them a few things they have said. Doing this will prove to them that you were really listening. When they feel heard and understood, they will trust you. Then, tell them what will happen next.

"Great, I have an awesome handle on what you're looking for. Now, let me get to work. I'm going to find some great homes for you."

End the conversation by making them feel like they are in control. Ask them when they would like you to start working for them? Tonight or this weekend?

If you instead ask, "would you like to look at houses this weekend?" you are shooting yourself in the foot again. While you want to create a sense of urgency, you want the client to feel in control.

"When would you like to look at houses?"

"Well, I don't know. I don't know if I'm really ready…"

Do not ask open-ended questions but rather yes or no questions. Instead ask yes or no questions. If you leave open ended questions, you'll never get to the end goal. You have to be the one to lead them down that path. You have to ask them and tell them.

"Does this weekend work for you?"

Tell the client: I'm going to go get to work. I'm going to find some homes. I'm going to send you everything available that's within the criteria that you told me.

Set yourself up for success by setting expectations from the get-go. This is what will happen next and then this will happen. Oh and let me tell you: Now, there probably won't be a lot of homes on this list because what you're looking for, a lot of people are looking for.

Does that create some urgency? It sure does. It is setting the expectation that there will not be thirty homes for them to choose from. And shame on you if you send them 30 homes. You're going to confuse them. When a client has 30 to look at, they cannot decide. Instead send them less than 12 homes and tell them to pick the best five homes.

You already told them that the first tour is the best tour. You told them that the majority of your clients actually buy on the first tour.

Be smart in your approach because the discovery is what leads to the next step, Tour Day. You have earned the right to tour homes.

You were likable on the initial call. You then learned their needs, wants and motivation on the discovery call. You successfully created a sense of urgency. Now, when you take them on tour, they're prepared. You have foreshadowed and set the expectations for your client and now, they are ready to write an offer when they see the house they want.

PRO TIP: Oh, and by the way, when you get to the closing section of the critical path, you are not going to ask them, "what do you want to offer?" You're going to tell them what to offer. You are the professional here. They choose to work with you because they think you are the best, and you are.

Week 4 day 2 WORKSHEET

Create a plan for your discovery call. This is an intake form that you will use every time with every new client.

During the discovery call you will find out their needs, wants, and motivations.

Three questions you will ask to identify their needs.

1

2

3

Three questions you will ask to identify their wants.

1

2

3

Three questions you will ask to identify their motivation.

1

2

3

Identify ways you will set expectations for your clients.

1

2

3

Week 4 Day 3
DAY 18: TOUR DAY

We are now at Tour Day on our critical path of sales. This week, we have talked about the initial call and being likable. We've spoken about discovery, finding out the client's needs, wants, and motivations. and then preparing.

Everything you have done up to this point is preparing for tour day. The ultimate goal is to get to show someone a home. It seems like the first step to making money as a real estate agent. You can close your clients on Tour Day if you set up your tour correctly.

Hopefully, you've created urgency and a fear of loss. You've set the right expectations. By now, you and your clients have picked out the four or five best homes—not 12 or 15. You do not want to be a tour guide. You do not want their head spinning. They won't be ready to buy because they won't even remember which house is which.

A tour should be three hours, and you should look at four to five homes. If you properly prepare them that the first tour is the best tour, there's an excellent chance that you can close them today.

I have made it clear that you should be working with a purpose. The purpose of tour day is to sell a home. Do not confuse tour day with a tour. It's not your job to be a tour guide. We are in the business of sales, yet I see so many agents out there who want to be friends with their clients.

Would you ever say to your client, "Tomorrow, let's go look at eight houses with no plan of attack. Let's just aimlessly go look at homes together."

No! What an utter waste of time. Yet, that's what hundreds of real estate agents do.

The power of no comes into play on tour day.

Plan of attack. Most agents set up their tours like the following. "Here are the three addresses of the houses, and my office is here. Now, the most logical route would be the following." No! Shame on you.

Do not set up your tour based on geography. Are you kidding me? Set it up so that the house you think they will buy is the third house you see. Rarely, if ever, do I close someone on the first house we tour. Very rarely does this happen. If I know they like Cape Cod the most, I will not take them there first.

How do I know they like the Cape Cod the most? They told me. In the world of real estate today, they have access to photos, virtual tours, and more at the tip of their fingertips. Use the internet to your advantage. The more familiar they are with a property, the more likely they will write an offer. That's the goal here. The goal is not to spend all day with this buyer. The goal is to get their offer accepted.

First step, set the tour up strategically—not geographically. Be strategic. Don't take them to the best home first. I don't care if the house is around the block. Tell them there was a scheduling conflict—whatever you've got to do. Do not show the best home or what's perceived the best home first. Don't do that.

Instead, pick your top two, and leave them for close to last. Now, it does not have to be the last house you tour. In fact, I would argue it shouldn't be the last one. It is better to show them the house you know they will like and should buy in the middle of a tour. When you visit the worst house for last, you can point out how great the house or houses before were compared to this one.

If they don't end up buying on that first tour day, yet you do everything right, they will likely close on the second tour.

If they look at more than 12 homes and don't like any of them, then they're probably not serious. You don't get to look at 12 or 15 houses with not one of them working for you. That's not reality. Be smart.

The power of no comes into play on tour day. Let's say you take Mr. and Mrs. Bowles to three houses, and by now, they are starting to say, "I think I could live here," but you know that the next house or the last house was a better fit for them, tell them.

Say, "Hey, I actually think you can do better."

You know what you just did? Do you see the power of telling a consumer not to buy something? Now, all of a sudden, they're comfortable with you because now you're not just trying to sell a home.

The power of 'No' is at play here on Tour Day.

More discovery happens on Tour Day. You get to see the reactions of your clients. Being a good listener also extends to being mindful of their body language, comments, and looks between a husband and a wife.

Ask follow-up questions. "Why is having an oversized kitchen island important to you? Oh, do you cook a lot? Do you have friends over when you cook? No, then why is that important to you?

"What don't you like about this master bathroom? What do you like about this backyard? Is it the way it's laid out? Is it that it backs up to green space? It seems that you don't want our master bedroom next to all guests bedrooms, is that correct? Good news, the next house we are looking at is set up with the mother-in-law suite on one side of the house and the master bedroom on the other side of the house."

If you hear the same objection come out of their mouth each time, prepare for that. "Now, I know the kitchen is crazy important to you, and this house doesn't have the large island in the kitchen that you're looking for. However, it does have the square footage in the kitchen to add that in before you move in. What do you think of that?"

Or you affirm their objections. "Yeah, you know, I'm not feeling this one either." Or you add, "In fact, it's pretty, it's probably overpriced as well."

When you can say that you do not like a particular house, you are using the power of no again. "Let's forget the home and move onto the next one."

They are thinking, "This Jason guy isn't just trying to sell every house to me. He is listening to my feedback and my wants and needs. He is doing a really great job. I trust him."

You're not going to convince somebody that doesn't like a home that they should buy that home—nor should you. But if you agree with them, and you say, "no, we can do better," you will build trust and rapport

Gauge your client. Then, at some point, you're going to go into a home that they really, really like. You're going to know this, because they're going to take a second and stroll around the house. If it's a couple, someone's going to end up outside; someone's going to be inside. They're going to cross paths.

Then, when you get to the house that your clients like, I want you to encourage them to retake a stroll around the house. "Hey, let's go check out the master again" and "Hey, let's go check out the guest bedrooms, make sure they're big enough." "You know, I really want to go see that great room again; I want to see if your TV would fit on that wall."

Get them to picture their life in that home.

When you can see that someone's standing there and they're in deep thought, that's the sign they are ready to buy.

It is your job to add credibility around other every component during this process: "You know what I also like? I love the neighborhood." "I love the location." "I love the price. I think they're right in the ballpark."

Guess what we're doing right here, setting them up to write an offer and sign a contract. Tomorrow, we're going to talk about this next step, the closing. A lot of times, closings happen in the home, on tour day. Now, you are done talking about the home. The home has done its job. It has sold itself. It is now your job, as the real estate professional, to do the rest.

You also tell them, "I like this house." You know if I didn't like the house, I would tell you. They believe you because you proved to them on Tour Day that you do tell them when you don't like things. You built trust with them earlier in the tour because you were preparing for this moment. You were preparing them for the time when you say, "I like this home. I wouldn't lie to you."

Next, I want you to talk about other selling features. Talk about the neighborhood, the commute to the office, the feel of the community and the school districts. This will build credibility around the home. You will talk about the amenities in the area including the best restaurants and the attractions. This is part of the resources package you created back in Week 3. You have marketing materials not only for yourself, but also for your market. You can sell to your clients: "This price is in the range you mentioned you want to stay in. Great, let's write the offer. That's the next step."

Week 4 Day 3 WORKSHEET

Are you even looking at homes that you think they're going to buy? Do you even know if your clients are serious about buying, but you're going to spend an entire day with them.

Think about the last Tour Day you had. Identify five things you did well.

1

2

3

4

5

Now, identify five things you did not do well.

1

2

3

4

5

Identify five things you want to do on your next Tour Day.

1

2

3

4

5

Week 4 Day 4
DAY 19: THE CLOSE

Yesterday, we talked about Tour Day best practices. A lot of times, closing the client happens on Tour Day. Today, we will talk about closing your client, and I will share the best practices.

How do I get them to say, "let's do it"? First, you have to set up the close. You do this by making sure that your client actually likes the home. Next, you don't talk about the home anymore. But rather discuss unique things around the property, such as the school district, the community, and the amenities.

After you identify a home that the buyer likes, do not let them tell you what they're going to do or tell you their next steps. No, you are the professional here. It is your job to tell them what is going to happen next.

If you allow them to tell you then the buyers are going to say, "Well, we're going to think about it."

You lost the sale. If you allow them to go home and think about it. They will not make an offer. They won't pull the trigger on their own;

you have to make them pull the trigger. If you allow your client to go home and think about it, you have lost. The client will say, "we'll call you later and get back to you."

Guess what? They're not going to call you later. The buyers will get into their car and talk themselves out of writing an offer entirely. They will go home and get caught in their daily life. Buying this house is going to become secondary instead of it being critically important.

It is your job to tell them what happens next. You need to prepare your buyers for the order of operations. You are the expert here. They will not know that it's time to make an offer. Reiterate the reasons why they should write the offer. The home has already sold itself. You need to reiterate the following: it's everything you want; interest rates are crazy low; you want to get out of your home right now.

You have to step in immediately once you build additional credibility around the home and everything else that it brings. You speak first. Once they find a home they like, immediately tell the buyers, "Here is what I think we should do."

You tell your client that the seller is currently offering the home at $425,0000, and the home has only been on the market for a few hours. You explain to the buyer what is going to happen next.

"I need to first make sure it's available. I will call the agent and make sure it is still available. I need to make sure I can still submit an offer. Then, if it is, we are going to make an offer."

In doing so, you are creating a fear of loss. If you create a fear of loss, the buyers will say, "Well, I don't want to lose it."

"From there, my suggestion would be to offer $419,000 because this home is actually priced pretty well at $425,000. But if I can save you $5,000-10,000, we might as well."

I am not setting the expectation that they will try to steal this home because you're not going to steal a home. Do not set yourself up for failure. Don't let your client tell you what they want to offer.

"First, I need to make sure the home is available. If and when it is, my suggestion is to offer $410k or $415k. The seller may come back and say they want full price, and quite frankly, it's probably worth the full price. But don't worry about that, the appraisal will dictate price. The appraisal is going to dictate if we're overpaying. But I'm telling you right now, I don't see an issue with the appraisal. If I can save you five, ten, or fifteen grand, then why not, right?"

Then, the client is going to say, "yes, let's do that. I trust you. You're the expert. You do this all the time. I've only bought a house once or twice or three times twenty years ago. I trust you, Jason."

You set the expectations here. Not the other way around. You told your story to the buyer and walked them down the path. You have to set up the closing process. If you foreshadow and set up this process correctly, you will close a ton of homes. You will get people to say "yes" without them even saying it. It's easier than that. They simply need to agree with you.

Now, prepare your buyer for the next step. That way, there are no surprises. Prepare them that there might be a counter offer. If they're thinking that they will submit an offer for $410k, yet they're not prepared for the seller to counter, then a counteroffer could knock them off course. So, instead of a counteroffer derailing the sell, you prepare the buyer. This is foreshadowing.

"The seller may counter. The house is priced well, and they might counter our offer. But if I can save you $10,000-15,000, I am going to try. Does that sound good to you?"

Again, the buyers don't have to even come up with an answer; they can simply agree with you.

"The seller may counter for $425k, and we may end up landing on $420k, but we, at least, saved $5,000. Then, we open escrow. I hope that sounds good to you, because it sounds great to me!"

If you haven't prepped for a counter, then the buyers might walk. There's no reason for that. You are a true professional who has been preparing for this moment. And in turn, you prepared your client for this moment. You set up the sale by setting clear expectations.

In everything we do for our clients, we should be foreshadowing. In the initial call, we foreshadow the discovery. In the discovery, we foreshadow the tour. From the tour, we foreshadow the submitting of an offer. We foreshadow the entire process from contract to close.

You will foreshadow the entire process to prepare your client mentally for what will happen throughout the transaction.

"They're probably going to counter us, and we'll see where that comes in at. But I firmly believe that we can get this deal done. I think we're going to be close enough, or we can make a deal. but first, like I said, let me make sure it's available,"

You have to reinforce a fear of loss, especially if a home is priced well. Reiterate that the house hasn't been on the market that long to create that fear of failure and loss.

Now, you're talking about the next steps. You have already talked about how you are going to negotiate.

"But now this is what we need to do , I'm going to call, I want you guys to go home and go do your thing. This is where I come in, let me do my job. Hope that sounds good to you. I'll call you in a couple of hours. Now, I am going to get everything drawn up."

"I'm going to call the agent, make sure it's available. And then I'm going to write up a contract. Once we know it is available, we're going to put a contract together, and submit it. It may take a day for a response. Hopefully, we can get a response tonight, but it might be tomorrow. Once we get a counter or when we agree on a price, we're going to open escrow at the end of the day. Then, our inspection period begins."

You are putting the buyers in the mindset that you are going to get this deal done. You are going into the next steps of the process because the negotiation portion is scary. You don't want to talk about the negotiations period and repairs a whole lot. You want to give the clients the roadmap to what you're going to do and how you'll accomplish it together. Then, you want to immediately get off that subject because that part is scary. What's not scary is talking about the next steps. The home inspection period. And then you're foreshadowing again.

"Now, keep in mind, Mr. Bowles, every home has its issues. There'll be a handful of things that we need to get repaired. The main thing is, is that there are no major ticket items. If there are, we have to request that they are fixed."

Why am I saying this right now to the client if we don't even have a deal yet? We haven't even submitted an offer, yet I am talking about the inspection because I'm putting them in the mindset that we will get a deal done.

When the inspection report comes back, the buyer expects things on that report because you told them to expect these things. Then, when there are ten things, they're not freaking out. Or better yet, where there's nothing on the report, you can say, "Wow! This house is in great shape."

Plus, we are now talking about the inspection report even though we are in the thick of the scary part: submitting an offer. Next comes an even scarier part: negotiating an offer. But your buyer isn't even thinking about that. They are mentally four steps ahead, thinking about the inspection report.

Throughout the entire transaction, you're in the driver's seat. Your clients are along for the ride, and it is your job to keep them buckled in and inside the car at all times.

Next, tell the buyer that if the appraisal does come back low, we can renegotiate the contract.

"Mr. Bowles, if you're not comfortable, you can walk now, but I don't think we're gonna have an issue." and then tell the buyer, "Once we clear the appraisal, we're waiting on the lender and title to deliver documents. Next, we will do our final walkthrough to make sure they repaired everything we asked them to repair. Lastly, we're going to close, and I'm going to give you your keys."

You are in the driver's seat. You foreshadowed the whole process to your buyer. Most importantly, all that scary stuff of negotiating the offer, which you're in the thick of right now, doesn't seem so frightening to the buyer because for them, it's already in the past.

You reassure your buyer that you are going to have a great experience closing on the home. They are already picturing the day where you hand them the keys.

Week 4 Day 4 WORKSHEET

Think about your last Tour Day. Did you build credibility around the home? Identify four ways you can do this.

1

2

3

4

Write out the steps of the process, so you have them committed to memory.

What are the three key takeaways from today's lessons?

1

2

3

Week 4 Day 5
DAY 20: THE FINISH LINE

This week is all about the journey to get to the closing table. The initial call, the discovery, tour day, and submitting an offer all lead to the closing table. Closing day is the best part of being a real estate agent. You get to help someone find and buy their next home. The home where they will spend years of their lives, growing a family, and making memories. It is exciting and beautiful!

I believe that we have one of the best jobs in the world. We get to help people find a new home and let them move on with their journey in life. Closing on a home is fantastic. It's an unforgettable experience.

Damage control, foreshadowing, and ensuring we have a smooth process is part of your responsibilities as a sales professional. So make sure that getting from contract to the finish line is done tactfully. Be smooth, and be smart.

If you recall, we've told our clients exactly how this is all going to play out. During the process, we foreshadow every step to eliminate surprises.

Being a professional means, leading them down the path that gets contracts. We took the lead; we did not let the client lead us.

Do not count your money until that deal closes because anything can happen.

We've talked about the inspection, appraisal, and walkthrough. It is all a part of the closing process that we've gone through with our clients. The good news is that you've mentally prepared your clients for everything that's coming up.

> *Do not count your money until that deal closes because anything can happen.*

After negotiating the offer and getting your client under contract, the inspection happens. A lot of deals get ruined here. If you've adequately prepared your client for issues that may arise with this home, the inspection should not kill a deal. Yes, the goal is to get repairs fixed. Make sure your buyer knows that the goal is not to nickel and dime the seller. Focus on the big-ticket items and set this precedent with your buyer before they get the inspection report.

Unless the house is in shambles, which is rare, do not fight it. Tell your buyer that they can walk, and you will find them another home. If it's terrible, don't fight it, be on your buyer's side, and sell them another home.

But this is rare, and the more you do this, the more you know what common issues are in your area. If you're in Kansas City, some homes have wet basements. If you are in parts of Tennessee, your houses have foundation issues because of dry soil. You will start to learn your market, and guess what? You can foreshadow specific problems with your buyers.

No matter how new or how expensive a home is, there are always more items that the buyer wants fixed, than the seller is willing to repair. But this is not a problem.

You set expectations that you're not going to nickel and dime the seller, yet you want to make sure that the seller fixes the significant items.

I prepared my buyer not to worry about a valve pipe or a random item not being up to code as long as it's not a safety concern. Instead, we will focus on big-ticket items and costly repairs. First, let's make sure the home is safe. Then let's make sure the house is clean.

Part of foreshadowing is telling the buyer that the inspector's job is to point out every single thing that is wrong with the house.

"The inspector is going to show up tomorrow and it usually takes three or four hours. To clarify, this is never and in and out in one hour kind of thing. If it takes five hours, that doesn't mean something is wrong with the house, and you shouldn't buy it. Do you understand? Then we're going to get a report from the inspectors, usually the next day. Then, together, you and I are going to determine what we're going to request from the seller."

I don't have this conversation on the morning of the inspection. I have this conversation with the buyers days before the inspection when possible. I don't want the buyers to get an inspection report and freak out and call me and say, "No, we're walking." Instead, I'm putting them in the mindset of we're probably going to ask the seller to make some repairs. You are telling the buyer not to stress when they see items on the report. This is normal.

The next step is the appraisal. There is nothing worse than a bad appraisal. If you've been in real estate long enough, then you have experienced an up market and a down market. Personally, I don't think one person's opinion of value should dictate whether or not a person should buy a home. The fact is, appraisals can come in low sometimes. Hopefully, when they do come in low, you have prepared your client that this stuff can happen. So again, they don't freak out. You are in charge of damage control at all times. That is your job as a real estate agent, just in case no one told you.

Foreshadow to your client that if the appraisal comes in low, your job is to renegotiate the contract. Assure your client that you are an expert negotiator. That's your job as a real estate professional. You don't just sell homes. You steer the ship from contract to close, and this includes negotiating and renegotiating the deal. Maybe, we get the seller to shave a few dollars off of the purchase price.

In any case, you're going to win. Now, if the buyer says to you that they're not paying anything above appraisal, you walk them back to tour day when they fell in love with the house. You walk them through repair negotiations.

Then you go back to the buyer and say, "Look, I've been doing this a long time." Or "Look, just because one person says it's worth x doesn't mean it's not worth y. The listing agent told me that there's multiple offers on this place, or the fact that there've been a ton of showings, it's clearly not overpriced." The point is that we can try to save money too, if there is that opportunity. The first step is calling the listing agent.

> *Just like anything in sales, he who speaks first loses.*

"Hey, look. Unfortunately, I have some bad news. Your client is not going to like this. But we're $15,000 short, what do you want to do?" Put it on them? Do not tell the listing agent what your plan is. Let them come to you and tell your client it's because you're in a power position.

Just like anything in sales, he who speaks first loses. Let the seller's agent talk first. Be sure to tell your client that you get to report back; in short, tell your client, "Look, this is what we're going to do, I'm going to let the seller decide what he's comfortable with doing. Then, when I get that information, I can play on it. But we're not going to come to them and tell them to shave $10,000 off. We're not going to do that. I want them to tell me what they want. Because then I'll have something to play with."

Talk to your client first, then go to the sellers agent and say, "What do you want to do? See what your client's comfortable with doing."

Let the seller's agent talk first.

Let them come to you and tell your client it's because you're in a power position.

Now, hopefully, you've worked all this out. Or better yet, you don't have these problems in the first place. But if and when you do, those are some tactical strategies to get out of that mess.

Maybe the issue isn't with the appraisal but instead with lending. Perhaps your client doesn't qualify for that loan anymore. Maybe the loan they were supposed to get isn't a loan that they can get now, and maybe their loan becomes more expensive. That happens a lot, and when it does, it is not a good feeling for your buyer. It is your job to smooth the rough seas and mitigate losses where you can.

At times, clients have to switch from FHA to conventional loans. Or perhaps they have to put down an extra 5-10% down that they weren't expecting. Sometimes interest rates change from 3.25% to 3.75%.

Let's say, for example, the interest rates go up. Now, their payment goes up $80 per month.

If you allow your client to dictate their comfort levels, they may freak out and cancel because they just don't want to do it anymore. Instead, you can mitigate that by saying, "Look, it's a shame what happened, but you will have an interest write-off on the home. So, take it into consideration that $80 really isn't $80. Also, that's probably...what? A couple of meals? Don't let a couple of meals get in the way of this home that you love. That would be foolish."

You can be frank with your client now. At this time, you built enough rapport with your clients where they like and trust you. They like that you can shoot them straight on a few things.

"Look, I know you don't want to spend $2,000 a month on a payment. I know you wanted to be at $1,850. But you can't let $150 bucks a month get in the way. Imagine the alternative, Mr. Bowles. The alternative is you're not going to buy a home. Because it's not the home that's the problem. It's the loan that's the problem. That's not going to change with this house or the next house. It is what it is. So, what do you do? Continue to rent and throw money away? What would you do to not sit in a house that you don't want to be in anymore? Let 150 bucks be the deal breaker? That's crazy, Mr. Bowles."

Your job as the real estate professional is to go back to the basics, the fundamentals. Remind the buyer of the reasons they want to move into this home.

Those are some tactical strategies to get through some of the issues that will happen if you're in the business long enough.

Your goal is to get your client to get to the finish line.

Another problem you will have is ego. This time, it's not your ego. It is the client's ego, the seller's ego, or possibly the other agent's ego.

When the seller refuses to make any repairs, your buyer may say, "Look, I'm not moving forward with this house solely on principle."

As long as you have a willing seller and a willing buyer, those items ultimately get ironed out. It is not a smooth road, sometimes during inspection and repair negotiations, your buyer is dead set on getting a $10,000 credit. At the same time, the seller is only willing to budge $7,000. You're playing this game with the seller and the other agent. Suddenly, you have to tell your client that the seller is only willing to give them $7,000. Now you're making this process ugly. Before you go to your client, getting them all upset and frustrated, and potentially losing a deal, why don't you try working it out?

Listen, I would never go back to my client over $1,000 or $1,500. Never. Yet, I see so many deals ruined over $500-700 because it's not even about the items anymore. It's not about the credits. It's about ego. Sellers not giving in, and buyers not giving in. "I gave him my best and final," they say.

If you allow $500-1,500 to get in the way of taking this thing to the closing table, shame on you. The buyer may never buy a house with you. They will blame you for letting this deal fall through, or you might have knocked him out of the market. Maybe they decide that they're going to rent now. So, you're telling me that you're going to let a seller and buyer's ego get in the way of you getting a paycheck. That's crazy.

What if you save the transaction? What if you flip it to where the buyer didn't even know about the $3,000 discrepancy until the end of closing? Then, at closing, you say, "Actually, you know what the other agent and I did? We didn't even want you or the seller to lose the deal over $3,000, so the seller's agent and I, we ended up making up the difference."

That's right. The seller's agent said, "Hey, look, just pay me $1,500 less commission and pay the buyer's agent $1,500 less commission. I want to get this to the closing table."

Then, you get to say to your buyer at the closing table, "I didn't want to bring it up to you during the process because I wanted you to enjoy your experience."

Now, you not only make it to the closing table. Now you get to tell your client, at the closing table, that you didn't want to do anything to hinder their experience. You felt like there was no need to ruffle any feathers.

You did something generous for the buyer; you didn't bother them during the height of their stress. You wanted them to enjoy their home buying experience. You now have a client for life. They will refer you more business than that $1,500 you ate.

Yet, agents get greedy. They don't want to give up $1,000 or $1,500. Don't let egos get in the way of a deal. Agents lose a $400,000 transaction over an $800 ticket item. Just pay the damn thing. First, ask the agent on the other side to split it with you. If that agent wants to be a jerk about it, then at the closing table, tell the client that you tried to get the listing agent to do it, but they wouldn't split it with me. "So, I just ate it." Well, guess what? If your buyer client ends up talking to the seller, which typically they do, they'll have this conversation:

"My agent, Jason, actually ate the cost of that because your agent didn't want to share. Did you know that?"

"No, I didn't know that."

The greedy agent leaves a bad taste in their mouth, and you walk away, helping another happy client. The goal is to make our clients happy. That is why we do what we do.

Week 4 Day 5 WORKSHEET

Think of your past five transactions, if applicable. What were some of the things that nearly derailed the transaction? Be as specific as possible.

1

2

3

4

5

As you reflect on the previous five items, what would you have done differently in each scenario?

1

2

3

4

5

Let's reflect on why you became a real estate agent. Revisit your reason and your purpose from Week 2. Rewrite it below.

Things will happen during the transaction that will frustrate you and your client. Remember why you do what you do and always remember to put your clients' needs before your own.

Week 5 Day 1
DAY 21: EXPECTATIONS AND FORESHADOWING

This week, we are continuing on what I call 'the critical path of real estate sales.' This week, I will be sharing more techniques to better prepare your client. As a real estate agent, you need to take your clients down the road. While you are not a tour guide, we established that you are meant to guide them from the contract to close.

This week's goal is to arm you with some excellent techniques around the critical sales path. When you're on the critical path with a client, you have to make sure you are using the right tools and the right psychology. You need to ensure that you are always saying and doing the right things.

Last week, we covered the initial call, or the buyer consultation call, and the discovery portion of getting to know your new client. I shared some best practices when it comes to Tour Day. I shared how foreshadowing and preparing your client for the bumps along the road to get them along safely. By now, you have an excellent understanding of who you are, who your client is, and how to prepare them for the transaction. This week, we will pick up techniques to make this even more successful for both you and your client.

This week, I will share more about the psychology around what we need to do to get somebody to take action, write an offer, and make it to closing.

...

You must understand there is a critical path to what we do. This week we will focus on the critical path of sales. The techniques behind that are what's going to help you be more successful with that critical path.

Today, we will discuss how to master foreshadowing and set expectations. I believe this to be the foundation and fundamental framework for any salesperson, not just a real estate professional.

Remember that you are in the driver's seat. You need to put your client in step five when we're in step two. We talked about this yesterday. Before you even submit an offer on a property, you are talking about the client's inspection and appraisal. You are putting them in the mindset that this offer will be accepted, you ignore the scary part about negotiation, or better yet, you touch on it briefly without lingering long enough to scare the client into not submitting an offer at all. You are putting them in step five when we're still in step two.

The more that somebody wants it, the more valuable that becomes.

With your client, you are laying the groundwork for the future because the more we set expectations for what we're doing, the easier that process becomes. You are always preparing your client for that next step. Recognize that when your client is ready for some of the disappointing steps along the way, they are less disappointed? They knew the seller would likely counteroffer because you told them that would probably happen. They knew the inspection would be this daunting laundry list of things wrong with the house because you said to them that might occur. They won't freak out and walk away from the deal when the lending details change. They are disappointed, sure. I've mentally prepared my clients to expect issues on this property, so when they get a report, and there are issues, they're not surprised by it; they don't freak out. That's why I bring up the appraisal before the appraisal happens. I mentally prepare them that if the home doesn't appraise, that's okay. We're still in the driver's seat; don't worry about it.

Prepare your clients for the bumps along the road. That is your job as their real estate agent. Your job is to prepare them for what's ahead. You'll do this by setting expectations in advance and using foreshadowing to mentally prepare the client.

For example, Scott is in Indianapolis. He works with dozens of buyers looking for properties. When Scott is preparing to go show properties to a buyer, especially an out-of-state buyer, Scott needs to let them know before they even start looking at homes or before he even sends them a list, that they need to be prepared to not see many homes. You can tell your client that there's not going to be many homes available. Emphasize that what they're looking for is what many people are looking for. It is your job to show them that houses like the ones they're looking for do not stay on the market long; thus, they won't see many of them.

Then, a week later, when Scott's buyer sees something they want, they know to make a decision quickly because Scott told them houses like this one do not stay on the market long. When the clients' offer doesn't get accepted because they were in a multiple offer situation, the client is bummed and a little disappointed, but they are not discouraged. The buyer is also not angry with Scott because Scott prepared them for this moment. Next time, the buyer will make an offer even faster and maybe even offer a little bit more to ensure their offer is accepted.

Like Scott, you are setting expectations throughout the process. By laying the fundamental groundwork, you are creating scarcity. If there's an abundance of something, it's that they don't make decisions quickly or even at all. Plus, you always see that the more somebody wants it, the more valuable it becomes. From the beginning, in your initial call, you are laying the foundation of this critical path. You listen to what the clients want, and you educate them on what's out there and what's available.

> *If there's an abundance of something, clients don't make decisions quickly or even at all.*

You begin to foreshadow the house they're describing is what everybody else is looking for. Then, when you go on tour, you won't see 14 homes; you will see four. And because the first tour is the best tour, we will offer the home you like the most. You want to give your client control, but to be clear, they are not running the show. You are. You want to make sure that you are the ones that are in charge of the process.

You explain to your client, "Here is what is going to happen. I'm going to send you a list of homes—probably no more than ten. Then you are going to tell me which five you like. From that list, I want you to decide what three you like the most. Remember, there's not going to be a whole lot of homes to choose from because a lot of people are also looking for what you described. However, we are going to find you a home you love because that's my job, and I am really good at my job."

On the initial call, you are laying the process's groundwork. Tell your clients that 80% of my clients buy on their first tour.

We're already placing them in the next phase of our critical path. Take the client away from where we're currently at, and take them to the mindset of where we're going to be. The goal is to go from the offer accepted to repairs negotiated to the loan approved to the closing table.

When we're talking about putting together an offer. We're already talking about the inspection because we want to get the client in the mindset that they will buy this home. When you layout expectations and foreshadow these processes, everything else becomes more manageable because they've already mentally prepared for the next phase.

While you can not control the emotions of others, you can mitigate poor responses.

While you can not control the emotions of others, you can mitigate poor responses. If your client freaks out when the seller counter-offers, you didn't do your job well enough. Now you're stuck, and it's your fault because you didn't prepare them for what was coming next, and what possibly could come. You always have to be preparing them for what's ahead on the road to the closing table. That is your job.

"Hey, there will be issues with this home because every home has its issues," I tell my clients well before the inspection even happens.

I'm walking them down the path. I am explaining the next phase well before it happens. That's how we get to the finish line. I'm laying that groundwork before I've even finished my phase I'm currently in. Practice this, so you can master the art of foreshadowing. When you do, you are going to win. You are going to close more homes than you ever thought possible.

Week 5 Day 1 WORKSHEET

Write out the phases of the transaction. By now, you should have these committed to memory.

Think about your last two closings. How did you foreshadow with your client?

Think about your last two closings. How did you set expectations with your client?

Write the name of three current buyers.

1

2

3

Now, underline their names if you feel you have successfully foreshadowed and set expectations with that client.

If you did not underline all three names, write three ways to set expectations with the client this week.

1

2

3

Identify four times when you felt in the driver's seat during transactions this year.

1

2

3

4

What are three ways you can improve your ability to foreshadow and set expectations with your clients?

1

2

3

Week 5 Day 2
DAY 22: DON'T BE SALESY

There's a difference between selling and being salesy. As a real estate agent, your job is to sell a home, yet it is essential that you are not coming off as salesy—quite the conundrum, right? You have to sell without being salesy? Today, I will show you how.

> *There's a difference between selling and being salesy.*

There are ways to apply pressure, and there are ways to take away the stress and create a level of comfort with your clients. The key to not being salesy is recognition. You have to recognize when you're applying a little too much pressure, then you have to ease off. And I've trained thousands of agents on this, right? If somebody is trying to make a decision on a home, and we say, "Hey, listen, Mr. Bowles, it's time to move forward. We need to do this. As you know, we've looked at five homes today and seven homes last Tuesday. This house, you clearly love it. This is the perfect one. I'm telling you: this is the right home for you. You need to make a decision."

That is about the pressure point. You are clearly laying it on, which you should be, by the way. You have to sell. Yet, there's a fine line between the right amount of pressure and pushing it a little bit too far. When you push it a little bit too far, you have to back up.

You need to apply pressure, but you also need to be conscious of the pressure you're using. When that pressure seems too much, you may be laying it on a little thick, pull it away in a discreet manner.

So, let's say here you are with Mr. Bowles on Tour Day. He is wavering back and forth a bit. This is where you start asking the right questions.

"Why didn't you like the house?"

We start going back and forth.

"Oh, you did like the house. What did you like about it?"

"I agree. I think it's in a great school district, and the neighborhood is like what you describe you wanted. The master bedroom is as you described. Tell me what else you like about the house, Mr. Bowles."

> *There's a fine line between the right amount of pressure and pushing it a little bit too far.*

At some point, the rubber meets the road because there are ways to get them to make a decision. Know that when you force that decision on your clients, you're ultimately forcing yourself into a cancellation. They have to be comfortable with the decision to buy or sell a home.

As you know, it is the largest purchase most of your clients will ever make. It is your job to make them feel comfortable.

Make sure your clients always know and understand that you're still on their team. When you start laying it on thick, be sure to pull away from that a little bit because your clients must know you're in this together. Don't be salesy. Be smart about what you're saying, and how much pressure you're applying. When that pressure becomes too great, make sure to pull away.

The key to not being salesy is recognition.

Now, let's talk about how to apply pressure when prospecting. It's on the phone where oftentimes agents use too much pressure losing the prospect before meeting them in person. Instead, create reasons for the prospect to want more information from you—not the other way around. Here's an example. Imagine you are calling through your database and Ms. Nilsen and her boyfriend were thinking about buying a condo downtown, ultimately they decided to keep renting.

"Hey, just calling to see how things are going," you start the call. "I wanted to see if you're still in the market to purchase a condo?"

You start building rapport again, and say, "Hey, listen, I'm sure you're seeing that interest rates are really low right now. So, you know, it's time that we get back out there and go look for a home."

You already know they wanted to take a break from looking, and that's what she tells you on the phone now.

"Well, why are you considering taking a break? Have your plans changed?"

Always keep them talking by asking great questions.

"Why hold off? You know that the rates are 3.5%. Pricing looks like it is going to continue to go up? Why are we waiting?"

At that threshold, as a salesperson, you have to take yourself back. When you're laying it on a little thick, you must step back and say, "Now listen, Ms. Nilsen. I'm not saying you have to buy a home tomorrow. What I'm saying is we need to get out there and take a look soon, because we're missing out on an opportunity. That's all."

Then, you have alleviated some of the pressure. Ms. Nilsen can sit there and think, "Oh, okay, well, that's comforting. This agent is not smacking me in the face by saying, 'you better buy a house today!'

You're saying to Ms. Nilsen, you need to buy a home, and then you're taking it back and saying "now, I'm not saying you have to buy tomorrow. But, I am saying that we need to get back in the car. We do need to look at more property because the time is right."

Step back from being salesy for a minute. You throw another jab in there by saying, "we do need to get out there soon."

The more your client lets their guard down a little bit, the more you can go in and hit them one more time, then two more times. That's the jab. The jab sets up the knockout. The knockout is when you go on tour, and you close them. Be smart about the amount of pressure you're using.

"You know, I just want to make sure that you and your boyfriend make the right decision. You know, I'm not saying you need to buy tomorrow. What I am saying is it's the right time to start looking again."

Week 5 Day 2 WORKSHEET

Identify three times where you applied too much pressure with a prospect or client. Be specific.

1

2

3

Think about your last two closings. How did you sell them without being salesy? Write three examples of applying the right amount of pressure.

1

2

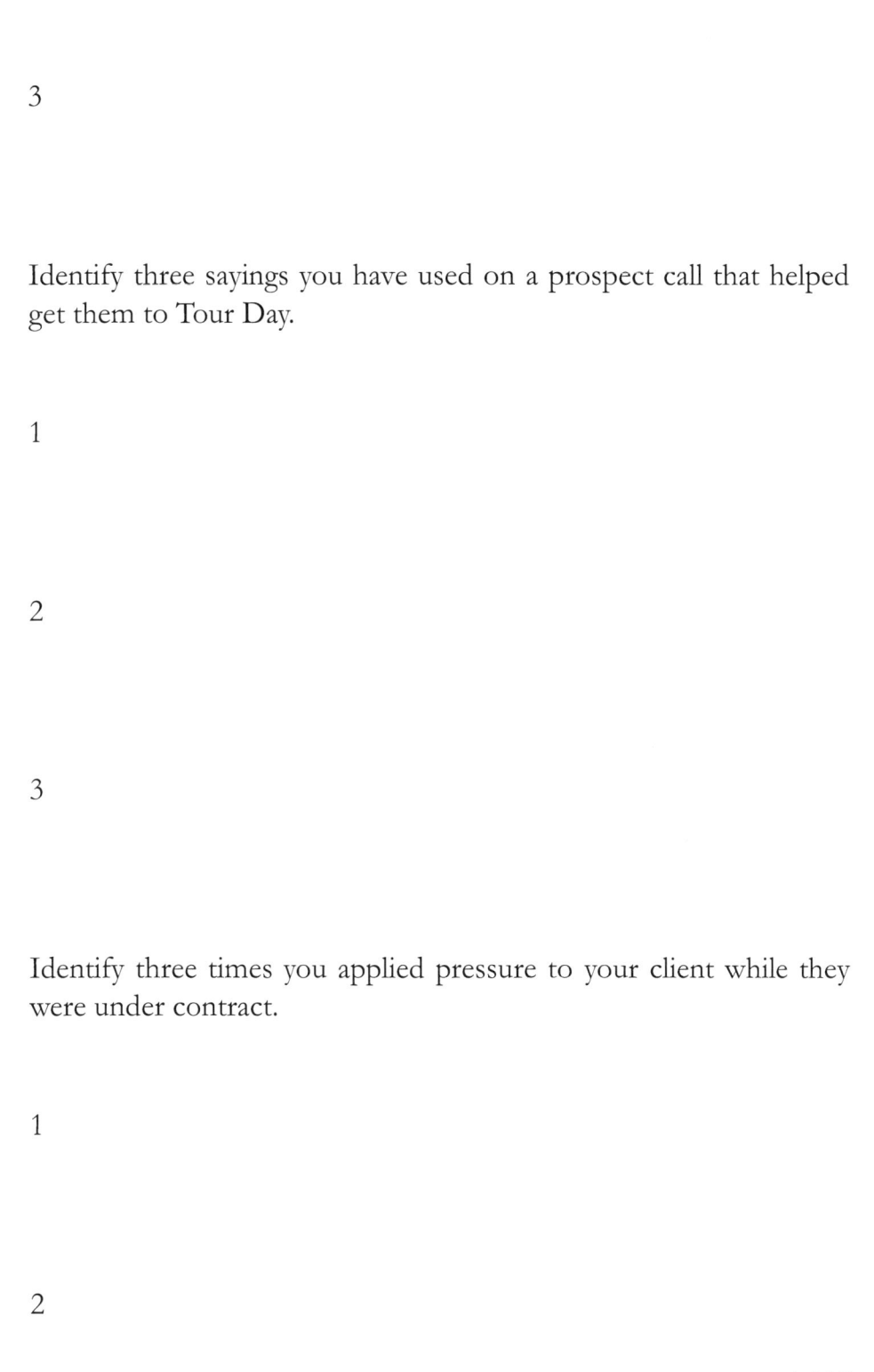

3

Identify three sayings you have used on a prospect call that helped get them to Tour Day.

1

2

3

Identify three times you applied pressure to your client while they were under contract.

1

2

3

Looking at the previous above, how did the client react when you applied that pressure?

1

2

3

Week 5 Day 3
DAY 23: MAKE IT THEIR IDEA

This week, we have learned about setting expectations, foreshadowing with our clients, and techniques on how to not be salesy. This allows us to mentally prepare our clients for the critical path to the closing table. Today, we will talk more about mentally preparing our clients.

Today, we're going to be talking about making your clients submit an offer or close on a property thinking it was their idea. One of the most extraordinary things you can do is make it seem as if they are the ones that thought of it themselves. We're conditioning our clients. Corporations have been using this sales tactic for years. It is called subliminal advertising. Corporations are telling you something by making it seem as though you already knew it. Think about it, an advertisement tells you that a chemical is harmful, and that's why their product doesn't use that chemical. You need a product to make your life easier. You know you have this problem? Well, we can solve it.

You may have never even heard of that chemical they mentioned avoiding. But now, you think, "oh yeah, I knew that!" Next thing you know, you are ordering that product that you didn't even know you needed.

It's all a game. Making someone else's idea sound like your own is conditioning. Today, we are going to talk about conditioning our clients. This will allow you to close more homes with more clients.

When you master this, you will win. When you talk to clients about interest rates, you are using statements like, "I know you see how low interest rates are." and "I know you already are seeing a 50-year low, Ms. Nilsen." "You are seeing what's happening in the market, Mr. Bowles."

The more you can work on that technique, the more you can make somebody feel as though they were the ones that thought of it in the first place. The more you can do this, the faster you're going to put people into homes, and the easier it will become.

> *One of the most incredible things you can do is to make it seem as if they are the ones that thought of it themselves.*

You are dropping little seeds when you are in conversation with your clients.

It's very subtle, but you'll hear it.

"Mr. Johnston, I know that we've been looking at a couple of properties, and we haven't quite found what we're looking for yet. I want to make sure that you know, we're still in this together, that you're still in the market and you're focused on purchasing a home?"

"Well, I am, you know, my wife and I, we just kind of decided that when the time is right, the time is right. And, we'll know, right?"

These people are on the fence. Now, your job is to make seriously looking at houses again their idea.

"Listen, Mr. Johnston. You can see what is happening, so I don't need to tell you. You know these interest rates are at all-time lows. I'm sure you've seen it in the paper and on the news as well. The housing market is doing well."

Mr. Johnston starts to agree with you.

"Well, then we shouldn't be waiting. I've never worked with someone who has regretted purchasing. I've only had people that regret not purchasing."

Then, Mr. Johnston starts to think. You dropped subtle things in the conversation, such as, "I'm sure you've seen interest rates are at an all-time low." "I'm sure you've been reading in the paper how well the markets have been doing?"

Mr. Johnston is nodding along, but the truth is he probably hasn't been reading the news. He probably hasn't heard that interest rates are at an all-time low. But now Mr. Johnston has. And now, he thinks he already knew that. All he is doing is agreeing with you. You are putting Mr. Johnston in the mindset that he already knows what's right. You're not telling Mr. Johnston what's right; he already knows.

"You know, the last time we were out looking at houses, you mentioned to me that the house you're in is just too small for you now. You told me you have a bigger family, and you want a little bit more room. I have to tell you, I want to make sure that we find that right home for you. I'm sure you've seen in your portal that about five of those ten homes are already pending. It goes to show you the urgency of the market. As you know, if you wait, you're going to ultimately pay more. I know you're noticing that. And that's what I don't want you to miss out on."

I don't know if he has checked their portal, and Mr. Johnston probably hasn't. But I just told them that a lot of homes are selling right now.

"I don't need to tell you that because you already know," I say. Saying this, creates this mindset in Mr. Johnston. He now gets off the phone and starts thinking, "Yeah, I know homes are selling fast. Yeah, I know when I look around at my current house, it is too small. I do want a bigger house. I know that."

All of a sudden, your client thinks that they thought of it themselves. It wasn't them! You told them that. You told them what to think; you told them they were smart. You said to them that they know the market. You said to them that you know how low interest rates are, and it's a great time to buy. You told them that homes are selling like crazy.

"I know that you know."

It's an automatic head nod. Yes, I do. I do know.

When you put people in the mindset that it's their idea, it creates this automatic nod. We spoke last week about how the client simply needs to agree with you. They don't need to say yes because it is easier to get them to say, "yeah, I agree."

When you plant the seed into somebody's mind to make it seem as though it's their idea, that now's the right time to buy, then you have mastered this technique. Once you have mastered conditioning your client into adopting your ideas as their own, then you will win.

Week 5 Day 3 WORKBOOK

Identify three clients who are not taking action.

1

2

3

What are the five most common reasons these clients are not making a move?

1

2

3

4

5

For each reason above, write two sentences about how you can turn this around in the client's mind

1

2

3

4

5

Identify three times you made a client think something was their idea. Describe what happened.

1

2

3

Week 5 Day 4
DAY 24: FORCING THE OCCURRENCE

Today, we're going to be talking about something unique that I call "forcing the occurrence." It is vital to your success as an agent and your ability to close a client. Forcing the occurrence is about control.

Your job as a professional is to ensure that you are in charge of the process. I see so many agents out there that want to help people buy or sell a home, yet they allow the client to dictate the entire home buying process. The consumer dictates where and when to look at houses. The agent is playing "follow-the-client" instead of taking the lead.

The buyer is telling the agent how much they want to offer when writing the offer. Stop that. As the real estate professional, the ball is in your court. You are meant to be in the driver's seat. We talked about this on Day 20.

Do you tell your accountant how to do your taxes? Do you tell your attorney how to defend the case? No, we trust these professionals.

Yet, for some reason, in our industry, it's different. I am here to tell you it shouldn't be that way. You need to be in control of the whole process.

Forcing the occurrence is about control.

Morgan went to the mall yesterday, and when she walked into the clothing store, a female associate approached her and said, "Can I help you with anything?"

And what is your immediate response?

"No, I'm good," Morgan said.

Every time, in nearly every store in America, this is how the conversation goes. Today, let's examine the difference between great salespeople and average salespeople. An average salesperson allows the customer to dictate the outcome.

"Can I help you with something?"

"No, I'm just looking."

"Okay, let me know if you need anything."

Well, that's not being in control. That's allowing a customer to dictate the outcome of what happens at that store. And if you're a salesperson, that shouldn't happen.

On the other hand, a great salesperson finds a way to get the consumer to do something. A great salesperson is polished and tactful. They force the occurrence.

Morgan walks into another store. Instead of asking Morgan, "Can I help you?" the salesperson asks, "Are you looking for jeans today?"

"You know what? We got a pair of jeans that arrived last week that are not on the shelf here. But they're amazing. Let me go get them for you," the salesperson says with confidence.

"Go try these on for me," she says to Morgan with a smile.

The salesperson forced the occurrence. She controlled the process.

Now, when you are preparing to take your client on tour, you should say, "We're going to go look at this one, this one and this one, and here's why."

Then you start foreshadowing. "When we go on tour, you're going to pick your best three. Then, we're going to narrow it down. Does that sound good to you?"

"Okay, great. I'll see you on Saturday," you tell them. You are forcing the occurrence.

Then, when you see that the buyer likes this house, you tell them, "you need to buy this home. This is the right one."

You tell your client, "you are not going to get better." because the power of no is at work here.

We had our initial call and our discovery. We got the buyer in the car. We have toured homes, and they know that there's not a lot out there.

They said no to the first couple of homes that we've already toured, and we've agreed with them. Those homes were not the right fit. Now, together, we get to say, "yes." You set up this whole process. From start to finish, each transaction is the same process. While each buyer and home has its own nuances, the process and the techniques are the same.

You are in charge of controlling the sale. If you're not in control, you will lose more clients, contracts, and deals. Do not give your client a reason to say no; they need a reason to say yes.

When trouble arises in the transaction, and it will, you look at your client with confidence and tell them: "Don't worry about it, let me take care of it. It might take me a day or so, but we will get you what you want."

You foreshadowed that it might take a day or so. This ensures that they won't freak out when they don't hear back from you within a couple of hours. You reassured them that it is your job to handle these problems. Plus, they were anticipating problems because you set the expectations that there was potential for them.

You're in control. You will direct your clients to do more of what we want them to do, like buying a home, which is what they want to do.

Week 4 Day 4 WORKSHEET

Identify three times you have successfully set an expectation with a client this month.

1

2

3

Identify three times you have foreshadowed for a client this week.

1

2

3

Identify three times you have made a client think something was their idea this week.

1

2

3

Identify three ways you can force the occurrence this week with your clients.

1

2

3

Week 5 Day 5
DAY 25: GETTING PEOPLE OFF THE FENCE

Today, I will share two techniques you will use on your critical path of sales. The first is what I call 'getting off the fence.' The second is what I call "to third party".

Your job as a real estate agent will be to get your clients, both buyers and sellers, off the fence. When clients are in limbo, your job is to push them to make decisions.

First, eliminate those who are not ready to buy. People like that are not on the fence; they're not buyers. Stop wasting your time on those people. We spoke this week about controlling the situation. This is critical when it comes to your time. Do not waste your time on people who are not ready to buy. If they don't really want to sell their home, walk away and work with someone who is ready.

I see it all the time, especially with newer agents. They become tour guides, instead of becoming a true sales professional. You need to not be afraid to ask these direct questions. Ask the buyer if they are prequalified. Ask the seller if they want to sell your house in the next four months.

Newer Agents: They become tour guides, instead of becoming a true sales professional.

If you don't know by now, you will not be able to force someone to buy a home. It's not going to happen.

What if a client says to you: "You know, we were not really quite ready to buy yet, but we just want to go see what's out there."

It is your job to determine if they are just wanting a tour guide or if they are seriously looking yet dragging their feet. You do this by asking good questions.

Why is it that you want to take a look at the market now if you're not interested in making a move for another year? If you're simply wanting to get a gauge of what's out there, I totally understand. It's just that the market is so unpredictable. The houses and the prices you're looking at today are not going to be the same next year. They are likely not even going to be the same next month.

What we're going to do is give you a list of properties. I'm going to set you up on these alerts. That way, when a home comes on the market, you can take a look at it. If you have a question about the home, you can call me about it. Instead of us spending time touring around looking at multiple homes, I think we should have you visit some open houses. I can give you my opinion anytime. That's the best plan.

You controlled the situation by telling them what is going to happen. You just saved yourself days and hours of showing homes that they're not going to buy. Ask direct questions and stay in control of the conversation. Don't waste your time with people that aren't buying. How do you know? You ask the right questions.

To 'third party' means a message is not coming from you; it's coming from somewhere or someone else. Third-Party allows you the opportunity to say things that you necessarily wouldn't be able to say on your own because it would be too salesy. I have said it before and I will say it again: get testimonials and reviews from your clients. You're not the one telling your clients how wonderful you are to work with, other people are.

Another technique is using outside resources and news articles to send your message. You can tell a client, "I'm sure you saw today's interest rates are at a record low."

You have to be strategic because if your client isn't thinking you're pushing them, they may do what you want them to. Use facts and figures to integrate the third-party technique. When you're working with clients, make sure you integrate what others are saying or what you may have seen in the news. Use that to your advantage. Master the approach of utilizing third party testimonials within your process of the critical path and watch your success rise.

Week 5 Day 5 WORKSHEET

Identify three times in the past where you allowed a client to waste your time

1

2

3

Now, looking back, how could you have avoided those situations?

1

2

3

Identify five ways you can use the third party technique with your clients this week

1

2

3

4

5

Week 6 Day 1

DAY 26: CAPITAL AND MEASURABLES

As you travel down the critical path of sales, you have started to pick up many new techniques.

First, you identified who you are. Next, you determined who your customer is, and this week, we will look at how to target them.

This week we are focused on marketing and promotion. We will talk about things like where to spend money and how to tackle self-promotion properly. You will determine your minimum standards of marketing and strategy and create a content calendar. You will examine if your business is using old school strategy versus a new school strategy. By the end of this week, you will know the importance of marketing and promotion. It is critical that we understand the value of marketing and learn how to measure the results.

Rome wasn't conquered in a day. You must focus on improving small amounts each day. It's incredible what you can accomplish when you look back six months, a year, and two years. To get better, you have to have a system in place. After this week, you will have a roadmap. We will begin by building it out, but then it is your job to make sure you're consistent. Once you have a strong foundation, you can build from there. As you grow, you can add people, and, all of a sudden, it just starts to grow exponentially.

…

This week we will examine what is working and what's not. In doing so, we must look at money in and money out. As a real estate agent, you are running a business. Everyone who runs a business must know how much money is coming in and out. Spending money will become necessary as you grow and scale your business.

Both new and experienced agents ask me: Where should I spend money?

First, you need to examine what is working for you in your business. Do you know where your leads are coming from?

By now, you know your niche. Are you working in a particular neighborhood? Are you working with divorcees, veterans, high-end luxury buyers in a specific zip code? This is your niche.

If you focus your business on working with families in a particular neighborhood, you should find and build relationships with representatives in media organizations that target that same market. Roxanne, an agent in Kansas City, has listed 30 homes in the suburbs of Kansas City in the last year. There is a magazine in Kansas City called the 435 Magazine that targets the suburbs of Kansas City. Roxanne called someone from the magazine and built a relationship with the editor. She not only inquired about advertising in the magazine but also asked about upcoming community events.

Keep in mind that the magazine will know the in's and out's of what is happening in the community. They are the eyes and the ears of that community. Become friends with them and be a resource when they need it.

Once you build a relationship with someone in the media organization, send them a quick text, "hey. did you see home prices went up 11% this month?" Always be looking to give valuable information to them as you do your clients.

What can you do to build a relationship with someone in a media organization in your market? Maybe it's not a local magazine but instead a radio station. You know local radio stations attend events, have local booths, and know everyone. It would help if you became their go-to for everything real estate.

PRO TIP: You know those real estate magazines where every single page is of an agent. One-fourth of the page is jammed packed with eight of their listings. There are so many magazines out there like that. The ad itself is one picture of the front of the house with the description. There are dozens of agents doing the same things within the same magazine.

Guess what? This is not driving business. There is a lot more you can do for your clients than spend $1,000 or so to put your listings alongside 100 other agents' listings. Do you want to be like the 30 other agents advertising there? Stand out. By now, you should know your niche so well that you can capitalize on it.

I find it valuable to be the only agent in a specific media category, or one of few, because my message could resonate. I never wanted to be in the cluster. That's why I am also not a big fan of doing broker opens. New agents come to me asking about broker opens, usually after watching reality television on a network like HGTV or Bravo.

The new agents think, "All I need to do is hold a broker open. I'm going to get a hundred or so agents in to view the house. I'll spend a reasonable amount of money on food, just enough to make it look nice. Then, the next thing I know, I will have seven offers, all over asking. Then, when it's all said and done: Bam! I will make a commission of, at least, $150,000."

I wish it were that easy. I've sold thousands of homes, and I've never sold one at a broker open. You end up spending $1,000 on beverages to gather together real estate agents for free food and gossip.

"But, Jason, my clients watch those same reality TV shows, and they expect me to do a broker open."

First, ask yourself: are your clients in the driver's seat? Or are you? As a professional, it is your job to control the situation, drive the conversation, and set the expectations. We have talked about foreshadowing since Week Two. Tell your client that you will sell their house by holding open houses three times a week. You know the best photographer in town, so their listing photos will put the best foot forward on the MLS and through our social media efforts. You will drive customers to their home by marketing the home to your extensive real estate network. Likely they won't even ask about broker opens because they will see you are in charge and know what you're doing—that's why they choose you to list their house. You're in control. Be sure to act like it.

When it comes to marketing, doing nothing will result in nothing.

If you're a new agent, start small and track what is working. If you have been in the business for a while, you, too, need to track what is working. If you sold the last ten homes to people in one organization, then spend time, money, and energy getting in front of more people in that organization. If you met the last seventeen buyers at open houses, continue to hold open houses. Find a buyers' agent who can replicate your formula so you can have some leverage.

There are different levels of marketing and advertising. In Week 8, we will talk about the Levels of Real Estate Sales Professionals. Today, I want to talk about levels in marketing and advertising. If you are starting your career, you may need to start with free social media marketing. If you are at Level 5 in your business, you will be getting your message out to more people through more advertisements.

Let's focus on what to do for the newer agents if you don't have a lot of money to spend on marketing. First, you must be willing to work hard. If you are not diligent, this will not work. While social media marketing can be free, it takes time and effort. If you did not know, Facebook and Instagram are free, and email marketing is almost free. However, you must be willing to create the content. If you are not doing this already, you need to be sending out a Newsletter to your inner core. Then, the moment you can afford it, also send the newsletter to your outer core so you can bring them into your inner core, too.

A newsletter can include community updates and market news, but it must always have a market trend report. You are establishing yourself as an expert in the field of real estate.

In Week Three, we went over your schedule. You are now committed to keeping to your schedule. This week, I want you to create a marketing schedule. Marketers call this a content calendar. The success of this relies heavily on your willingness to stick to the plan. You will need to create blog posts and email marketing. Keep in mind that this does not need to be completed by you. If you can afford to pay someone to do this for you, by all means, do that.

Back in 2011, I created my own newsletter. I remember hovering over my keyboard for 12+ hours, making this newsletter perfect down to every last punctuation mark and photo. I printed the newsletter myself, and I paid someone to deliver them. It cost me less than $500 to have the newsletters delivered to approximately 2,000 houses in a specific farming area.

First, I created a content calendar as I am advising you to do. I was committed to sending out a monthly newsletter. Every single month, I had to sit down and bust this out. At the time, I could not afford to pay someone to do it for me. From there, I took the same content, and I created drip campaigns with follow-up emails. This was all done at a low cost. Did it take a lot of time? Yes, it did. Yet, it paid off because I was consistent. I did not start with one newsletter. I set out to do a monthly newsletter, and I did not skip a month.

Consistency is key. I didn't skip a month. There were no excuses.

As the business grew, I was able to offload some of these tasks to other people. While giving up control was difficult, the newsletter actually got better when I handed it to someone who had more time to devote to it. Plus, I hired someone who was a professional writer. Their expertise was writing and content creation. My newsletter improved, and I got time back on my calendar. I was still able to come up with the ideas and the content in collaboration with the writer.

Want to know the best free marketing in real estate? Open houses. They are virtually free. Once you have your signs paid for, there is no upfront cost.

Pro Tip: Have your name legible on a sign. I almost cannot believe I have to write this. Yet, I drive by neighborhoods all the time, and I see a broker sign pointing to an open house.

The agent is advertising their broker's name and not their own. That's brilliant.

Instead, if the new agent invested $400 on branded open house signs, know the whole neighborhood sees your name. Someone driving by can also read the name because it's not size 14 font in the bottom left-hand corner. Print your signs with your name big enough to read. Again, I cannot believe I am even writing this, but I feel I have to.

Remember Caitlin from Week Two, who farmed a specific neighborhood so hard she ended up buying her dream house in that very neighborhood. Do you think Caitlin had her name on her Open House signs? You better believe it. The neighbors knew her name before they ever met her. You know why? Because her brand was all over the neighborhood. "Caitlin is the neighborhood expert," people would say. Caitlin held an open house in that same neighborhood three days a week. Hundreds of people drove by her signs every single day. She became a staple in the neighborhood.

Her signs were not just her broker's name. Her name was not super tiny. Her name was visible, and she stayed consistent. Consistency and visibility were key for Caitlin, and they are also critical to your success.

I became so successful because I did open houses consistently. I wasn't on the radio station in that town, in the magazine, or in this part time and haphazardly holding open houses. I was mindful of what I wanted and where I was going with my business, and I stuck with it.

If you're holding open houses 45 minutes in that direction and 20 minutes in this direction like Matt or if you're abandoning your schedule like Devin, you are going to fail.

I imagine that if you are reading this book, you do not want to fail. You very much want to get to Level Five, which I will talk about in Week Eight.

You want the same people seeing your newsletter, social media posts, and open house signs. Stay consistent and stay in front of people.

In Week Two, you identified your niche and your ideal customer. Now, let's focus on ways to stay in front of your ideal customer. Once you build credibility within the community, you will get referrals, and your phone will begin to ring. First, you must build credibility by getting your name out there consistently.

Remember Matt? He was holding houses open all over town. He was so burnt out that he didn't make it as an agent. You know why? He was trying to be everywhere in front of everyone. First, you cannot be everywhere. Just like you learned that you could not work with everyone. You cannot advertise everywhere.

Now, let's talk about measurables. Today, we are talking about spending money on advertising, so I would not be doing you a favor if I didn't explain this adequately. First, you need to understand that not every dollar in advertising will be easily traced to a dollar in commissions.

When you are allocating money to advertising, do not look at it as one for one. If you spend $12,000 this year on marketing and that brought you a $400,000 listing, or $12,000 in commissions, I don't consider that a break-even. Why? Because real estate is not a one transaction business. One transaction leads to many transactions. Here is an example. I post an ad in a local magazine. I get an inbound call from that one ad, and because my listing appointment is on point, I get the listing. Then I sell that listing, and I get a referral from that seller. Then that referral refers me to their aunt and uncle. Then I doubled up the house, and I represented the buyer and the seller. Or I got a buyer from holding the house open. Then, that buyer sends me a referral.

Thus, you cannot possibly look at an advertisement and say, "Well, I got one listing from it."

We're in the business of selling homes. If you can genuinely break even from your marketing spend, you're way ahead of the game.

If you aren't already, get your signs made, create content consistently and do the work. Set aside time this week to write marketing content.

In Week Eight, I will share with you the five levels of real estate sales professionals. If you want to get to level five, you need to do the work today.

Week 6 Day 1 WORKSHEET

Are you creating content consistently now? Circle Yes or No.

If Yes, how can you continue to put out good content?

If No, what are three pieces of content you can commit to making this month?

1

2

3

What are three free ways to get in front of your ideal customer?

1

2

3

What are three ways you can spend money to get in front of your ideal customer?

1

2

3

What can you do today to build a relationship with someone in a media organization in your market?

Do you know where your leads are coming from?

Where are you marketing now?

What's most effective?

Week 6 Day 2
DAY 27: TWO SIDES OF MARKETING

We talked about marketing yesterday, and we will continue to talk about it today. Now, you know you can't do everything and be everywhere.

You must know the intent when spending money on marketing. There are two sides of marketing. First, there is marketing to drive new business opportunities. Next, there's marketing for the brand. Some would tell you they go hand in hand, but that doesn't mean that's your intent. For example, just last quarter, I put something out there, and I knew I wouldn't get a lead from this piece of marketing. Instead, I'm doing it for what I call a brand play. I'm doing it for awareness, so I become a household name.

That's why branding comes after you've created something. However, you can create your brand before you have a business. I mentioned your open house signs yesterday and how your name must be big enough for people to read. Hopefully, you have ordered those by now. These signs are your first piece of branding. Next, your newsletter becomes a part of the brand. The best way to start branding yourself for free is through social media. This is all advertising and marketing for your brand.

Next, you may be ready to start spending some money. So, you start with Google ads to drive traffic to a new listing. This is an example of advertising for a new business opportunity. Once you can bring new revenue in the door, you can continue to build your brand from your marketing and advertising.

Branding comes after you've created something.

Building your brand will take time. I think of it as this little snowball that we continue to roll down the hill. As we roll it down the mountain, it just keeps getting bigger and bigger. The significant part about pushing something downhill, rather than uphill, is that it gets easier as it picks up speed. First, you may need to spend money, and it hurts. You may notice when the money comes out of your account because it doesn't fill back up as quickly. Over time, you will start to see the tables turn. Your account balance will start to increase even as you pour more money into your marketing efforts and your advertising budget.

Brand awareness is more powerful than trying to rely on merely new business from advertising. Once you build a brand big enough, people will not question you and your ability to list their home. You're a brand name. You have this massive team, and you have become a huge agent. If that's your goal, and it should be because you serve more clients and make more money, branding will be critical to your success.

Start where you can and grow over time.

Now, what happens when you have been spending money with the intent to drive new business, yet that new business does not appear. If you have been trying consistently for six or seven months and it's not working, you need to advertise elsewhere.

After you have reevaluated where you're marketing, look at your messaging. You are in one of the most competitive industries. There are thousands, if not hundreds of thousands of agents looking to work with the same consumer. Are you making it clear why they should pick you? Are you standing out? Why should someone list their home with you? Why should a buyer buy with you?

When you're in a pool of some of the most competitive people in the world, you have to step up to the plate. Don't come to the listing appointment with some generic folder from your brokerage. Spend the $3.99 to have a sharp-looking folder. Better yet, spend the money to have your entire listing presentation digital and available to the client before you arrive.

Why does someone list with me? Because I am the best. I am King of my market. I am the King of my city. Then I become the King of my state. Now, my goal is to become the King of the country.

You must know that it's a process, and you have to understand that process. It takes time. You might find yourself in the middle of it right now. You might find yourself toward the top, where you are starting to have a vast empire. Or maybe you're at the very beginning. Either way, your branding needs to reflect where you are going. Decide where you want to take your business and make your branding reflect that.

If you want to dominate in New Home Sales, start branding yourself as a New Construction expert. If you're going to own a particular zip code, spend your marketing dollars strategically in that zip code and brand yourself as the expert in this neighborhood.

Now, listen, I admit that I advertise in many magazines, and I don't get many calls from those magazines. Instead, people in my community pick up those magazines, flip through them, and set them down on a coffee table or a bedside table. Sometimes, they set them face down. Who is smiling back at them on the back of that magazine? You guessed it: my team and me. Our branding is inside that magazine, too, just in case the person sees our advertisements. It continues to add credibility. When the reader thinks of real estate, they will think of our team.

But again, I admit they don't pick up their phone and start scrolling our Instagram or pick up their phone and dial our number. Instead, the next day, they might attend an open house, or maybe they're not in the market to buy a home, but they see my branded signs as they drive home from work. Next year, when they are ready to downsize or move across town, they start attending open houses. To clarify, people don't go digging for a magazine from last year to find my number. That doesn't happen either. Instead, he gets into his car and walks into an open house. Who is there to greet him? A buyers' agent from my team. The young, hungry agent hands the gentleman a card. He smiles because he recognizes the name, Jason Mitchell Team. "Man, you guys are everywhere," he may say to my agent. You see what I've done for that buyers' agent? I've added credibility to them.

It's my obligation as a team leader to ensure that my agents have the best opportunity to close business. When I spend tens of thousands of dollars on advertising, this is the moment I am thinking of. I have ensured our branding is on point and consistent. It is pointed toward the people we want to serve, so we have the best chance of representing them in their next real estate transaction.

You can build your brand with a little bit of money if you're consistent in what you do. This will pay off. While it does not happen overnight, I can tell you this: it can happen a lot faster than you think if you're consistent with what you're doing. It can snowball. Over time, after consistently putting your name out there, you will successfully build your brand. Tomorrow, we will talk about promotion.

Week 6 Day 2 WORKSHEET

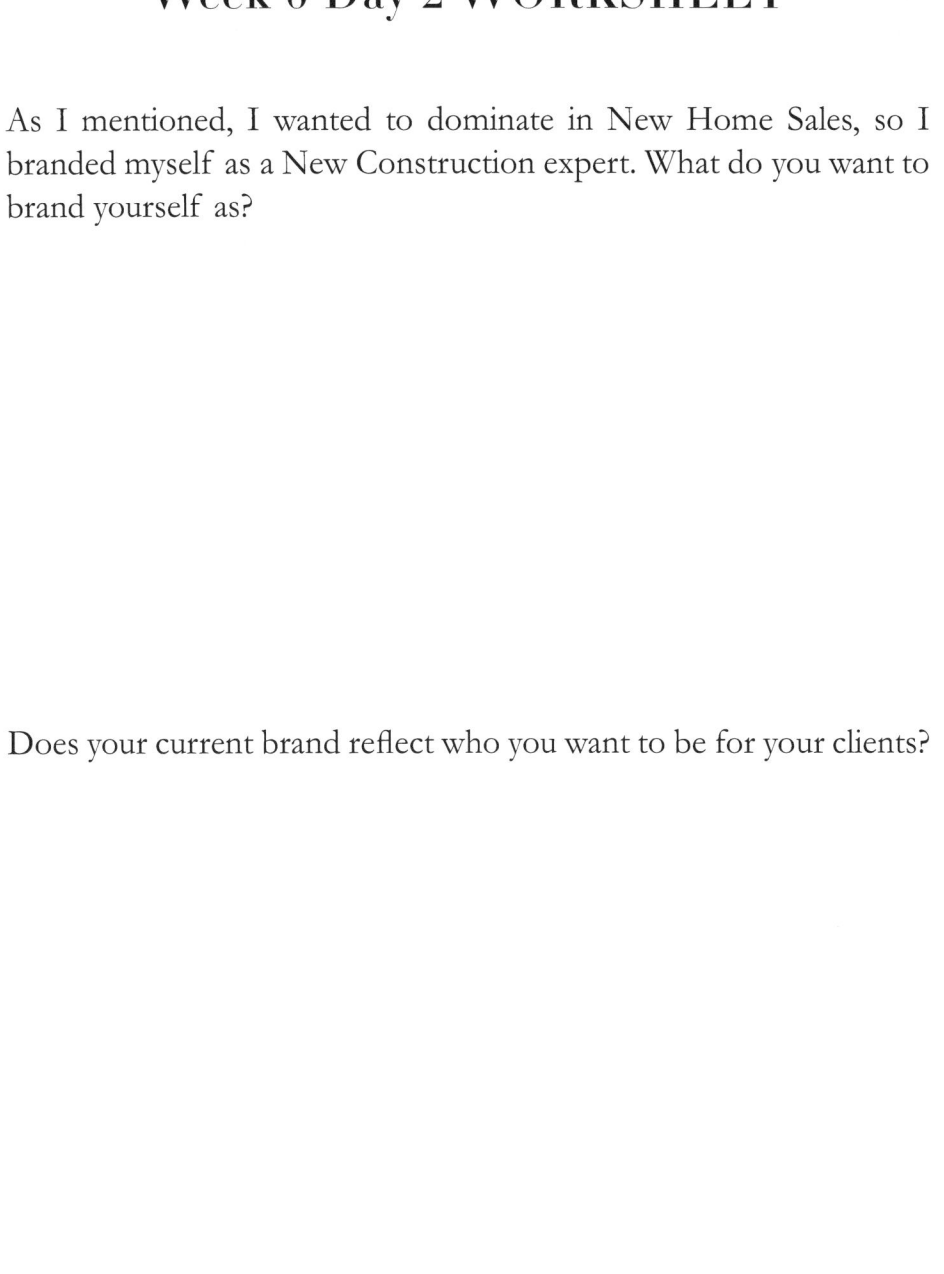

As I mentioned, I wanted to dominate in New Home Sales, so I branded myself as a New Construction expert. What do you want to brand yourself as?

Does your current brand reflect who you want to be for your clients?

If yes, identify three ways your current branding reflects who you are.

1

2

3

Identify three ways you can improve your branding.

1

2

3

Week 6 Day 3
DAY 28: SELF-PROMOTION

Today we're going to talk about self-promotion. Before we do, I was hoping you could think of the most arrogant person you know. Whether it is someone you know personally or someone famous, who is the most arrogant person you know?

When you hear their name, how do you feel? What do you immediately think of? What would it look like to be friends with this person? Would you trust them in business?

Today, as we talk about self-promotion, I will do my best to guide you away from being like the person you're thinking about. There are methods to self-promote in a way that you do not come across as arrogant. People won't believe you have some massive, unchecked ego. Instead, they admire you for your accomplishments and commitment to greatness and, in our case, as real estate professionals, our commitment to serving our clients.

When I hear that term self-promotion, the first person I think of is Floyd Mayweather, a boxer who made billions of dollars because he was a master self-promoter. To clarify, this is not who I think of when I think of arrogance and cockiness. Whether you like Floyd Mayweather or you don't, he's what I call must-see TV.

He is the Tiger Woods of boxing. Mayweather is must-see TV because he's a master at self-promotion. Now, I'm not here to say that Mayweather's way is the right way; what I'm saying is that it was effective.

Promotion is critical because we have to be the ones that tell the story. Once we can tell our story, others will start to hear it, believe it, and spread it to achieve success. As we're working our way up, or while we find ourselves in the middle of selling $20-$30 million a year in production, self-promotion is critical.

You have to be the brand. The brand is you. It is such a lost opportunity when I see signs with real estate agent's names in small print. Your name should be big and bold everywhere the public can see it.

You're the brand, not your broker. You're the brand. You're the Rainmaker, so we have to make sure that that self-promotion is something that you take pride in. And there are right and wrong ways to do it.

> *"Some pay to see me win, some pay to see me lose, but they all pay." - Floyd Mayweather*

In real estate, you don't want to come off cocky and arrogant. Not only will agents not want to work with you, clients will not want to work with you. And then they're going to talk about how you are cocky, arrogant, and they're not going to refer you to others. When you're truly humble and give thanks, and, people feel that.

When you are talking on social media, you talk about your clients and not about yourself. Is your brand centered on kindness and appreciation, or are you continually bragging about yourself? There is a fine line, and you must learn to walk it. In Week Three, I told you that random acts of kindness would allow you to talk about your wins, too. If your marketing is shining a light on your clients, naturally your wins are being showcased without coming across as arrogant. Focus your marketing on how wonderful your clients are, and then every once a while, you can mention how wonderful you and your business are doing.

Then there's my brand. There's my name, which resonates with people, but you have to be your biggest fan.

> *My name started to become recognizable by those in my brokerage and those in my community. This was all before I was selling as many houses as they perceived. That's the power of perception.*

Self-promotion also deals with the old theory that perception is reality. When I first started out in my career, I posted my new listings everywhere, every single time. Posting them everywhere made it seem as though I had more business than I probably did at the time. Then I started promoting other people's listings, too. My name started to become recognizable by those in my brokerage and those in my community. This was all before I was selling as many houses as they perceived. That's the power of perception.

At the time, Facebook was still new. I'd get messages on my walls, back when people did that. The messages would read, "Man, you're crushing it." This was years ago.

Then, I would post my numbers front and center. At the time, I was still in my 20s, and I found out that I was the number one agent under 30 in the state of Arizona. So, I used that as my tagline.

Jason is Arizona's number one agent under 30.

Over the years, I was also the number one agent in a couple of zip codes, so I put that front and center. I wanted everyone to know this, so I put these credentials in every ad I sent out. I'm number one here, and I've sold the highest price per square foot in this community.

I did that, and then I told people about it. That's self-promotion. If you want to continue to grow your career, you have to develop creative ways that make you stand out. Maybe you have sold the most homes in this area, neighborhood, or zip code, you're the gorilla of that neighborhood.

Try a creative spin, letting your community know where you stand. If you are not number one in your market yet, what can you say about your accomplishments? Are you the go-to agent for graduates of Blue High School or the go-to agents for insurance agents at ABC, Inc. Whatever it is, promote yourself in one way or another. As you grow, change, and expand, so should your promotions.

It will not sound like bragging if you do it correctly, and what you say is true. That is key. If you are not selling more homes than most agents in one category, let that be your motivation. Once you get there, you need to be telling everyone that you sell the most homes here.

Lift yourself up. Be proud of your accomplishments. Be proud of where you're going and who you have helped along the way.

If you are going to make it in this business, you must become a self-promoter. Remember that perception is reality. Begin to craft your self-promotion today and let the people know who you are.

Week 6 Day 3 WORKSHEET

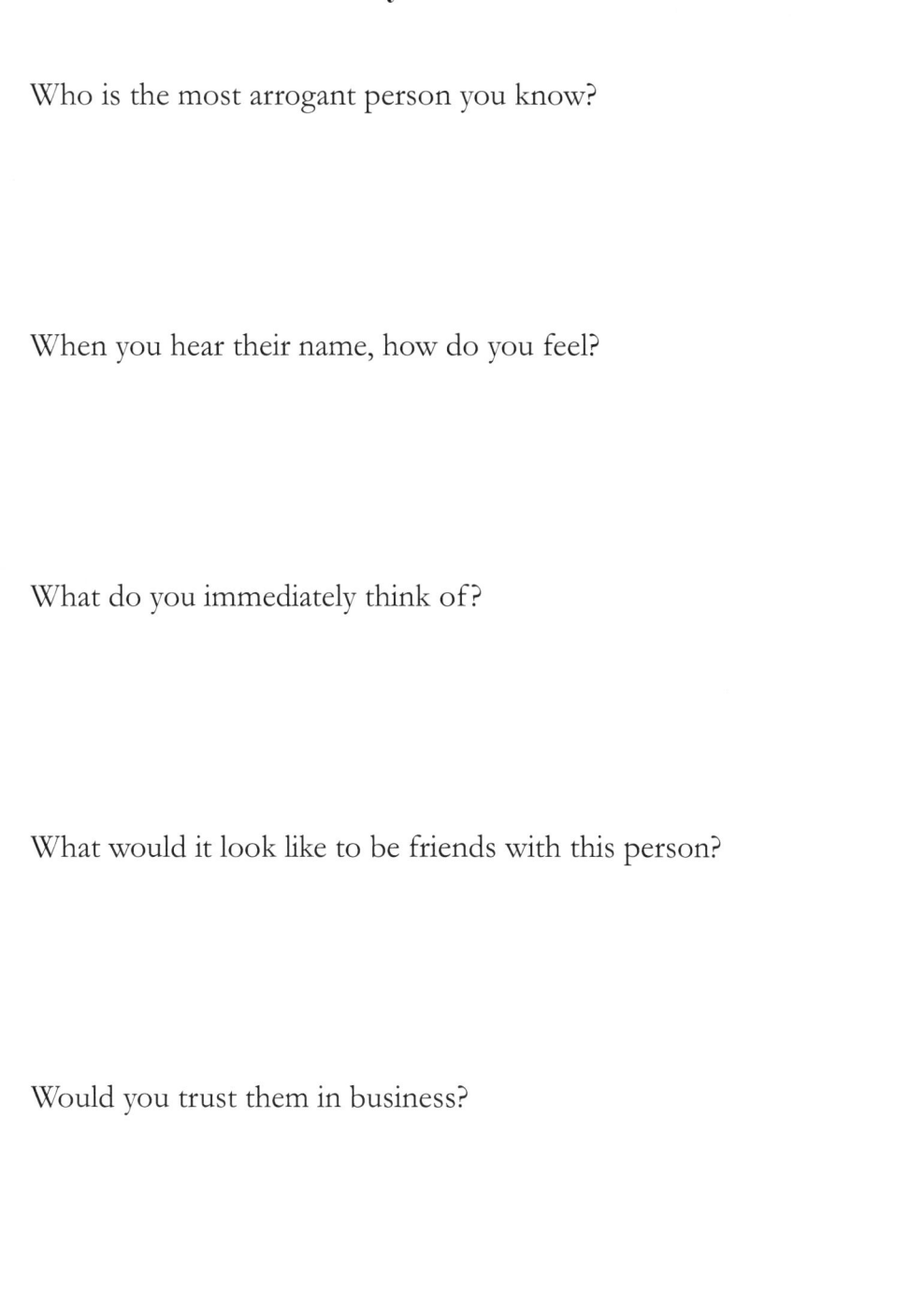

Who is the most arrogant person you know?

When you hear their name, how do you feel?

What do you immediately think of?

What would it look like to be friends with this person?

Would you trust them in business?

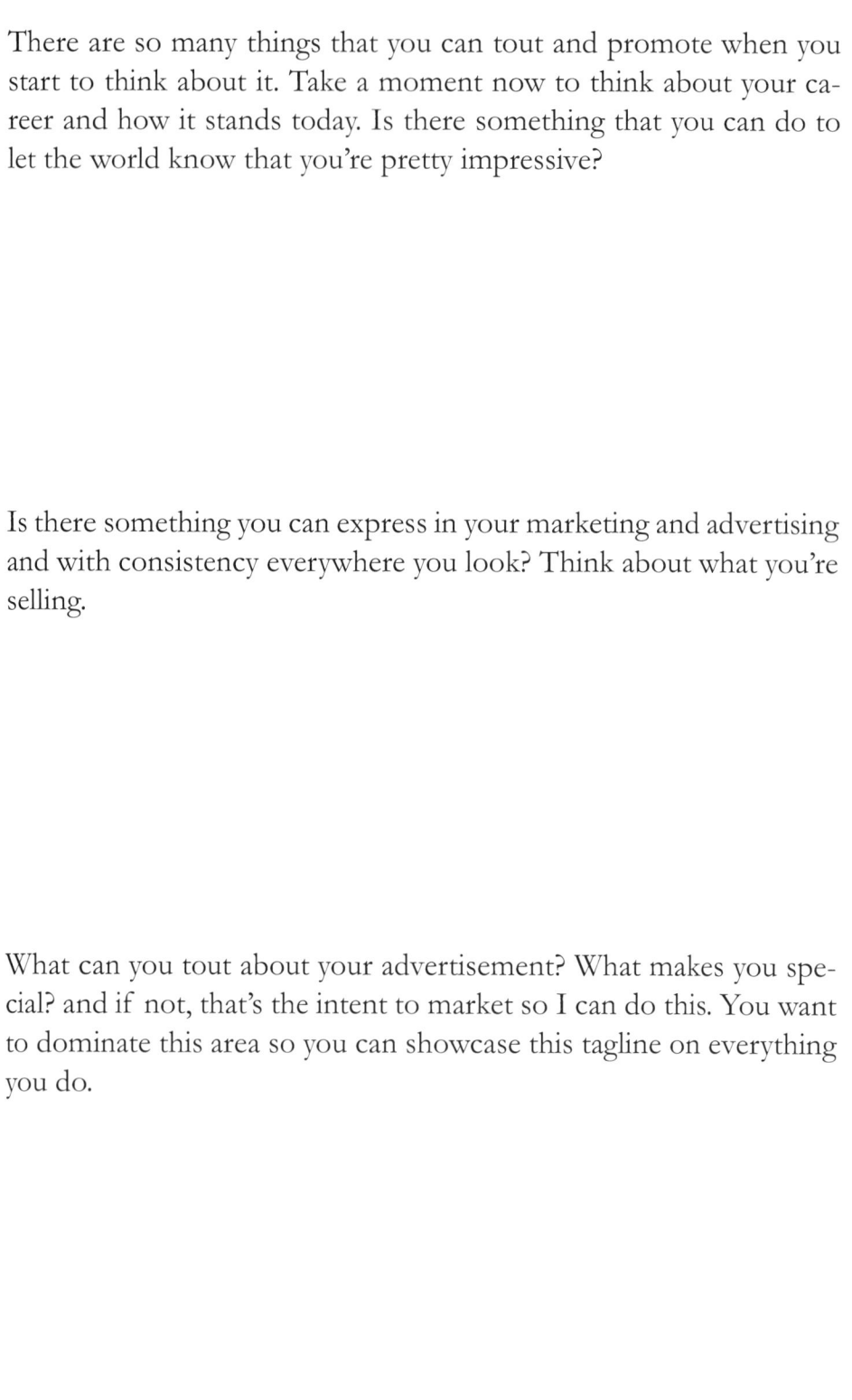

There are so many things that you can tout and promote when you start to think about it. Take a moment now to think about your career and how it stands today. Is there something that you can do to let the world know that you're pretty impressive?

Is there something you can express in your marketing and advertising and with consistency everywhere you look? Think about what you're selling.

What can you tout about your advertisement? What makes you special? and if not, that's the intent to market so I can do this. You want to dominate this area so you can showcase this tagline on everything you do.

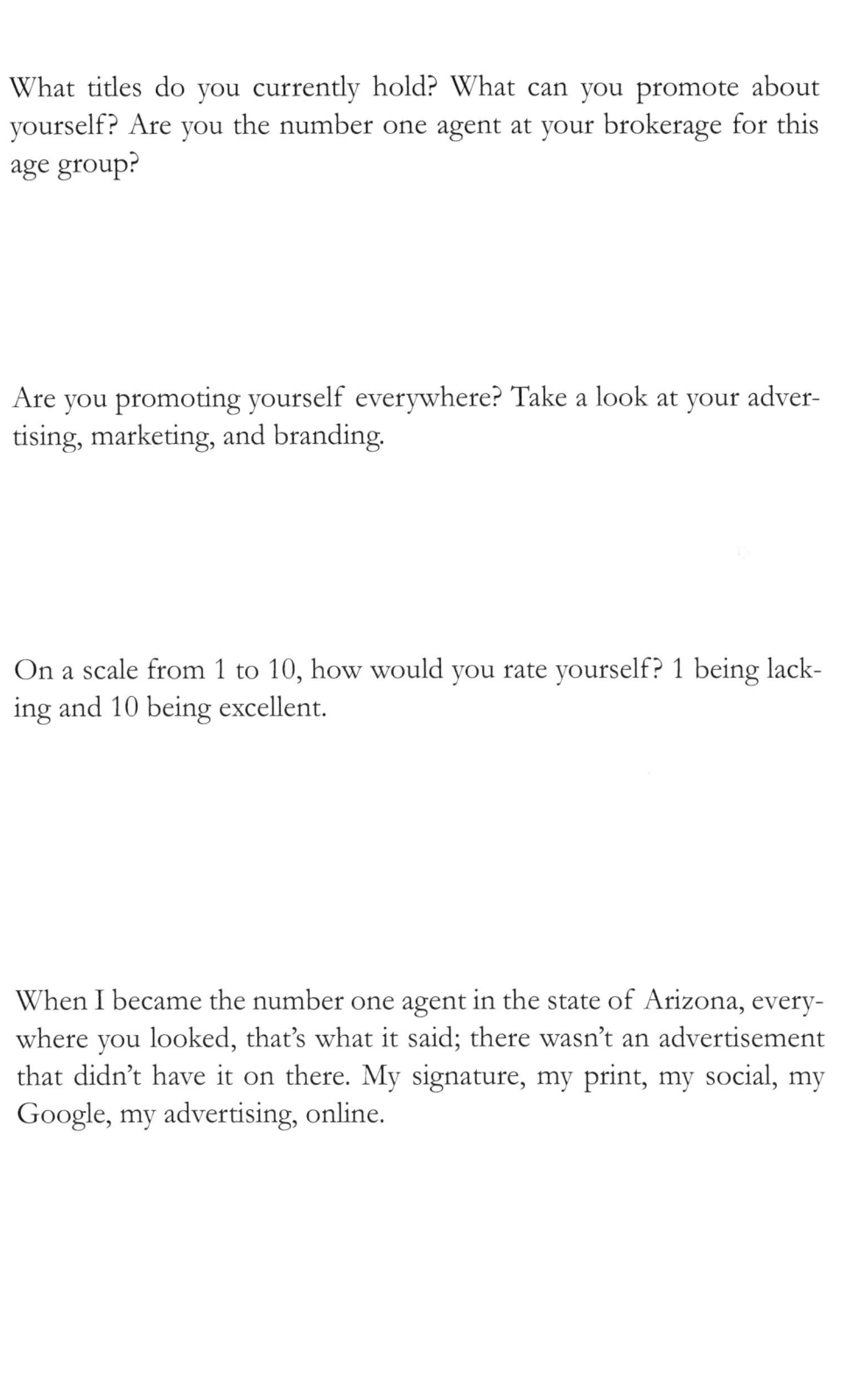

What titles do you currently hold? What can you promote about yourself? Are you the number one agent at your brokerage for this age group?

Are you promoting yourself everywhere? Take a look at your advertising, marketing, and branding.

On a scale from 1 to 10, how would you rate yourself? 1 being lacking and 10 being excellent.

When I became the number one agent in the state of Arizona, everywhere you looked, that's what it said; there wasn't an advertisement that didn't have it on there. My signature, my print, my social, my Google, my advertising, online.

If you rated yourself six or below, what are three ways you can improve?

1

2

3

Week 6 Day 4
DAY 29: MINIMUM STANDARDS OF MARKETING

Today, we are going to go back to Week Two where you discovered your ideal customer, inner core, and your niche. That all comes into play today. Your marketing needs to reflect who you are as a person and as a business. Too often I see agents are simply throwing things together and making marketing their last priority. If you want to not only survive but thrive in this business, you need to meet the minimum marketing standards.

There are two pieces of your marketing. Analog and Digital. Analog marketing encompasses the physical marketing assets you have.

This is your collateral, including your buyer packet, seller packet, and a listing presentation. Inside these packets, you have professional business cards. These are what I consider to be the bare minimum of real estate analog marketing. If you do not have these pieces yet, put together a plan to create each piece over the upcoming months.

By now, you know that you cannot take this on all at the same time. Instead, set aside one hour each week to move the needle, starting with a business card. Next, compile your listing presentation. Everything should be consistent. When a buyer sees your business card sitting on a kitchen counter, they should know it's yours right away from the look and feel of the card. It is the same font and color scheme you are using on every piece of your analog marketing and collateral.

The next thing we are going to look at is your digital marketing. Your email signature, your brand content online, and a website, are the minimum of what we must have, because no matter who you are, if you don't have these things , you're going to lose the battle. Now, what else? Well, we have to have a business Facebook page, and an Instagram, that's a given, we must have a social presence. You must also have a LinkedIn profile, at the very least.

Everything should be consistent.

My business page is about business. It's not about my girlfriend, and it's not about my kids. That's what your personal page is for. Your business page is about you, and what you do in your business. Those who visit your website should understand a little bit about your work culture, too. Your website should tell the audience your value proposition, too. Your website should answer the question, "Why should I list or buy with you?" To add credibility, include trend reports, facts and analysis. Tell people that you are an expert at what you do.

Your Instagram needs to boost beautiful imagery of homes and happy clients. While your LinkedIn tells the story of where you've come from, and where you are, what you aspire to be, and what your goal of connecting with them is.

Business is done in the digital world, and there is no hiding from it. Play the game or leave real estate. And remember, you don't need to be a pro at this. That's what we are talking about today. Get to a point where you are meeting the minimum threshold, then as you grow and as your revenue grows, you can start to hire this out.

For the new agents out there, you likely cannot afford a team of marketing professionals yet, and that's okay. We have been talking about hard work since Week 1. By now, you are committed to working hard, aren't you?

If you're not willing to grind in this business, in your first several years, get out of the business, you will get swallowed up.

From Week Two, I have told you that we can't do it all, it's impossible. However, there are specific minimum standards that we must make sure are meeting. No matter where we're at in our career, you must have standards you are committed to meet in every section of your business, including marketing standards.

As our career progresses, we can undoubtedly empower and employ people to manage those things for us. But if you do not have the resources to do it, you must grind and do it yourself.

You're building the culture and foundation of your organization.

Now, let's talk about what to do if you aren't the number one in your market or if you aren't the top agent under 30. Your buyer's presentation may not say that you have sold the most houses in this zip code. That's okay. We all have to start somewhere.

Your buyer's presentation should answer this question: why should this buyer work with you? If you don't have the numbers, talk about yourself and what you will do for them. As your numbers grow and you gain some experience and merits, you can improve your presentations.

You may say things like: I'm just going to work hard; my job is to make sure you don't make a wrong decision, or say, no one's going to work harder than me.

If you know you're the type of agent who will answer your phone at nine o'clock at night, tell the client that. Tell them that story.

Pro Tip: Let me tell you the wonderful thing about this industry: it gets easier. It comes to a point where you will make more and more money year after year, but also becomes easier because you built the foundation of your organization.

Week 6 Day 4 WORKSHEET
Part 1

Do you have the marketing pieces you need to succeed?

Analog marketing checklist. Circle the items you have ready to go.

- Seller packet

- Buyer packet

- Listing Presentation

- Business cards

Are there other items you have that you want to include? List them here:

Digital marketing checklist. Circle the items you have ready to go.

    Email signature

    Landing page

    LinkedIn Profile

    LinkedIn Business Page

    Facebook Business Page

    Instagram Business Profile

Are there other items you have that you want to include? List them here:

Next, please examine each piece of marketing, both analog and digital. Do they have the same font, color scheme, and branding throughout? If not, make a list of the items that need to be improved.

After you have that list, set aside one hour each week on the same day of the week. Simply take one hour and commit to improving one piece of marketing each week until all components have been created and improved. Focus on consistency and the bare minimum marketing standards. In the beginning, the pieces do not have to be perfect. They must be error-free, and the branding needs to be consistent. That is the minimum standard.

Part 2

Today, you will write your mission statement. Your mission statement should tell your clients what you stand for, who you are, and who you want to help.

Let's start by identifying your core values. Take a moment to brainstorm a list of 10-15 values.

1

2

3

4

5

6

7

8

9

10

Now, I want you to circle the five values you would never abandon. These five values should be your guiding light as you make daily decisions and big milestone decisions.

Now that you have your five top values, I want you to craft a mission statement. What do you and your real estate business stand for?

Week 6 Day 5
DAY 30: OLD SCHOOL VERSUS NEW SCHOOL

By now, you are making significant progress with your marketing and promotion.

Simply put, the most significant part of marketing and promotions is creating awareness. After today, I want to have clear standards for your branding and marketing. Start with the bare minimum and grow from there. As I have said before and I will say it again, don't overload yourself. If you are overwhelmed, it could cause paralysis, and no movement will happen.

This week, we revisited what your niche is. Today, I want you to zero in on where your inner core hangs out and where they consume information. Your job is to get in front and stay in front of your inner core.

You must know where they are and how to reach them because if you're marketing and promoting to a black hole, it doesn't matter how much money you spend.

I see marketing in two ways: one school versus new school. One isn't better than the other, yet it is crucial to understand what is working in business. That's why yesterday, we talked about measuring what is working . Today, we will further explore marketing and promotions by looking at old school versus new school.

I started my real estate career in 2003. So, it's not like I started in 1984. Did you know people were still using fax machines in 2003? It is not the same real estate industry as it was even ten years ago.

We should never be faxing documents in today's business, yet sending handwritten notes and door knocking can still be effective today. I consider Postcards and sending market updates in emails old school marketing tactics.

The problem is that postcards are expensive. Another thing that agents still do is meet face to face with clients and talk about everything for hours. This is not a fair use of your time. It also sends the message to your clients that you are not busy finding them properties or working on marketing theirs.

Another strategy we should say goodbye to is wet signatures.

The game has changed, and so should you, if you haven't already. Now, let's explore new school marketing.

This week, you developed a content calendar. Today, I want you to build a digital strategy.

If you stay consistent, your audience is going to get the message. Your goal is to build a brand.

Do people read newspapers still? Yeah, but not a lot. The demographic who is reading the newspaper is getting older. Most of the clients you are targeting are online. When they want to buy or sell their house, the first place they look is online.

The best part of the new digital age is that marketing to a specific audience becomes more effortless. The social media platform allows you to say I want to target my marketing campaigns to this particular type of person within this specific area. Marketing on social media also allows you to run relatively inexpensive ads. You can even target particular IP addresses now. You know where your inner core lives, and online marketing will enable you to target them directly.

The critical element of digital marketing in the new school is video content. Like anything, practice makes perfect, so you must be willing to get in front of the camera even when you're not comfortable. Clients are expecting video content these days. As you build out your branding and marketing, you must be willing to spend some money on excellent videos about your business, who you are, and why clients want to work with you. Video marketing is an excellent investment in your business. You want these videos to be polished and professional. Once they are, get that message to everybody.

From there, you can set up SMS campaigns. If someone sees a sign in front of your listing, they can text this number. When they do, they receive an automated text message that includes a link to the polished video mentioned above. From there, a drip campaign is triggered. They receive access to a virtual tour of the property. This will save you time. If they are not interested in the property after watching the virtual tour, they will not require a showing. Then, you have an email set up to trigger them to sign up for your newsletter. After that, they can tell you more about what they are looking for or what they are in the market for. Maybe, it triggers a task for you to call them.

Today, focus on ways to get in front of people with the right message. Your job is to craft a compelling digital story that is available to anyone who inquires. If you focus on building that, you're going to be ahead of 90% of people because 90% of agents know they need to do it but don't. If you're scared or nervous to be on video, push through the fear. Big rewards are on the other side of fear. If you don't know how to create video content, ask for help. By now, you know you cannot build a Level 5 real estate business on your own.

If you decide to add video content to your marketing, find the right person to create some effective content. Maybe you're reading this, and you have video content, but you don't have an SMS campaign, find the right SMS company that can help you deliver these messages.

I would much rather spend the money to have predictable analysis and measurable analytics than throw stuff to the wind hoping for the best. Today's exercise will help you evaluate where you're at with old school versus new school marketing. Make the changes and stay consistent.

Week 6 Day 5 WORKSHEET

In today's exercise, you will write out all the current marketing materials, strategies, and content you currently have.

What pieces of your marketing is Old School?

What pieces of your marketing is New School?

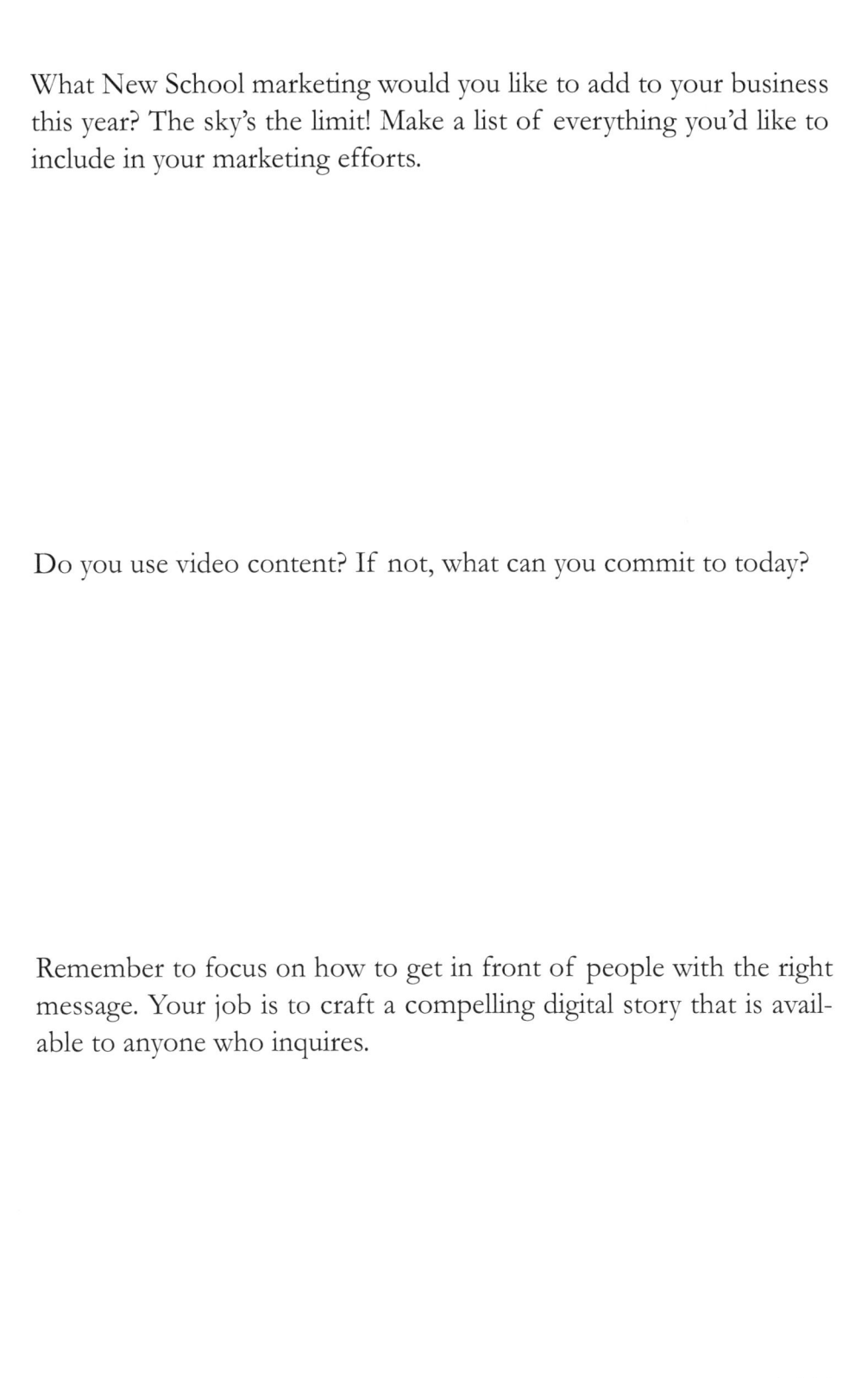

What New School marketing would you like to add to your business this year? The sky's the limit! Make a list of everything you'd like to include in your marketing efforts.

Do you use video content? If not, what can you commit to today?

Remember to focus on how to get in front of people with the right message. Your job is to craft a compelling digital story that is available to anyone who inquires.

Week 7 Day 1

DAY 31: PROSPECTING AND APPOINTMENT SETTING

This week, you will learn to master the listing strategy. I will share the critical elements step by step to become a master at getting and selling more listings. This week, we will cover prospecting and how to set up that initial appointment. We will also talk about marketing strategy even further. By the end of this week, you will know how to create a scalable listing model.

In Week Two, I asked if you could take on nine listings today. Would that negatively affect your business? Could you handle the volume? If the answer is no, we have some work for you. As a real estate professional, you should be able to take on nine listings in one week without disrupting your flow, your business, and your sanity. However, most agents do not have a strategy in place to handle this massive influx of business at one time. This is baffling to me as a top agent. The goal in real estate sales is to sell more homes, make more money and serve more clients, right? This week, we will ensure you have a listing strategy in place so you can take on nine new listings today. Heck, let's get to a place where you are taking on nine new listings a week.

At the peak of my career, I had 111 personal listings at one time. This week, I will share how you can, too. I will show you how to go from two listings to 20. In Week Two, I shared the importance of time management. This week, it will make more sense of why it's so important as you grow your real estate business.

Listings take time, and the more efficient you are, the more you can take on. Keep in mind that there are some listings you will not want to take on. I will show you how to steer clear of the listings and sellers that won't sell.

If you want to go from Level 1 to Level 5, you cannot only be a buyers agent and only want to work with buyings. You can't create a massive real estate business without having a significant portfolio of listings.

"List to last" has been a timeless adage in real estate and for a good reason. Listings create opportunities to work with buyers.

Fifty-percent of the time, the seller should become your buyer client. For every home you list, you should generate 25 buyers from that one listing. It could be by holding opens homes or calling off your signs, or even calls from the online listing.

An excellent listing strategy is so critical within your business. All it does is create more and more and more opportunities. This week, you will learn to master your listing strategy so you can list more homes and make more money.

…

Today we're going to talk about prospecting, along with setting up appointments the proper way. I will teach you what to say when your phone rings to ensure you get the listing appointment or set the buyer consultation. How do we get the phone to ring, you might ask.

First, let me tell you what not to do. Do not try to work with everyone. In Week Two, you determined who your ideal client is and who you want in your inner circle. Next, you determined your niche. Casting a wide net isn't the way to go about it.

At the beginning of my real estate sales career, I focused on using the open house strategy. I held open houses three to five times a week. By doing that, I mastered a community. People saw my signs every day. Just like Caitlin, who I mentioned in Week Three, I become the neighborhood expert. People were used to seeing my signs, meeting me at open houses if they attended and I waved at them when they drove past. This was perception versus reality at the beginning. Like Caitlin, I wasn't the top-grossing agent in my brokerage, market, or even that neighborhood yet. I was determined to become the best agent in that zip code, and the community, just as Caitlin was determined to become the expert in that neighborhood. So much so that she wanted to move into her dream neighborhood, and she did.

My whole business was organic in that way because I started my business focused on holding open houses. Next, I created and delivered newsletters to that community once a month. I did this every single month without fail. Soon, I became the name people thought of when they thought of a real estate agent. From there, I expanded to the adjacent communities. I sent my newsletter to those community members and I started marketing in those communities, too. It grew as time went on. As I listed more houses, I started bringing on more Buyer and seller clients. I will show you why.

A misconception in the business is that getting buyers is easier. I disagree. Getting listings is actually easier than getting buyers.

Prospective clients start to desire to be a part of your story.

Once you become a staple of a community like Caitlin, getting the listing appointment is easier. If they know you sold Mr. Martin's home for over asking or in less than a week, they will want you to do the same for them. How do they know this? Caitlin told them. Caitlin told them the story with Just Sold postcards and in her monthly newsletter. By becoming a staple of that neighborhood and that community, Caitlin was able to get her phone to ring organically without spending a lot of money. But in addition to that, once that phone starts ringing, and you get more signs in the yard, everything gets easier. You are telling the story that you are the expert. This is perception versus reality initially, but over time, as you sell more houses, it becomes your reality. Once it does, you can start to expand into other communities.

Over time, more people see your name both on signs and in their mail, maybe even online through email marketing or online advertisements if you are targeting their IP addresses. When they visit your website and your social media, they see you raving about your clients and cheering them on. Prospective clients start to desire to be a part of your story. They want to win with you. As you see, this does not have to cost a lot of money. It will take time and hard work, yes, but you have committed to doing that by now. You have set up a strategic plan where you are not wasting time and money. By doing so, you become more purposeful with your time.

The phone has started to ring more. You have started selling more houses. As your revenue grows, you will reinvest in your business and expand your marketing efforts, and the phone will continue to ring.

The key is knowing what's working and understanding what's not. For agents like Caitlin and me, open houses worked. As I was closing more buyers, they referred me to friends and neighbors. The beauty of listing houses is that once you list the house, you get buyers. For every house you list, you should acquire at least 25 buyer leads. Not only will people call off the sign but they will also attend your open houses without representation. The first question you ask someone who walks into your open house, "are you working with an agent?" Nowadays, more and more buyers are attending open houses without agents because open house listings are available online. Those prospects can become your buyer clients.

The easiest way to pick up a buyer from a listing is to help your seller buy their next house. Statistically, a little over 50% of people that sell their homes will buy immediately. If you do a good job listing your seller's home, you will most likely represent them as their buyers agent, too. This is yet another reason why I love listing properties.

Your job is to become likable.

Every time you sell a house, you should ask the seller if they know anybody else you can help. You must ask for a referral. Every buyer you are working with, you should ask them if you know someone who is also looking to buy or sell. You must ask. Never assume they will refer you to business. You have to ask for it. You did such a good job serving them and making it about them that it should be no problem to gracefully yet directly ask for referrals.

When the phone rings, you must first ask, "how did they hear about you?" Maybe they saw your sign, or they met you at an open house. If they are a referral, be sure to circle back and thank the person who referred them to you as well. You must find out where your leads are coming from because you need to replicate what is working. There is no need to reinvent the wheel with real estate. Find out what is working and do more of that.

If a seller calls you and that's how you snagged the listing appointment, you have this in the bag. You should be able to win this listing with ease. They called you. They were referred to you by someone they know.

Let's talk about what I call 'psychological credibility.'

Before attending a listing presentation, you will have an initial call. Your initial call for a listing appointment is short and sweet. You have a few goals with these calls. You want to build rapport, set expectations, and be likable. I see many agents spend 80-90% of their time talking about the home. Walking every room and focusing on the features of the house. Instead, I want you to spend less than 10% of the discussion talking about the home. The other 90% should be about them. What are their goals? Where did you hear about me?

Your job is to become likable. People like talking about themselves, feeling heard and understood. If you spend twenty minutes talking about the upgrades they have made over the last ten years, that's not really about them and their desired results. Ask them what motivates them to sell? Are they looking to move closer to their grandchildren, are they upgrading into a nicer neighborhood, are the sellers downsizing to spend more time traveling the world now that they are in retirement.

If they tell you that they are moving to the other side of town, you tell them, "Oh, yes. I know that neighborhood really well. I just sold four homes in that community last month." or maybe you tell them: "It's great. In fact, I am working with a client right now that's looking in there."

They start to think, "oh, he already knows the community."

End the call or the visit by telling them, "I'm looking forward to helping you. I'll take great care of you."

Your job is to gather information. But once we have enough information, don't go down a rabbit hole of continuing to ask more about the living room.

You should tell the prospect what you will bring for your appointment. Prepare the prospective sellers that you are looking forward to having a chance to sit down with them and hear about their goals. You want to listen to their goals and needs. Then, you will give a genuine opinion on what you think you can sell the house for. Tell them during the call that you want to be on the same page.

You want them leaving the call, even before you arrive at the listing appointment, feeling and believing that we're a team. Ask the prospective client, "How does that sound for you?" You are getting them to agree with you before they even meet you. This is all psychological.

The initial call on the listing appointments don't require a ton of discovery like buyer consults do because you have to go to the home; that's where the discovery takes place. The discovery portion of the listing process takes place at the home. The discovery on a buy-side takes place on the initial call. Remember that discovery on a buyer is the initial call. Discovery on a listing is not the initial call but when you view the home.

As you wrap up the call, you will enforce psychological credibility. You reassure the client that you know their community and confirm a time that you will come to their home to meet them in person. You are setting expectations for what they can expect when you come by.

You are now starting to master the psychology of sales. If you do those things, you'll get every appointment.

Week 7 Day 1 WORKBOOK

Identify three ways you can use psychological credibility in your prospecting calls.

1

2

3

Identify three ways you already using psychological credibility in your prospecting calls.

1

2

3

Identify three ways you can improve prospecting calls.

1

2

3

Week 7 Day 2
DAY 32: APPOINTMENT SETTING

Today is day two of mastering listings. Yesterday, we went over prospecting and setting up the appointment. Today, we will talk about the appointment.

You will bring the necessary information to each appointment. This includes comparables (comps), marketing strategy, marketing materials such as your sellers packet, and your listing packet.

Keep in mind that every listing appointment is relatively the same. With that, also know that every agent showing up to that seller's house is presenting the same information. If it's not a referral, you're not the only one being interviewed. It is your job to stand out. You don't know if you are the first agent or the fifth agent the seller has interviewed.

Today, I will share with you how to stand out because you have to separate yourself from the rest. Most agents will share their marketing strategy with the clients. Do not think that you'll impress the seller by telling them that you post on social media, have excellent email marketing and postcards. That's what every agent interviewing for this listing is telling them.

Instead of sharing a marketing strategy, you must share what I call a 'timeline strategy.'

No one uses a timeline strategy, and that's why this will become an essential aspect of your listing presentation.

Likability is extremely important, as I have shared throughout this book. You will stand out by sharing what I call 'timeline strategy.' A timeline strategy is not a marketing strategy.

A timeline strategy is a strategic plan that you share with your seller at the listing presentation. You will tell the seller what will happen on day 1, 2, 3 all the way to day 60 or 90 if you need to. You will tell your client: "ideally, we won't need to get to day 30, 45, or 50, but in case we do, I created this strategy to focus on execution and getting you what you want."

If you think the house will sell quickly, tell them that. If the home is unique and it may not sell soon, prepare the client for that. Do not sugarcoat it; it will shoot you in the foot later. You will stand out by being truthful with the client.

Likability is extremely important.

Protect yourself by discussing future price drops if the home doesn't sell.

Devin, an agent in my office, came to me a few years ago upset because his seller was starting to resent him. He listed the house 33 days ago, and they had less than five showings. The house was not only unique but also overpriced. I asked Devin if he prepared his seller for future price drops at the listing presentation. Devin had not. Devin skipped this step because he was fearful that he would not have gotten the listing. After thirty days on the market and virtually no showings, Devin knew it was time to drop the price. However, Devin had not prepared his client. Thus, when it came time to make that phone call, the seller was upset with Devin. He was resentful.

I have told you that at one time, I had 111 personal listings. Not all of them sold right away. A few of them, I had to price drop. Instead of being upset with me or resentful like Devin's client, they were disappointed yet prepared. Why? Because I set the expectation during the listing appointment. I foreshadowed this possibility in my timeline strategy that I shared with them.

On Day 30, they were prepared that I may call to drop the price. I was doing my job because, remember, I do this every day. I sell hundreds of homes every year. I am the expert, and I tell my clients what they need to do to sell their home.

Instead of being prepared, Devin's clients were upset. His sellers felt he was trying to take money out of their pocket. They questioned Devin's ability to sell their home. They felt Devin wasn't doing his job right.

My clients know what is coming.

Clients often feel the money is coming out of their pocket when they take a price reduction when, in fact, it is the markets rejecting the price of the home. We know that, but the sellers don't see it that way.

Instead, my clients know what is coming. I can pick up the phone and simply tell them: "Hey, it's day 30. We got to stick to our execution strategy."

You won't have to fight for price reductions like Devin. Instead, you used foreshadowing and set expectations like I have taught you.

When you put that plan in front of them from the very beginning, sellers are happier with you, and you sell more homes.

When you walk into your listing appointment, this is the story you need to tell: I do this every day of my life; this is my career. I will work harder for you than any agent that you're thinking about hiring, I promise you.

Within three, four months, or six months (depending on the type of home or the current market), if you're not happy with what I'm doing, you can walk away. No harm. No foul. Other agents will walk in here and ask you for a six or twelve-month commitment from you. I am not asking you to do that. Why? Well, for one, I am really good at my job, and I will show you that. Secondly, I want my clients to want to work with me. I do not want them to feel they are imprisoned or contractually bound to work with me. I am the best agent in this town, and I want you to want to work with me. Look, I'm so confident that I can sell this home. If I don't sell it, within 90 days, we can walk away from one another. This is why I sell so much real estate because I am different. My strategy is better. My approach revolves around you and me as a partnership, as a team to sell your home. How does that sound?

Note: This works more in a conventional listing environment and works less with a luxury listing because luxury typically takes more time. But if you're confident that you can sell that home and 60-90 days, give them a guarantee.

During the listing presentation, ask the seller if the other agents they have interviewed had a strategy laid out. Ask the seller if the other agents had this strategy. Did the other agents have a plan in place if the home does not sell? The answer is going to be no, and that's where you're going to win. Now, you have a marketing strategy and timeline execution strategy. Plus, you're super likable, and you made them feel comfortable because you didn't lock them into something uncomfortable like a six-month contract. Then, ask the seller, "do the other agents have these things? Or are they merely talking about fancy photography, videography, and social media? Because you have those, too."

Your job in the listing presentation is to show the sellers that you are different. They are likely interviewing other agents, so you need to stand out. That's why you have a timeline strategy.

Week 7 Day 2 WORKBOOK

What makes you different from other agents?

Do you have a marketing strategy? Yes or No. *Circle one.*

If not, create a plan to complete your marketing strategy in the next four weeks.

Do you have a timeline strategy? Yes or No. *Circle one.*

If not, create a plan to complete your timeline strategy in the next two weeks.

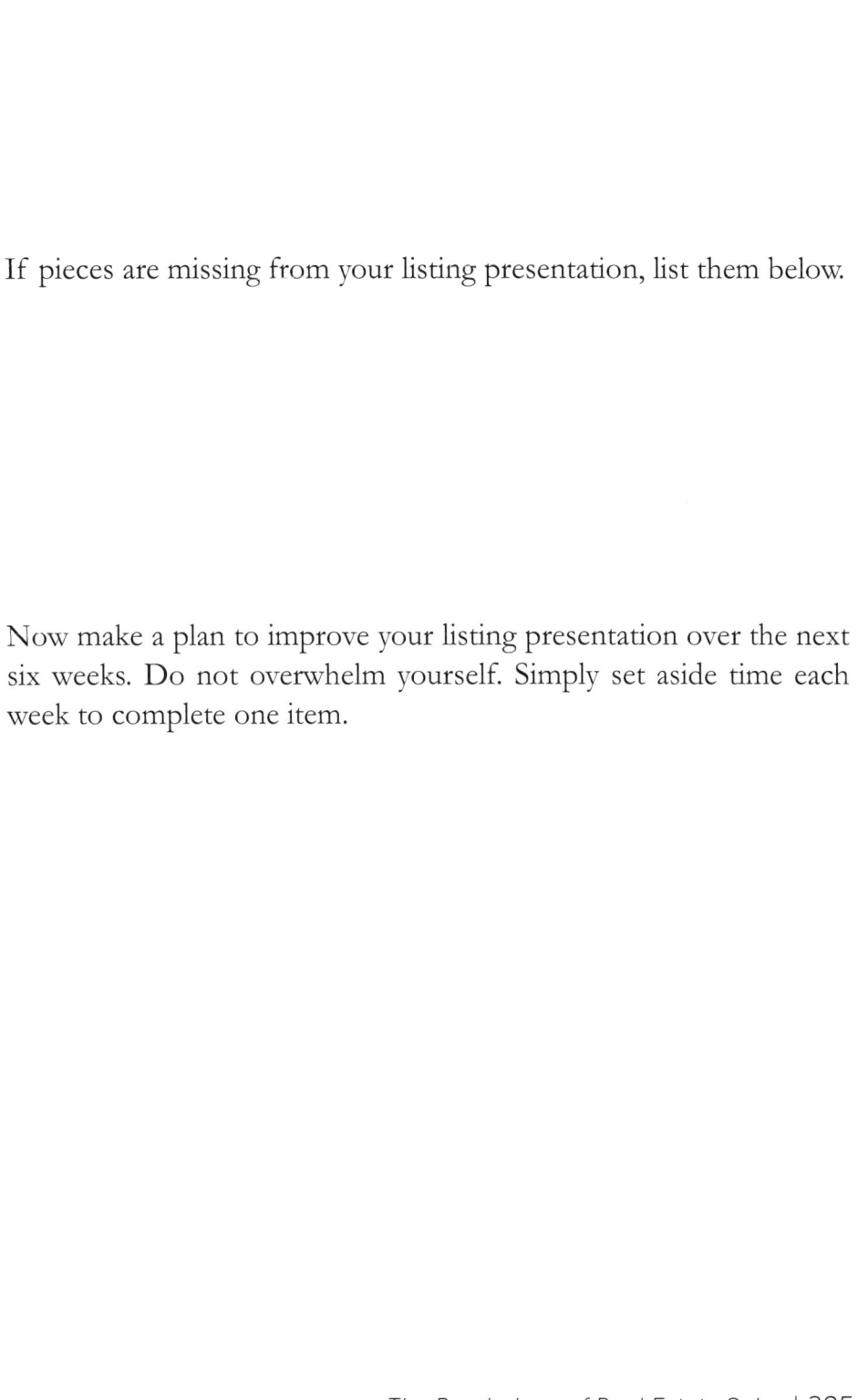

If pieces are missing from your listing presentation, list them below.

Now make a plan to improve your listing presentation over the next six weeks. Do not overwhelm yourself. Simply set aside time each week to complete one item.

Week 7 Day 3
DAY 33: CREATING A SCALABLE MODEL

This week has been packed with practical action steps for you and your listing presentation. You are well on your way to mastering the listing process.

First, we talked about prospecting and the initial call, which leads to getting the appointment. Yesterday, I shared a practical strategy to take with you to the listing appointment.

Now, you know how to separate yourself from the other agents Interviewing. The listing side is critical in real estate because you will secure buyers to work with every time you list.

You are the Rainmaker.

By now, your goal shouldn't be to get one or two listings a month. Your goal should be to become a listing machine. You should have a dozen listing appointments a week, and your conversion rates should be really high, depending on your level of experience. Once you are here, you need to ensure your business is scalable. If you still cannot take on an additional nine listing without pausing prospecting, messing up transactions, and dropping the ball with clients, you have a problem.

If you continue getting all these listings, at some point, you won't have enough time in the day. If you are attending 12 listing appointments each week, you don't have enough time to show 15 buyer clients around town. You won't have enough capacity to call Expired listings and For Sale by Owners (FSBOs). You will run out of time in your day to give all of your sellers showing feedback.

Michelle, an agent in Denver, was starting to pick up momentum. She had six listing appointments and listed five of them. However, Michelle was running her business without structure. She was living in chaos. She was excited to have five new listings, but her buyer clients started to feel neglected. She skipped prospecting and stopped calling FSBOs. The listings sold within 45 days, but she found herself with nothing coming up in the pipeline. Her broker took her aside and told her that she needed to create a scalable, efficient model.

At the peak of my career, I had more than 110 listings that I was personally managing. I didn't stress once because I had a plan. I not only had an action plan but also a strategy.

If you don't already have a plan and your business is looking eerily similar to Michelle's, I want you to make a plan this month. Then ask yourself, will this plan help you go from three, four or five listings to 20 and 30 listings?

If you're afraid to do the work, then then you should not be in this industry.

By now, you are starting to master sales. You have been learning new sales techniques, and you are beginning to implement those into your business. Now that you're mastering those sales techniques, you must ensure that your business becomes scalable. Otherwise, you will be like Michelle. Get five listings, have nothing. Get another five listings, have nothing. Your business does not need to experience these peaks and valleys. You can handle 100 listings at one time. Let me show you how.

You are the Rainmaker. You should be able to go on two or three listing appointments each day and capture 80% of them. Then, as you get more listings, you're going to sell more homes. At this point, you're going to hire some staff to help you out. That's the goal.

In Week Four, you created checklists for yourself to follow. You have a buyer checklist. Now, you have a listing checklist. Once you master this process and tweak it over time, you will be able to plug someone in to handle the checklist items, too.

When you secure a listing at the listing appointment, the next step is to order photos. Once you have the images, where are they saved? How were they uploaded? What needs to happen next before the listing is posted? Does the house need staging? Who calls and schedules the stager? Who lets the stager into the property? Who uploads the listing to the MLS?

It is the same process whether it's a $100,000 home or a $10 million home. There may be different marketing strategies at play with a luxury listing, but by the time you are listing $10 million homes, you have this strategy in plan and written out. You have someone on your team who is driving that ship, and it isn't you. If this home gets drone footage, your assistant or marketing coordinator or listing coordinator orders and schedules that.

The execution strategy behind the process is always the same. If you want to create a scalable model, you have to make sure the processes and systems that you're creating internally are the same every single time.

When I get a listing signed, I take the same steps every time. Then over time, you may realize that step six should actually be step ten.

That's great. The plan is flexible because you have learned to be flexible.

By now, you should have someone you can call to run lockboxes out to properties. If you are going on more than four listing appointments each week, it is time to hire a runner at the very minimum. You are not superman. You cannot do it all, and you should not do it all.

The number one question agents ask me is: when should I hire an assistant?

The answer is as soon as possible.

One $700,000 listing pays for half your assistant's annual salary for the year if you're paying them $40,000. If you are not listing $700,000 homes in your market, what is your average sales price? The average home price in the United States is $225,000. You would need to sell five or six homes at $225,000 in order to pay your assistant $40,000.

Let's say that you sold 25 homes last year, and you're on track to sell 32 homes this year. Could you hit 38 homes if you had an extra set of hands? Could you sell an additional six homes if you had help? If the answer is yes, write a job ad and hire someone right now.

But Jason, I want that extra $40,000. Do not be greedy, and do not dream so small. Imagine once you have your assistant up and running. Once they are adequately trained, you will sell more than six additional homes. You should be able to double your production if you have a scalable business. That's what we are building here, and you are well on your way to having a scalable real estate business.

You have checklists for every step of your business by now. Over time, those checklists are refined and improved. Now, your new hire can plugin and free you up to be a Rainmaker.

Now, you are not like Michelle experiencing peaks and valleys week after week. Every week is a good week. Over time, you are going on a listing appointment every single day of the week, and you're winning 80% of them. You are listing 20 homes a month before you know it. If you're doing that, you will hit $50,000,000 in sales volume if the average home price is $225,000 in your market. If you're starting to list homes twice that amount, guess what? You are closer to closing $100 Million than you thought. Congratulations!

Instead, you are Michelle, who is capping out at $10-12 Million because she is afraid to spend money on staff. She also wants to control everything. When you come from a place of fear, you will lose. Plus, your clients will lose. When I go on listing appointments, I talk about my staff and how they are central to our success. When you call me, you will always have your phone call answered because it's not just me. I have a team here to support you.

In the last few years, I would wake up, and have two to three listing appointments set each and every day. I knew I was going to get the listings, too, because I had my plan. I went in; I looked the part, I shared my timeline and marketing strategy. I stood out because I was different, and frankly better, than all the other agents they interviewed. So, I got the listing. Then, I woke up the next day and did it again. I got better and better over time. Then, it became even more effortless because listing presentations were starting to become referrals. The seller wasn't interviewing three or four other agents because they didn't have to. They wanted to work with the best, and I was the best. My marketing told that story; my numbers told that story. They wanted to be a part of the success story, too.

To become scalable, you have to create an efficient model. Then over time, you will perfect it, and you'll get more listings. Then, inevitably you'll have more sales, and you'll be able to afford to bring someone on to help you.

Week 7 Day 3 WORKBOOK
Part 1

Can you take on nine listings today? Yes or No. *Circle one.*

If not, what are three things you can do to bring you one step closer to being able to take on more listings?

Do you have staff or part-time help?

If you do have help, are they familiar with your checklist?

If you do not have part-time help, why not? What are three things you can do this quarter to bring you one step closer to being able to hire someone?

Part 2

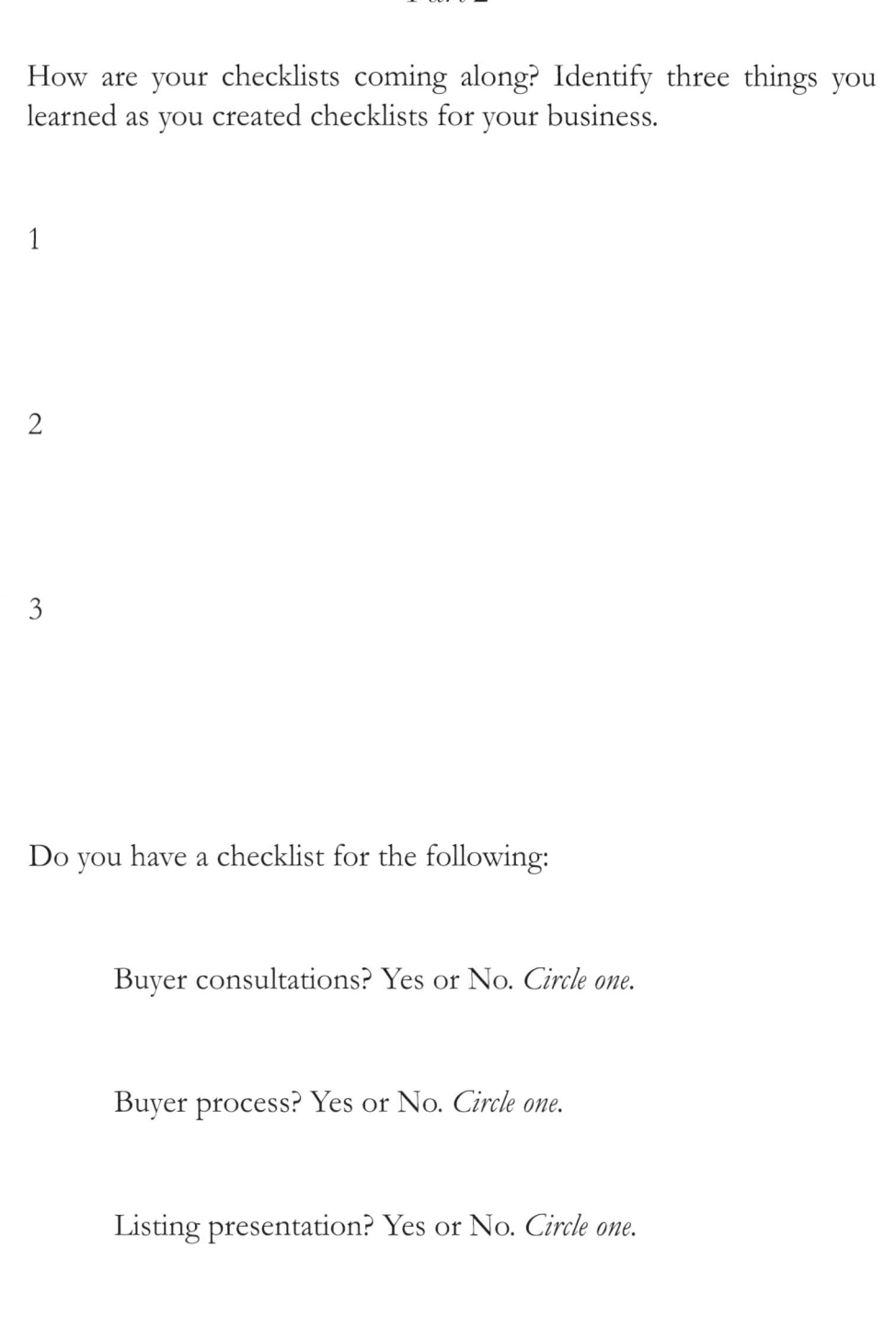

How are your checklists coming along? Identify three things you learned as you created checklists for your business.

1

2

3

Do you have a checklist for the following:

    Buyer consultations? Yes or No. *Circle one.*

    Buyer process? Yes or No. *Circle one.*

    Listing presentation? Yes or No. *Circle one.*

Listing process? Yes or No. *Circle one.*

Marketing strategy? Yes or No. *Circle one.*

Timeline strategy? Yes or No. *Circle one.*

If the answer was no to any of the above questions, take out your calendar and set aside time each week to create and complete each checklist. Do not overwhelm yourself. Start with the buyer side and then work your way to the listing side.

Week 7 Day 4
DAY 34: EFFECTIVE TIME MANAGEMENT

Today, we are going to talk about effective time management around listings. You will identify what doesn't have to be on your plate. The listing side of your business needs to be as efficient as you can possibly make it. I shared yesterday that you will get multiple buyer leads for every listing, and then because you have mastered the sales side of your business, you have turned those buyer leads into buyer clients.

As we continue to talk about structure, be honest with yourself about your ability to scale as a business. The level of efficiency in your business has a direct correlation to time management.

First, let's focus on some pain points. As I built my book of business with listings, I inherently became busier. I had to spend significantly more time on the phone with my seller clients, giving feedback on showings. As I showed more houses, I spent more time negotiating offers on behalf of my buyers. No matter what, I carved out time to prospect to ensure I wasn't like Michelle, who abandoned lead generated tasks the moment she got five listings. I kept my pipeline full not only by lead generating but also by asking my clients for referrals. As I mentioned in Week Three, I also built relationships with vendors who referred me business. From all of this, I inevitably had more listing appointments to attend.

With all of this growth came growing pains. I found solutions that worked for me and my business, and I scaled to a sales volume I had dreamed possible. I want you to do the same. Today, we will determine what things can come off your plate and what you can do to be more efficient with your time.

As you are starting your career as an agent, you will attend inspections because you need to become familiar with inspections. As we talked about in Week Five, you will foreshadow the parts of the inspections that can be scary for your buyers and your sellers. To understand inspections, you will need to attend dozens if not a hundred of them. When you observe them, learn what the common repairs are in your area or for the type and year of the home.

The more you know, the better.

Are basements dry or wet in your market? Do homes even have basements in your market? What are large ticket items that cost buyers a lot of money? What scares buyers the most but is not of concern? The more you know, the better. However, as you grow, that should be one of the first things to come off your plate.

When you foreshadow the process with your buyers, prepare them that you will not attend the inspections. They don't know that you used to attend them. You are in charge here, remember? Tell your clients what to expect.

Here is what I do and what every buyer's agent on my team does.

We tell our clients that we are going to order the inspections for them. Scheduling this for you is a service we provide. However, we do not go to inspections because I want it to be third party. I like the client to feel comfortable knowing that the inspector is not a part of my team and has no skin in the game. Their job is to point out everything of importance in the house. There will be dozens if not dozens and dozens of things indicated on the inspector's report. A robust report does not mean the house is a bad deal or that they should walk away. After the inspection is over, the inspector will provide us with the inspection report. We will schedule an appointment to go over everything that was on the report. From there, we will note the important items that we will be asking the seller to repair and/or credit us. This is not the part of the process where we nickel and dime the seller. This is not the part of the transactions where anyone needs to freak out or second guess anything. There will be things wrong with the house. It is our job to negotiate repairs or credits. Together, as a team, we will determine what is best. I want you to be happy, safe, and confident with your purchase. I have looked over hundreds if not a thousand inspection reports by now. I have your back. My buyers' agents or I tell every buyer this. I always end with, "Does that sound good to you?"

Again, this is getting your client a chance to agree with you.

Then, on the inspection day, the buyer knows that they will not be seeing me. They're happy, and I am thrilled because I got my time back. When I cut inspections out of my schedule, I could prospect more and attend more listing appointments. This led to listing more homes and making more money. This is what I want for you, too.

If you are struggling with this, you need to practice letting go. There was no reason for me to be there. If they had a question, they would call me. When I got the report, the buyers and I would discuss it. Then I trained my buyers' agents to do the same. If I had to, I would talk to the inspector on the phone while I'm driving to my next listing appointment or meeting my next buyer.

I took inspections off my plate because it wasn't necessary for me to attend. If you're looking for inspection summaries to fill the void of your day or to make you feel more productive, you're never going to make it to Level 5. You may never even leave Level 1. More on that next week.

Now that you have removed inspections off your plate, it is time to look at showings. If you have more than ten buyer clients actively looking at homes, you need a buyers agent to help you show properties. I am not going to expand on this because by now, you know my opinion. You need to get a buyers' agent the moment you can.

Now, let's talk about your listings that require showings by appointments. This means you have a listing that requires someone to be at the property to allow the buyer and the buyer's agent into the property.

Most of my higher-end listings require showings by-appointment-only, or maybe you're in a market where every listing requires someone to let the buyer into the property. This someone does not have to be you. It can be you or someone on your team.

As I was growing my business, I found myself having more and more high-end luxury listings. These would require someone at the property for every showing. Now, by this time, I realized that I couldn't be everywhere at once. The number of listings I had was hindering my business. After all, now I couldn't take on new listings because I had such a backlog.

I asked myself: what can come off my plate?

I realized that I did not need to be at the first showing. If a buyer saw the home for the first time, someone on my team showed the listing—not me. With these luxury listings, 90-percent of the time, the buyers would want to see the house a second time. Thus, the buyers were not writing an offer after their first showing. At first, I attended every showing because it was my luxury listing, after all. It became apparent that the buyers who saw the property for the first time did not make offers. Thus, I was wasting my time attending and prepping for the showing. We'll touch more on this in a moment.

Being present for every showing became another task I was able to remove from my plate. I had an agent on my team, who I trusted, show the listing. On the off-chance that the buyer did want to write an offer, the agent let me know right away. I would then follow up and start the negotiating process. However, 90% of the time, the buyer would leave the property and not write on an offer. When a buyer did want to see the property for a second time, I would attend those showings.

I completely took myself out of the first showings, which freed up so much of my time. It created a win-win for both the agent on my team and me. I was giving them opportunities to meet buyers. Also, if they showed the home and that buyer wrote an offer and bought the house, the agent on my team who showed the property received a bonus. That's right. I would give a bonus to the agent on my team as an additional incentive. I do not expect people to work for free, and neither should you. I want hungry, professional agents on my team.

Time management is everything in this business.

If you think your sellers would be upset that you are not attending every showing, that is your fault. You are not setting expectations during your listing presentations. The key is setting the expectations with the client.

I tell every seller, "The reason I sell so many homes is because I built an incredible team. On the first showing, I have one of my agents here to let the buyer in and ensure your house is putting its best foot forward. Then, if there's interest, I will immediately come in. If there's no interest, I'll get feedback to find out why, and I will provide that feedback. If they want a second showing, I will be here at the second showing to close them. Odds are someone will want to see your home a second time because 90% of buyers do not write an offer on the first showing. They want to see the house a second time. That's where I come in. Sounds good?"

Do you see what I did there? I built credibility because I am successful enough to have a team. I set expectations that I do not attend first showings. I foreshadowed that 90% of buyers do not write an offer after the first showing. Now, I don't have a worried seller asking why they have not received showings after the market's first day. I set the expectations to not only make their experience better but also to free up my time.

I think back to all the time I wasted before I made this shift in my business. I was showing houses to hundreds of people who never bought from me—what a waste of time. If you aren't already, you need to qualify buyers before the showing if it's by appointment only.

If you know the house has what I call disqualifying factors, let the buyers' agent know upfront. Does the house have a lot of stairs in it? Does the house back up to a school? Ask the agent if their client is okay with that. Let the buyer and the buyer's agent know so you are not wasting anyone's time.

There's nothing wrong with qualifying someone. If something you told them about the home turns them away from even looking at it, they were never going to write an offer. Do not waste your time showing the home to someone who will not buy it.

If you have a listing that will only accept cash-only offers, ensure the buyer knows that. Do not ever show up to an appointment-only showing unless you know the buyer can buy the property.

Pro tip: If you are at a point in your sales business that you have to say no more listing appointments, more buyers, or even more time prospecting, it is time to hire someone. By now, you should be finding help in the form of part-time or even full-time staff. Not only have you realized you are not superman. You can't do it, but you also do not want to do it all. You didn't get into this business to work every second of every day. You didn't get into this business to give your clients mediocre customer service. Your clients deserve white-glove and concierge-level customer service.

If you are doing things correctly, you are busy. Your time is spent working both on and in your business. From listing feedback, new listing appointments, marketing, showings, and buyers, it's impossible for you to do it all. You must invest in your business. There is no better investment than people.

The next thing I took off my plate was prepping for showings. If it was a vacant home or even sometimes when it wasn't, the house needed to be prepped. Lights need to be turned on; countertops need to be whipped down, heat or air conditioning may need to be adjusted depending on the time of year.

By the time I drove to the house and prepped for the showing, I spent hours of my week on these activities. That was another thing to come off my plate. I assigned this task to someone on my team along with closing and locking up the house after showings. I did this same thing with open houses. It took hours to put out open house signs in the neighborhood. That was one of the first things I paid someone to do. We call this person a runner. If you don't have a runner, ask the top agent in their office who they use or ask your broker for a recommendation. You will be amazed at how much time this saves you.

As you look at things to take off your plate, calculate how much time that frees up for you. Time management is everything in this business. It's up to you if you spend the time to bring in more business or stay chasing business that you have already closed.

Week 7 Day 4 WORKSHEET

With everything you do to show a home, how can you possibly be more efficient?

What can you do in your business to create more time for yourself?

Now, take a moment to determine how valuable your time is. If you spend five hours a day lead generating, how many listings appointments does that create on average?

How many listing appointments do you attend and close? What is your conversation rate?

On average, how much is your commission per listings?

Now, do the math backward. How much is each hour of prospecting worth? Is it $200 or $500? How much?

Now, list the $15 per house tasks do you have on your plate? This includes putting out signs, lockboxes, printing marketing materials, posting on social media.

Identify five things you can take off your plate.

1

2

3

4

5

Do you have a buyers' agent now? Yes or No. *Circle one.*

If not, why?

When are you going to get one? I will hire a buyer's agent by _____. *Insert Date.*

Week 7 Day 5
DAY 35: WHEN TO SAY 'NO' AND WHEN TO SAY 'YES'

Today is our last day of mastering listings. This week was full of tangible techniques you can start using today. From time management to task delegation, you should be finding multiple ways to make your listing process more efficient.

Every home that you list will require dedicated amounts of time. The more you list, the more time required of you. Eventually, you will run out of time and will need to hire staff. Some clients will also require more time than others.

As you know by now, some clients are super tricky while some aren't. I can't tell you how many people who were my friends that turned on me. The home buying process can be emotional; you know that by now.

Unlike professions like attorneys and CPAs, real estate agents do not require a retainer upfront. As a real estate agent, you're putting your time, effort, and money out there to the world without getting a guaranteed paycheck.

Would your clients call their CPA at nine o'clock on a Friday night? Probably not, but they will call you. They will demand your full attention, yet you have not received a dollar of their money.

Let's revisit time management. This is a theme throughout the entire book as you have likely noticed. In Week 1, you determined when you work best in order to create a schedule as discussed in Week 2. Earlier this week, you looked at what inefficiencies you had in your business as you took things off your plate. Today, I want to explore what clients to take off your plate and what clients to not even take on in the first place.

The home buying process can be emotional.

There are some clients that you should not work with. You know your ideal client by now, and you know your niche. Does that mean you should say no to business that is outside your niche? No. That is not what I am saying. However, some difficult clients are never going to be worth your time.

At some point in your career, you will run into a seller with unrealistic expectations. The seller will want to sell their home for far more than what it's worth.

I had an agent who was on at my brokerage. He was notorious for saying yes to everything and everyone. He described himself as a people pleaser. Other people in the brokerage described him in different ways.

He would say yes to sellers and list homes for $40,000 to $80,000 more than he should. Why? Because he could not put his foot down when sellers requested to list their houses at these astronomical prices. Or maybe, he didn't know he could say no. Instead, he would spend his time, money, and energy listing these houses. He would pay for the professional photos and even the staging of the home. He would list the house and attend every showing. The house would sit on the market for months, sometimes up to a year. Like Devin, he didn't foreshadow or set expectations of price reductions. The listings just sat on the market.

Ask yourself what's the point if the home isn't going to sell?

There are going to be times when you take a listing that may not sell. Maybe the house is in a great area, that gets a lot of traffic. You will have dozens of opportunities to get your name out there. Plus, with every listing, you will have potential buyers calling you to inquire about the listing.

Before taking a new listing, it has to be worth the headache. You are going to endure the pitfalls of a listing that sits. Your seller will be upset with you if you do not manage their expectations. Even if you try foreshadowing and setting expectations, they will still likely be upset with you because you cannot sell the house for the price they want. They don't want to hear that the price is not realistic. You knew this when you listed the home. So, only take this on if the benefits outweigh the headache. If you are going to get a lot of foot traffic or if the signs will get a lot of eyes on them, maybe you will take this on.

But know that you're going to get backlash. You will likely lose that client and the listing. You risk your reputation as you lose that relationship.

The seller will certainly not have the best things to say about you. You must ask yourself is this worth bringing on potential buyers from this listing.

I have done this. I've listed homes that I didn't think I was going to sell, but I thought I could drive some excellent opportunities on the buyer side. That's not to say I don't try to sell the home; of course, I do. It's just to say that I knew I was walking into a really tough situation.

I knew the open houses would get a lot of traffic. I would never do this on a rural property where no eyes are seeing my sign. There would be little to no point in that. Again, this is only in the situation where the seller has unrealistic expectations, and there is no room for negotiating the list price.

In yesterday's homework, you determined how much your time is worth. Today, I want you to decide when it is worth taking on a headache buyer or a headache seller.

Saying yes to listing a home that you are confident you can sell is an easy decision—meanwhile, saying yes to a unique property that may not sell is a tough decision and one that you should not take lightly. An upset seller can ruin your day, your week, or even your reputation. So, be strategic when saying yes or no to different sellers.

Not every home is a yes.

It is okay to tell a seller that you do not want to list their home. You want to be strategic and graceful. Do not be blunt and say, "your house will never sell for that." However, you can tell a potential seller this: "if the home doesn't sell, I want the real estate professional that was honest with you about price and honest with you from the very beginning. I do not want to waste your time, and I run my business on honesty. I truly would like an opportunity to sell your home when you and I are on the same page about price. Does that sound okay?"

I really have said this to sellers. You would not believe the number of times my phone would ring months later. Sometimes, not as often, of course, but other times, my phone would ring the next day. It turns out I was the only agent who was honest and upfront with them. While I refused politely to list their home at that price, other agents agreed to list. Or maybe the seller had listed their house for that price, and sure enough, it sat for months. They had to put their pets outside every time there was a showing just to never sell the house. They had to live their lives differently, keeping their home spotless and tidy in case another showing came up. They lived like this for months and then finally picked up the phone to call me.

One seller told me that if I was not willing to take their listing, they must be wrong about what their home is worth.

I tell them that I don't want just to take a listing, I want to sell your home. I am in the business of selling homes, so I do not accept listings that I do not think will sell. I never like setting myself or my clients up for failure. More often than not, sellers decide to trust my judgment.

Sometimes being the second agent to list the house is even better. The seller gets rid of the first listing agent and always blames that agent even if the seller was the one with unrealistic expectations. They will always blame the first listing agent. The seller will swallow their pride and call and list with you and agree to a large price reduction. Now, you can sell the home.

The seller tends to be a little more motivated and maybe a tiny bit more realistic because they've already been through the wringer.

Then, you get to come in as the saving grace. You come in and sell the home in 30 days. In their eyes, you're a superstar.

Not every home is a yes.

Be wise with your time because listings take time. Sometimes, it's not completely about if the seller wants to hire you or not. You must ask yourself if you want to spend your time and energy on a home that you may not be able to sell.

If you take on a problematic listing, do yourself a favor and set the expectations that you still want to work with the seller if and when this doesn't sell. Let them know that you are there to help them, even if that means a price reduction.

You must be on the same page. Know when to say yes and know when to say no.

Week 7 Day 5 WORKSHEET

Identify the four worst clients you worked with in the past three years.

1

2

3

4

Now, identify at least three common traits of these clients.

1

2

3

4

Now, identify at least three common traits of the transactions or properties.

1

2

3

4

Identify the four best clients you worked with in the past three years.

1

2

3

4

Now, identify at least three common traits of these clients.

1

2

3

4

Now, identify at least three common traits of the transactions or properties.

1

2

3

4

Identify a time when you said yes, and you should have said no.

Week 8

Congratulations, you have made it to Week Eight. Over the past seven weeks, you have learned more about yourself, your ideal customer, and your business. By now, you should have a clear vision of goals for yourself and your real estate business.

Now, it is time to evaluate what Level your business is at today. Over the next five days, you will learn the Five Levels of Real Estate Sales. Where you are today does not have to be where you are tomorrow. It is possible to move up; it's also possible to move down or even never move at all. It is your decision if you want to level up—not your clients. You must decide if you're going to be a Level Five then you must do the work to get there. They go hand and hand. It is not possible to become a Level Five without doing the work.

This week, we will examine each Level and how to get to each one.

Even if you find yourself in Level Four or Level Five, I recommend taking the time to read through Level One, Level Two, and Level Three. It will give you a chance to reflect on how far you have come and maybe reminisce about the times when you were just starting out. It may even be possible that you, too, can pick up a trick or technique along the way.

Determining what Level you are at has nothing to do with ego and everything to do with self-awareness. Since Week One, I have been reminding you to let go of your ego. We have covered greediness, selfishness, and ego because these three things get in the way of agents making it from Level One and Level Two to Levels Four and Level Five. This week is about determining what Level you are to decide which part of your business needs attention. If you don't know where you are, you don't know where you are going.

I specialize in what I call 'Levels Coaching.' First, know that anyone can teach, inspire, and motivate. However, to put action plans in place, we must understand your Level. I would train a Level One agent entirely different from how I would train a Level Four agent.

Before you know it, you'll start doing deals. And then, hopefully, you start doing one or two deals a month, and then it builds from there, but where you're at right now, learn as much as you possibly can. And ask questions.

First, here is a quick guide:

Level 1 - $0 - $5 Million a year in production

Level 2 - $5.1 million to $14.9 million a year in production

Level 3 - $15.1 to $29.9 million a year in production

Level 4 - $30.1 to $49.9 million in production each year.

Level 5 - $50M+ a year in production

I encourage you to read every Level, not just the one you think you are at today, based on sales volume. Depending on what market you're in, you may be monetarily a Level Three but running a Level Two business in reality.

Week 8 Day 1
DAY 36: LEVEL ONE

At Level One, you are here to learn. The industry has so many moving targets, and by now, you know that 70+ things can go wrong in any given transaction. It is your job to sell houses, but it isn't always that simple.

Agents at Level One have likely been in the business for a year or two. You're just getting your feet wet or starting out in the business. Maybe you have been licensed for longer than that but haven't been entirely focused on your real estate business. Perhaps you're still holding onto a full-time job because you're scared—you need the security of a salaried position—or so you think.

Levels Coaching aims to take you from Level One to Level Five.

First, know that the money will come, but you have to learn, and you have to be willing to learn. Agents who act like a know-it-all or worse yet aren't even self-aware enough to recognize that they are a know-it-all will fail.

A Level One is closing zero to $5 Million a year in production. The most important thing you can do as a Level One Agent is learn.

Hungry driven real estate professionals will want to run out and pound the pavement the day they get licensed. I am here to tell you real estate is a marathon, not a sprint.

> *The money will come, but you got to learn, and you got to be willing to learn.*

Real estate is a game of longevity; it's about year-over-year growth. We often look at the next few months as a full-speed-ahead sprint, but that's wrong. Take this time to learn. You are doing the right thing by picking up this book and showing up. If you are reading this, you should have completed the homework for Weeks 1-7. Do not skip a day; do not rush through the worksheets without doing the work. If the worksheet tells you to examine your schedule and commit to a structured schedule, show up and do the work. It doesn't help your business to identify that you need a new listing packet but then never do the work to complete the new listing packet.

Do the work.

Don't get me wrong. I love working with Level One agents who are hungry and driven—ones who do the work. They get their real estate license and immediately think they will light the world on fire. And I will tell you that I hope you do. But the reality is, this is a game of longevity. So at Level One, we have to make sure that we are doing everything in our power to learn as much as possible. Your job in Level One is to learn the contracts and the transaction process. Almost just as importantly, you also need to learn the market so you can guide your clients.

It's not about setting the world on fire; it's about consistent hard work.

Third and arguably most importantly, you need to master efficiencies. It is important to build a foundation of good habits that will allow you to level up as you wish. Basics like sticking to a schedule and maintaining a content calendar really matter.

Take your time.

Have you ever noticed that large successful corporations have a structured onboarding process for their new employees? There is a reason that corporations take months to train their new employees. Corporations want their employees to be fully ready when it's time to hit the field. The same principle applies to Level One agents. It's about learning and understanding the work ethic you will need to get to Level two.

Partner or find a mentor.

As a Level One agent, one of the quickest ways to grow is to partner with an agent you respect. We mentioned this in Week One that you should be paying attention to who makes the Top 10 List in your brokerage, in your market, and your state. Your mentor can be two steps ahead of you or twenty, but it is crucial that you look up to them. You have seen how they communicate with their clients and how they treat the agent on the other side of the transaction. If you like what you see and they are successful in the business, I recommend approaching them to partner or build a mentor relationship.

Learn as much as possible, and don't be afraid to ask questions, and surround yourself with the right people. Look at their habits, their personality traits, and their work ethic. You should measure yourself against how you want to be ranked. If you observe top agents in your market, they have similarities.

If you are determined to be a solo agent, you don't need to partner but instead ask them if they're willing to mentor you. Don't expect anyone to work for free, so be ready to offer value to them.

You want a mentor because there are so many things that can go wrong on any given day in any given transaction. It is invaluable to have someone you can reach out to when you have questions or need help in your business. Maybe this is your broker or another agent in the office. Be sure to build the relationship slowly and genuinely. Don't only reach out when something is wrong, and be careful not to make every little thing feel like an urgent matter.

Once you find a mentor, pay attention to their habits. Observe how they work. Are they showing up to the office every day? Are they prospecting for 20 hours every week? Notice how much they are available to their clients. How are they foreshadowing? When they do speak to their clients, are they setting expectations?

> *Don't only reach out when something is wrong.*

It's not about setting the world on fire; it's about consistent hard work. Your job as a Level One agent is to learn as much as possible, and the deals will start to come. However, you must be willing to put in the effort.

First, are you at a brokerage that is setting you up for success? I don't believe that switching brokerages is always the solution; however, I have seen agents held back by being at the wrong brokerage or on the wrong team. Don't merely hop from brokerage to brokerage, thinking that's the easy fix. First, evaluate your work and the actions you are taking. However, if the problem is your brokerage, consider making a strategic change.

I want to be around an agent or an agency that gives me the tools to be successful. When I coach Level One agents, I ensure they have what they need to get out of Level One as soon as possible.

For a lot of agents, joining a team is the right answer. Sure, you may give up a portion of your commissions, but if you gain access to tools you don't have as a solo agent, it is often worth it.

Things a team should offer you:

Teach sales skills, even if it is merely observing the Lead Agent or other successful agents on the team

Access to administrative support - such as paperwork and transaction help

Marketing support such as an established website that captures leads, an SMS campaign, or access to a speed-dialer

Week 8 Day 1 WORKSHEET
Level One

How much did you close in volume last year?

What are you on track to close this year?

Who are consistently the top agents in your brokerage? In your market? Name, at least, four here.

1

2

3

4

In your opinion, why are they number one? What do they do differently?

1

2

3

4

Who can you surround yourself with someone who can give you the knowledge you need to build your real estate journey? Identify at least three agents.

1

2

3

If you are currently closing under $5 Million in volume, do you want to close more next year? If so, how much would you like to close next year?

What are three action steps you can take this quarter to get you there?

1

2

3

Week 8 Day 2
DAY 37: LEVEL TWO

Level Two Agents close $5.1 million to $15 million a year in production. Level Two is where a majority of agents get stuck. In fact, 80% of real estate agents are at Level Two.

As evident from the sheer number of agents in Level Two, it can be difficult for agents consistently to exceed $15 million in annual sales. But once you do, it is not as challenging to go from Level Three to Level Four.

Like America's middle class, there is an Upper Level Two and a Lower Level Two. Upper Level Two is $12-14 Million in volume. This Upper Level Two is not yet Level Three. There are specific roadblocks, including mental blocks that keep agents going from Level Two to Level Three. For some reason, that $15M marker is a hurdle for some. Today, we will explore a few roadblocks so you can breeze through Level Two and break through these roadblocks.

Agents in Level Two are what I like to call the 'questioning child.' They continuously ask things like: "should I do this?" or "Should

I spend money on that?" They are the first to ask, "Should I hire someone?" or "Should I hire him?"

They'll come to me and ask if they should hire an assistant. Even after I tell them, "Yes!" they reply with, "Well, I don't know."

"Should I hire a buyer's agent?"

"Yes."

"Well, I don't know."

"Should I invest money in advertising?"... "Oh, I don't know."

I understand agents at this Level agents are anxious to spend money. Level Two Agents feel as though they can't really afford to make mistakes.

Ask yourself: *where are you going?*

If you want to close more than $15M in sales, you will need to spend money, and you should hire someone so you can keep providing concierge-level customer service to your clients. Being too busy (or too frugal for that matter) is not serving you or your clients.

When I worked my way from Level One to Level Two, I first learned more about the business side of real estate sales. By this time, I had closed enough transactions where I knew what I was doing. I was navigating troubling transactions with confidence.

As a Level One Agent, tasks such as writing up a contract became second nature. It was in Level One that I learned to set up a tour properly by not showing the best house first. I mastered these skills because remember, you are mastering your craft. You are a professional.

You must decide if you want to Level up.

Now, at Level Two, it is about building your business. It was at Level Two that I asked myself: do I want to build a team?

If not a team, would you like to simply build a small little support staff and continue to close $10-12M in volume?

At this Level, agents have the process of their transactions down. Checklists are created and are being followed. Agents at Level Two understand the game and have a proven work ethic that brought them to here.

One of the most common questions I get from agents at conferences is: "if you had $2,000 a month to spend, what would you spend it on?"

Many gurus will tell you that you should spend that on marketing and advertising.

"Digital marketing is the way forward" is something I hear over and over. While I would not argue with that, that is not what I tell agents at Level Two.

The Number One thing you should be investing in is a person. The answer is to hire an assistant.

Find someone who wants to actively participate in your business. Do not simply hand over a salary but instead allow this person to become vested in you and your business.

Your assistant is helping you as part of your growth strategy.

The Number One thing you should be investing in is a person.

The best thing I ever did for my career was to hire an assistant and invest in a person to grow my business. I can confidently say that I went from Level Two to Level Three within 12 months because I hired the right assistant.

I gave them a piece of what I was doing, and they were fully vested in my success. Your assistant's job is to help you grow your business. As they take things off your plate, you must be committed to income-producing activities like lead generation and bringing in more business. Then at some point, as a Level Two Agent, you can bring on a buyer's agent.

Understand that to grow, you're going to have to spend money. While it can be nerve-racking, you need help. At some point, you're stretching yourself too thin. Along with your assistant, a buyer's agent is going to free up time. The right buyer's agent will allow you to focus more on the consumers you want to work with, not the consumers you have to work with. Imagine being able to hand off your least favorite client from last year to your buyer's agent. Wouldn't that be a game-changer in terms of freeing up your time and improving your happiness and wellbeing? Sometimes the mental capacity alone is worth freeing up.

The best thing I ever did for my career was to hire an assistant.

We spoke in Week Seven about attending inspections or first showings. Your buyer's agent, once trained, should be taking this off your plate. Your assistant is ordering signs and organizing showings. They or a transaction coordinator are handling all the paperwork. Your assistant is now managing the process and all the moving parts. They can likely take some marketing tasks off your plate, too.

Look at the agents who are consistently closing $20M+. They have support. They're not putting out lockboxes, opening the property for the stagger, attending inspections or photoshoots. They're focusing on Rainmaker tasks.

Your job now is to go out and get more business. You can't do that if you're bogged down.

Most agents find hiring to be scary. Once you hire someone, you are then responsible for someone else's annual salary. By now, you can handle it. You have proven yourself in the business if you're closing $5-15M a year.

You must decide if you want to Level up.

Less than 10% of Real Estate Agents are at Level Three. So, you have a decision to make. Will you stay with the masses (remember: 80% of Real Estate Agents are at Level Two)? Or will you do what it takes to get to Level Three? Then possibly Four and Five? If you make that decision, you must invest in yourself.

Decide now that you're gonna have to bet on yourself to get out of Level Two. If you want to stay in Level Two, that's great. You can make what most would consider a decent living closing $10-14M in sales every year.

I will explain more tomorrow, but know that being at Level Three doesn't mean you have to build a large team. However, to consistently close more than $15 Million, you will need support. Start today, if you haven't already, and once you make the decision that you want to scale, hire support.

Next, I want you to closely examine your business. By now, you should know where your clients are coming from and determine where you are getting a majority of your business. If not, that is your homework today.

At Level One, it is okay to not know where business is coming from. Some agents are simply grateful to have the phone ring. At Level One, maybe agents receive a call off of a sign or a referral here and there. To consistently close more deals, you cannot run your business like that. It does not help to simply determine where business is coming in from part of the time. Now that you are a real estate professional, you must track where leads are coming from, how many closings you have closed, and where those closings came from. Remember, this task does not have to stay on your plate. It is best to delegate this task to someone who has the time, energy, and skillset to best track this information.

You must decide if you want to Level up.

When I was at Level One, I admit that I bounced around, trying to find the best way to get clients. I had my monthly newsletter, which I sent out religiously. However, I was tracking if my clients were coming from that or from open houses. It wasn't until I hired my assistant that determining where business was coming from became easier. It was no longer my responsibility to track this—it was my assistant's.

Week 8 Day 2 WORKSHEET
Level 2

Where do you want your business to be in three years?

Five years?

Ten years from now?

Where do a majority of your clients from? Is it from a few channel accounts? Is it from relationships? Is it from your social network?

Where are you attracting the most clients from?

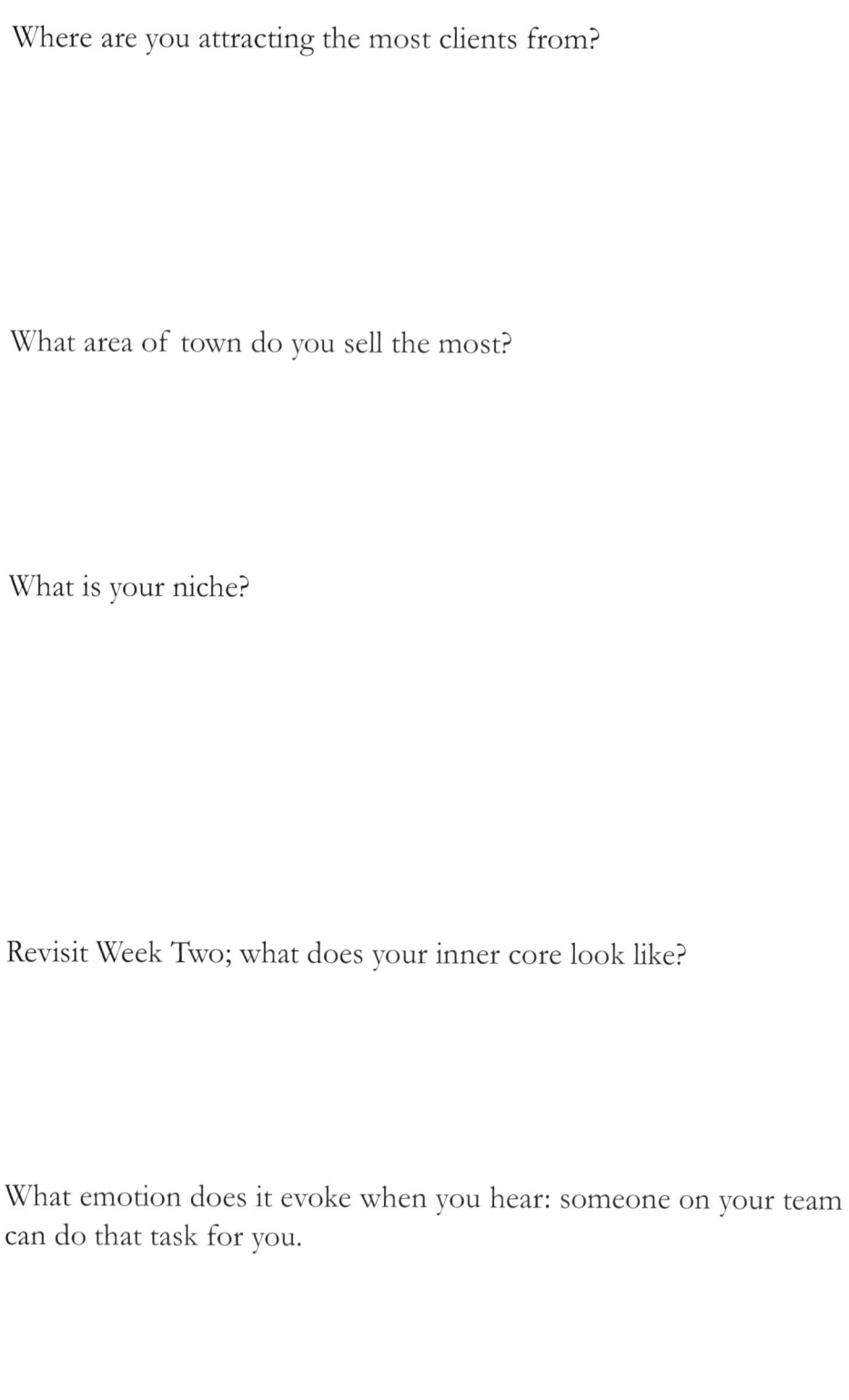

What area of town do you sell the most?

What is your niche?

Revisit Week Two; what does your inner core look like?

What emotion does it evoke when you hear: someone on your team can do that task for you.

Identify ten items you'd like to get off your plate in the next 60 days.

1

2

3

4

5

6

7

8

9

10

Week 8 Day 3
DAY 38: LEVEL THREE

Level Three Agents close $15 to $30 million a year in production. If you are closing more than $15 million a year, you can take a moment to congratulate yourself. Most people don't realize how hard the real estate business can be; they see the television shows and think it's easy. They don't realize that there's so much competition and so many things that can go wrong. It is a challenging field to not only be in but also to master. If you are consistently closing more than $15 million, congratulations, you are mastering your craft and succeeding .

You clearly have the drive. You're committed to putting in the time, energy, and money to grow a successful real estate business. It hasn't been easy, I know. It doesn't happen overnight or in a year. Agents don't go from zero to 30 million in a year. At the beginning of this week, I said that real estate is a marathon, not a sprint. If you are a Level Three Agent, you know that.

Only 10% of people in real estate make it to Level Three. There is an Upper Level Three closing $25-30M, and Lower Level Three closes $15-25M, similar to Level Two.

Some of you may be thinking, "Look, I'm content. I don't want that crazy lifestyle. I'm making $500,000 a year, possibly more money than I ever thought possible. I love my lifestyle."

If you don't have aspirations to be a Level Four agent, not a problem. The principles we will cover today still apply. However, that doesn't mean even you can't build efficiencies to make your life easier. That doesn't mean you can't build internal processes to make everything flow better for you, your staff, agents, and, most importantly, your clients. That doesn't mean that you cannot add a couple buyer's agents that can take the work on for you.

Mindset

Let's first talk about our mindset as a level three real estate professional.

The sets of problems that a Level Three Agent face are different and possibly new for you. First, you may feel too busy. If you still feel too busy, you are not letting enough go. Let's revisit something crucial we covered in Week One.

You're not Superman.

I told you in Week One that you cannot do it all because I want agents to practice letting go from the beginning. Also, this is one of the most common struggles among all real estate agents. We have likely gotten into the business for different reasons, but one thing is common ground: we like being in control. Letting go of that control will give you more freedom than you could have ever imagined. It is possible to close $30M and not touch every file. It is not only possible, it is necessary.

Real estate is a marathon, not a sprint.

A lot of Level Three Agents come to me to say, "I have more business than I actually know what to do with."

I tell them, congratulations. First, you don't have to work with that new client if you don't want to. You have buyer's agents on your team who can handle them from contract to close by now. If you don't want to go sell a $200,000 home anymore, you don't have to!

I should never hear a Level Three Agent say, "I am bogged down with paperwork." No, you need to have that entirely off your plate by now. Your assistant should manage a Transaction Coordinator. Paperwork should no longer be your responsibility or even take up your headspace.

Culture

Once you are at Level 3, if you want to stay here or, better yet, grow to Level 4 or 5, you will always employ support staff of some kind.

If you are a greedy agent, your team will leave you.

What do I need to do to bring in more of the business that I want to work, not just the business that's coming to me? I know when I was a level three agent, I would sit here and say, I'm working so much because I feel like I have to work everything. Or maybe now you have a couple buyers reps, which you probably do. And we have to find ways to give them more and pass that along. It's that internal struggle that "I can't do it all. But I still want to make all the money." I will tell you this,

If you are a greedy agent, your team will leave you. The more you can help, assist them with growth, the more you will succeed.

A Level Two agent looking to be a Level Three needs to improve their systems and processes. You should be focusing on building efficiencies. Build a blueprint for scalability, one that will allow the opportunity to create a machine.

If your systems are not ironclad and easy to scale, you will never get to Level Four. When you look at agents at Level Four, they are machines. Everything is the same. Each transaction is treated the same. Someone on the team is assigned to every piece of the process, from contract to close. Nothing gets dropped.

Level 4 Agents, you are not checking every little thing. You don't wake up in the middle of the night wondering if an inspection was ordered and scheduled or if this client dropped off their earnest money. That's no longer your job. Your job is to put the right people in the right places on your team, so you no longer have to worry about these moving pieces for every transaction. By now, hopefully, you have so many transactions in escrow, you can't rattle them off by memory, nor should you.

By now, there should be multiple agents within your team that can assist you on the list and buy side. If not, you need to look at recruiting and hiring this quarter. Do not wait.

Next, make sure that your organization's fundamental process is identical every single time an opportunity arises. When a potential buyer calls from a sign on one of your listings, what happens? How is that handled and tracked?

It should be the same every time. By now, you have multiple listings running at once. You can't have your assistant coming to you asking what to do. They should know their role and know it well. By now, they are fully vested in both you and your business. If you think you have the wrong people in the wrong spots, it is time to hire and fire.

Your team's culture is crucial. You may have been able to close $10M with a buyer's agent who wasn't a personality match or a culture fit, but I am telling you that you will never close more than $30M consistently if you have the wrong people on your team.

Once you are confident that you have the right agents on your team, give them more business. You and the agents on your team are out in the field producing. Now that you are at Level Three, you are producing at a really high level. But make sure you are not handling too many of the transactions and clients. Meaning, you need to be honest with yourself: are you giving them reasons to stay?

> *If you think you have the wrong people in the wrong spots, it is time to hire and fire.*

I see it all too often that agents at this Level spend time, money, and energy training buyer's agents only to see them leave within a year. Yes, you want to hire and mentor-driven, ambitious individuals, but that doesn't mean they should turn around and outgrow you or abandon your team within the year. You should be creating opportunities for them to stay. You should be crafting a culture of loyalty and growth for each and every person on your team.

If you are too busy to do this and commit time and energy to creating a culture, you need to give your buyer's agents more of your clients. You need your assistant to take more off your plate. As you look at growing from Level Three to Level Four, you need to step out of the field more and back into the office. You should be working on the business, not in the business 24/7.

Then, the goal is to get to a point where agents on your team are producing for you. Then, you can pick and choose what clients to personally take on. Not only does this help you, it incentivizes your buyer's agents to stay with you. They will think, "Whoa. My lead agent is giving me better and better leads. They are not taking all the listings every time. They're throwing me some quality leads now and then."

Why would a buyer's agent leave you if you are truly taking care of them? Hint: they won't.

In Week Seven, we went over marketing and promotion. Once you are a Level Three, you have the time and resources to start investing in marketing even more, and you should.

You need to take time to reflect on your business.

As a Team Lead in Level Three, you must focus on business development. This includes marketing. It also includes identifying the demographic of people that you want to work with. By now, you know who your inner core is and what your ideal customer looks like. From there, you know where to find them, market to them, and close them. If this is still a struggle, you need to take time to reflect on your business. This may mean you need to slow down and look at the business from a different angle. It is crucial to your success as a real estate professional. You will not continue to close $15M+ if you do not know who your customers are and where to find them. You surely won't close more than $30M.

Systems and efficiencies

Once you feel you have the right people in place and confidently know who your customers are, it is time to examine your internal processes. This step means you will explore each procedure of every transaction step.

Allow me to show you what this looks like in my own business. Today, we do almost 400 transactions a month or $1.6 Billion in sales in our business. I now have a well-oiled machine with airtight systems and processes. It would never be possible to close this many transactions and continue to have satisfied clients if I hadn't built a strong foundation.

Why are we talking about this now to Level Three agents closing less than $30 Million? Because it was here in Level Three, where I began to build the foundation of the processes and systems that I still use today as we close $1.6 Billion. When I was closing less than $25M, I took time each month to reevaluate the transactions we closed that month. I would always ask my administrative assistant how we can improve? Where did we drop the ball? Together, we made incremental changes to the process. We erased redundancy and improved our efficiency. It is the same checklists we used back then that we use today.

Level Three Agents, you are making enough money to comfortably invest in your business. I don't know why you feel you need to hear it from your coach or me or your broker, but many of you feel like you need permission to spend money on your business. that just isn't true. If you are continually closing $15-30M a year, you have enough money to invest in your business. Your CRM should be updated daily and not by you. Frankly, some of the country's top producing agents never even log into their CRM. That is the job of their assistant.

As I said yesterday, hiring my assistant allowed me to go from Level Two to Level Three in less than 12 months. However, Level Three was the most challenging Level to get out of. It took me a couple years. But I decided early on that I wasn't going to stop at $20M, $30M, or even $50M. I knew I was destined to own and run a One Billion Dollar company.

It was not the decision alone that propelled me forward. It was the relentless effort that made it possible.

Week 8 Day 3 WORKSHEET
Level Three

Today, let's examine your three pillars.

Mindset

Culture

Systems and Efficiencies

Mindset

In the last two weeks, have you told yourself or someone else that you are too busy? If so, you need to take things off your plate. Review the last question from yesterday's worksheet.

On a scale from 1 to 10, how good are you at letting things go? *(One being unable to let anything go and ten being excellent at delegating and handing off tasks).*

Culture

If you were to describe your business to your friends, what would you say?

If you were to describe your team to someone you wanted to recruit, what would you say?

Do you have agents on your team now? If yes, do you enjoy mentoring?

Do you enjoy the process of having people that rely on you?

If not, identify three things keeping you from adequately relying on your team?

1

2

3

Why do you have these reservations?

Systems and Efficiencies

Identify three systems in business that are helping you close more transactions?

1

2

3

Now, identify two systems you feel need to be improved in your business.

1

2

Identify three instances where inefficiencies have cost you money or cost your clients a transaction?

1

2

3

How can you afford these in the future?

1

2

3

Week 8 Day 4

DAY 39: LEVEL FOUR

Level Four is selling $30 to $50 million in production each year. Very few real estate agents achieve enough sales to reach Level Four.

Once you have achieved Level Four, you can take a moment to congratulate yourself on how far you have come. But before you pat yourself on the back, I know you, Level Four agents, have problems, too. Your minds are continuously going. You have proven you want to go all the way to the top, and not going to stop. You are relentless. Maybe your mind works at night. You are continually thinking of implementing and finding ways to drive more business because now you've created all these efficiencies.

Now, ask yourself: how do I get past $50 million a year in production?

At this point, you've built your business, and everyone has a different business. Everyone has a different model, you know what you need to do. The question is, how do you get there, because Level Four training to reach Level Five is all internal.

It's all internal.

Your job is now busy enough to match agents on almost every client you have because you're driving so much business into the machine. So now, to get to $50 million.

Now, you have to build the business.

When you first start out as a real estate agent, you are building systems and processes. When an agent reaches Level Four, they're building a company and a team. If you cringe at the word "team" or start to perspire at the thought of hiring more than seven employees, I have good news. An agent does not need to have a large team to close more than $50 Million. You can have a small, high-functioning team. Just know that there is no room for mistakes.

When I built my team, I grew it organically. I added agents when it felt right. I always had my foot on the gas. I see some agents get to Level Four and stop doing the work. They stop making the calls that brought in business. What happens then? Sales start to slip.

> *When I built my team, I grew it organically.*

Some agents at Level Four begin to make excuses as to why they haven't taken on as many listings this month. At Level Four, your job is to bring in more business—not less. When I was at Level Four, I knew my job wasn't to be in the field every day anymore. My job was to grow the company and ensure my clients and my team were satisfied. You are now the Rainmaker, and every day, you should be making it rain.

Culture

Yesterday, we touched on culture briefly. Today, I want to emphasize its importance in your success. If your team has a revolving door of Buyer's Agents, you need to address this. Agents will leave a team for various reasons, of course. Yet, the most common reason Buyer's Agents leave a team is because of the Lead Agent and their behavior. The second most common reason is because of the team's culture or lack thereof.

If you have created an attractive team and consistently added buyer's agents over the last year or two, it is time to examine your current agents and their production. Your job as the Lead Agent and Rainmaker is to ensure the Buyer's Agents on your team belong there.

That was one of my biggest struggles when I got to Level Four. Unfortunately, I had buyer's agents who were lazy, but I had an excellent internal support team. As I mentioned, hiring my assistant is the Number One reason I could scale so quickly. Also, I had two more support staff who handled things like processing paperwork and improving our systems.

My biggest struggle was internal culture. I had mastered the Rainmaker part of the job. I was bringing in business and creating opportunities for my buyer's agents, yet some weren't appreciative of the business. A few of them didn't want to work the deal once I brought it in.

"Did you call the lead I gave you this morning?" I would ask.

Then they were shocked that I was livid with them when they told me they hadn't gotten around to it yet.

My biggest struggle was internal culture.

The buyer's agents felt they could rely on me to always bring in business and leads; thus, they didn't value the leads I brought in. I knew, and they knew I could make it rain. Thus, they did not bother picking up the phone when a new lead came in. After all, another would come in a few hours later.

In today's worksheet, you will closely examine your organization. Be on the lookout for what or who I call 'culture killers.' A culture killer is someone who, despite your best efforts, brings the culture down on a team. Perhaps they are lazy, negative, or unhappy. Someone with a victim mindset can be toxic in the context of growing a successful team. You will need to remove Culture Killers and reward those upholding the type of environment you desire for yourself and your team. One easy way to determine the kind of environment you want for your team is to create a Standard of Excellence.

Standard of Excellence

Your job as a Lead Agent and Rainmaker is to establish the culture and the Standard of Excellence. If you allow agents to get away with behavior that does not directly reflect the culture you are trying to grow, you fail your team. It is easier to meet expectations when we know what those expectations are.

Hiring and retaining good agents is key to your success.

This also makes it easier to cut the fat. When an agent is not behaving correctly or does not add value to the team, it is easy to say you are not closing three transactions a month as per our Standard of Excellence. You do not attend our weekly team meetings on time, which is required for all agents in their first year. Whatever your Standard of Excellence is, make it clear and known to everyone on the team.

This also makes it easier to cut the fat. When an agent is not behaving correctly or does not add value to the team, it is easy to say to them, "you are not closing three transactions a month as per our Standard of Excellence." Or "You do not attend our weekly team meetings on time, which is required for all agents in their first year."

Whatever your Standard of Excellence is, make it clear and known to everyone on the team.

This also helps you hire the right people. If they don't fit the mold then you don't hire them. Hiring and retaining good agents is key to your success. Retaining agents on your team is important, so is client retention.

Client Retention and Portfolio Retention

I have witnessed great rainmakers in the industry make this mistake. These agents have mastered marketing, advertising, lead generation, and other avenues that ensure they can continue to bring in new business. These are typically high volume teams, yet they make one mistake: They neglect past clients.

The Lead Agents are so focused on being a Rainmaker that they are only looking forward full-speed ahead. They forget to stay in touch with past clients.

If you are this agent, don't stop what you're doing. Of course, you want to continue to push ahead and bring in new business, but hire someone on your team to follow behind you and look backward. They can spot opportunities that you don't make time for and miss. This can be a support staff member or a Buyer's Agent. You can call this person Client Relations. Their job should be to set up drip campaigns and systems around client follow-up. Their goal is what I call 'Portfolio Retention.'

Post-closing process

This can be easily implemented, but it will take work to maintain. Be sure to hire the right person for the job. They will create a process around post-closing. On average, 10 to 12% of your annual business should be with past clients.

How many closings from this year were repeated clients or past clients of yours?

Is there a systemized way your team is staying in front of past clients? Are you staying top of mind?

In Week Two, we talked about being an Information Junkie and how random acts of kindness could help you stay top of mind for your clients. However, the reality is that when you are closing more than $50 Million in sales, it is nearly impossible to remember every past client. This is why you must create a post-closing process. Find ways to better serve your clients even after they close. Maybe this is a newsletter full of valuable tips for new homeowners. You can create a neighborhood newsletter welcoming clients to their new community. Whatever it is that you decide to do, do it well and do it consistently. By now, you have staff, task one of them with owning this process.

Prospecting

Once you have a solid system for handling the post-close process, you should improve the ways leads come into your pipeline. When you start to close $30 to $50 million a year, you do not have time to do all the follow-up. When a lead comes in, it is imperative that it is handled quickly and professionally. If you are running a team and growing a business, leads will fall through the crack. Don't allow this to happen. Instead, hire someone whose job is to focus solely on Prospecting. Some call this an Inside Sales Agents or ISA. You will need to properly train your ISA or, better yet, hire someone to train the ISA for you.

Whatever it is that you decide to do, do it well and do it consistently.

In today's worksheet, you will examine the systems you need to hire an ISA if you haven't already. If you have been using an ISA already, you will examine and possibly improve this part of your business.

You may be in Level Four and think that you don't need an ISA or someone on your team to handle prospecting. Some agents believe that they are closing this much volume because they alone brought in the leads. Your hard work indeed brought you to where you are today. However, it will not be enough to propel you into Level Five. It may not even be enough to keep you in Level Four long-term. Consistently closing business will require you to establish new systems. It will mean doing things you are uncomfortable doing. But by now, you have spent the past eight weeks practicing things like letting go and getting out of your own way. You now know that you need help.

You are not Superman.

To go from Level Four to Level Five, you will need to master both Portfolio Retention and Prospecting. Hire someone to help you because you cannot do it all. When you do, you will add tens of millions in volume.

The added benefit of mastering portfolio retention and prospecting is that it will also help you recruit top agents; agents who will also bring in their own business and leads. Allow me to show you how.

After you master Portfolio Retention, 12% of your business is past clients. Then once you master Prospecting, you have a dedicated person on your team bringing in leads. Now, how does that look to a potential buyer's agent considering joining your team?

You mean to tell me if I join your team, you're going to give me buyer opportunities and listing opportunities. You have a skilled ISA who is adequately trained, and they bring in leads regularly.

Next, you're going to follow up with my clients for me? Your team already has a set standard of protocols? The team has established ways to stay in front of my past clients, too? If I join your team, you're gonna do all that stuff for me? Great, sign me up!

Now that it took me years to build the right foundation to where I knew I had the right team members beside me. I want you to develop a standard of excellence because I didn't have one, and it kept me from building and retaining talented agents on my team. Once I established a standard of excellence, it became clear who needed to go and who deserved to stay. It also helped us recruit the types of agents that would take us to the next Level. Greatness attracts greatness.

Once you have talent on your team, you start to grow organically. Our culture became one that others, like us, wanted to be a part of.

Week 8 Day 4 WORKSHEET
Level 4

Culture

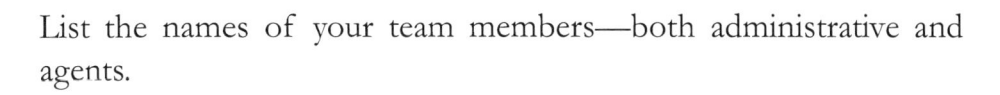

List the names of your team members—both administrative and agents.

As you look at the performance and the behavior of each team member, are there bad eggs? Are any of them Culture Killers?

If so, get rid of them. You will not get to Level Five with Culture Killers on your team sucking up your time and energy and the team's time and energy.

Standard of Excellence

Do you have a Standard of Excellence written out? Yes or No. *Circle one.*

If so, does everyone know where to find it? If not, take time today to write one.

Do you have a mission statement? If so, does everyone know where to find it? If not, take time today to write one.

Portfolio Retention

Are you maintaining a certain percentage of your portfolio business? What percentage of this year's closed volume is from past clients? How many closings from this year were repeated clients or past clients?

Or are you seeing past clients use other agents at this point?

Is there a systemized way your team is staying in front of past clients?

How are you staying in touch with past clients? Do you have an established automated system for Portfolio Retention?

Who on your team is in charge of Portfolio Retention?

Prospecting

What happens with a new inquiry?

Whenever a client hits a particular milestone, it triggers an email or an SMS. Perhaps after an inspection, you are notified that you need to have a follow-up call.

Who on your team owns this part of the business?

Do they have their scripts? Yes or No. *Circle one.*

Do they have their process written out if they can't come into the office or, worse, quit? Yes or No. *Circle one.*

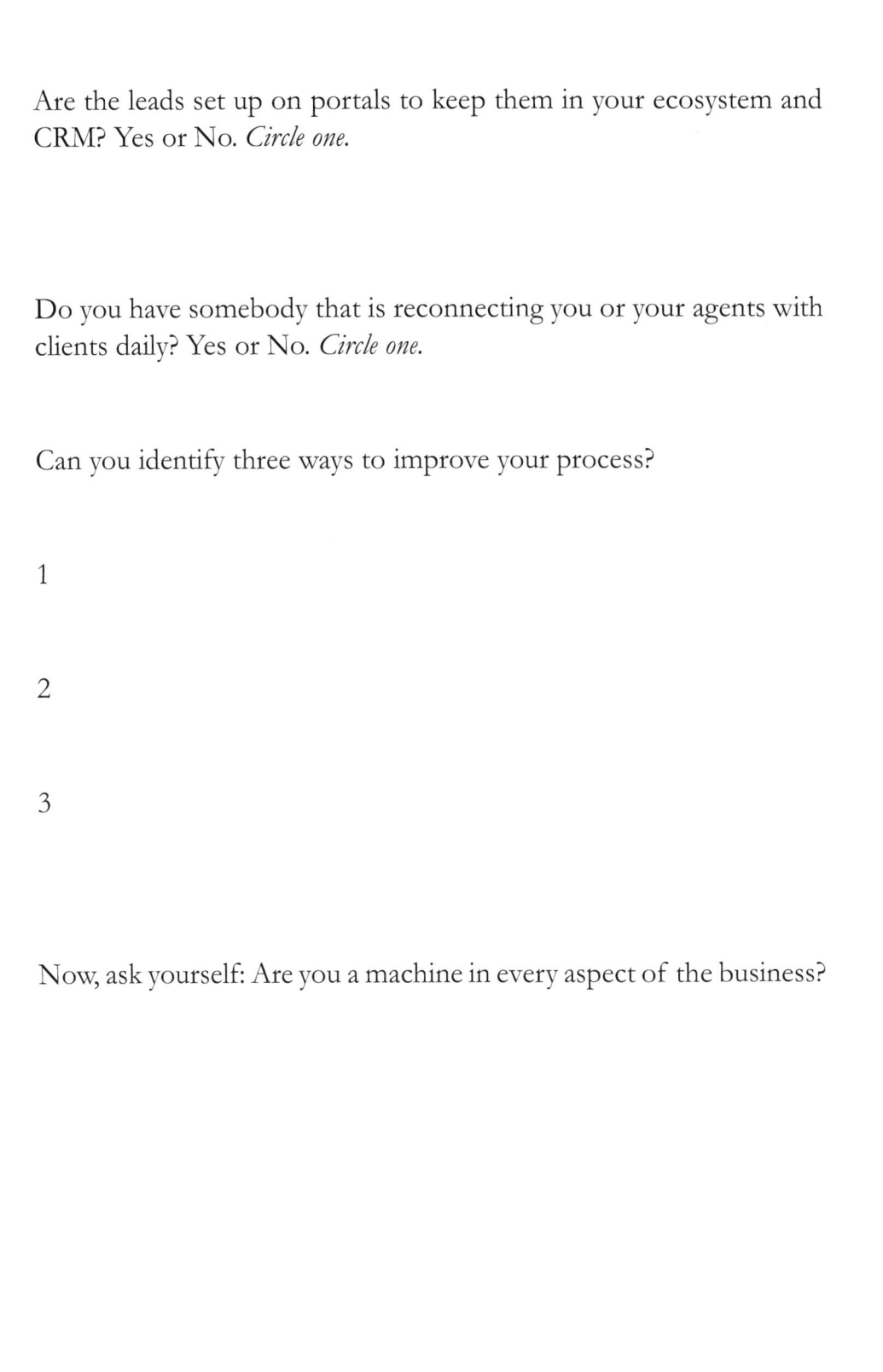

Are the leads set up on portals to keep them in your ecosystem and CRM? Yes or No. *Circle one.*

Do you have somebody that is reconnecting you or your agents with clients daily? Yes or No. *Circle one.*

Can you identify three ways to improve your process?

1

2

3

Now, ask yourself: Are you a machine in every aspect of the business?

Week 8 Day 5
DAY 40: LEVEL FIVE

If you are closing more than $50 Million annually, you have reached Level Five. Less than 1% of real estate agents reach Level Five. If this is you, Congratulations!

Even less agents close more than $100 Million in volume, yet there are many of you reading this who either have or who will close more than $100 Million in a year. It is possible. Allow me to show you how.

Depending on your market, reaching Level Five also means you are number one in your market. In some states, selling more than $100 Million in real estate sales could bring you close to number one in your state. Regardless of what market you are in, if you are selling $50 Million worth of real estate, you are at Level Five.

Level Five agents who are closing $50-52 million still have room for growth and need to focus on scaling. Be warned that just because you are in Level Five today does not mean you will always be here. A few things can push your sales below $50 Million in future years. Now that you've made it here, let's ensure you stay here.

First, you do not get to Level Five by accident. Take a moment to reflect back on all the hard work you put in to get here.

By now, you have spent years putting in the effort to build your business. Agents in your area have heard of you, and consumers in your market know that your name is synonymous with real estate both selling and buying homes.

Level Five agents are still looking for ways to improve and better serve their clients. With ever-changing technology and market shifts, there are opportunities for growth at every Level, even Level Five.

In Level Five, agents need to ask themselves these three questions:

1. Am I functioning as the CEO of my company?
2. How do I keep growing my empire? Know that if you are doing $50 Million or more in production, you've created an empire.
3. Do I want to be a mega agent or a mega team?

Over the past few weeks, we have touched on mindset, culture, and efficiencies in your process.

Before diving into Mega Teams, let's first explore your job as the CEO of your team. Even if you do not want a Mega Team, as a Mega Agent, you are now the CEO of the company.

The CEO Role

As CEO, your job is to drive more business. As a CEO, you are no longer attending showings, inspections, or even listing appointments. Instead, your focus is on how to scale the business. While the organization still has to grow, you can decide where you want to position yourself within your own business.

Whether you want to be a Mega Agent or a Mega Team, the day-to-day is not on you anymore. Your job is to be the CEO of your company.

At Level Five, you must determine what people your business needs. At Level One and Two, it was more about you and your ability to close transactions successfully, but now, it is about placing people in the right seats on the ship. You are the captain.

Once you are closing $50 Million and more, outstanding leadership will be a big part of your ability to scale and grow. Your assistant has been an instrumental part of your business since Level Two, but now you need more than administrative support. You need leadership support. Administrative staff will play more of a role in the day-to-day business functions, and the leadership team will be in charge of team management. It is the leadership team will play a large role in strategic planning for business growth.

I can't believe I even have to say this, but your leadership team and administrative support staff should be people you can genuinely rely on. If not, get rid of them. You must be able to step out of the sales side and focus on strategically growing the company. Your staff must be focused on the sales volume and closed transactions. They must also have the systems in place to do both.

> *Both your leadership team and administrative support staff should be people you can genuinely rely on.*

Now that you are the CEO, your leadership team should be fielding calls from agents. The agents will need someone to turn to and ask questions, especially the newer agents. With that being said, you need to be able to step away from this role as quickly as possible. Find someone you can trust for the agents to turn to and ask questions.

Remember: your job is to be the CEO, so you need to step away from previous responsibilities.

Your support staff is managing the processes and systems. Ensure your team understands their roles and responsibilities every single day, so you can truly step away as needed. At times, your support staff will have questions and need someone to turn to. At Level Five, this person should not be you. You need to find someone to be in charge.

Empower leadership to come to you with high-level issues but otherwise, keep things off your plate so you can focus on strategic growth.

Where to Put Your Focus

Ensure that you are stepping on the gas in the right areas of your real estate business.

First, your financials must be in order. The business financials are an indicator of where the business is going. You do this by looking at your Profit and Loss statement. Today's worksheet will have you examine your P&L Statement and ask yourself: what's working and what's not?

There are excellent resources to help you with this, too. Enable your accountant, processor, and bookkeeper to review your financials every month. Identify where the business is spending money. As we have explored throughout the previous weeks, you will spend money on your business. You must examine where the money is coming in and going out.

Becoming the Mega Agent You Want to Become

Some Level Five agents are still in production. Meanwhile, some Level Five agents have stepped out of production altogether. If you are still in production, it is easier and arguably more enjoyable because agents can pick and choose which clients to work with.

Either way, you're not coming into the office every day. When you do visit the office, it is just that: a visit. You're in and out. Your support staff and agents have avenues for communication. You have entrusted other leadership for them to go to for the support and the answers they need. It's not that they do not need you, but they are already set up for success because of you.

All you need to do is make sure things are being handled, but that's where your leadership team steps up and reports to you with any problems.

Growing a Mega Team

To grow a Mega Team, you will likely expand into other markets to build what we call 'expansion teams.' I am now in multiple markets, and I can tell you that it was not an easy road for me.

At the beginning, I looked at markets where I could duplicate my model. To date, this was one of the most challenging things that I had to do.

I started my team in Phoenix, Arizona. It wasn't until I was at Level Five, that I began to consider building an expansion team. At the time, we were doing more than $150 Million in production. Because of its proximity to Phoenix, Tucson was my first target market. It felt like the most natural progression. I would easily start a team in Tucson—or so I thought.

I admit I went down Tucson arrogantly, thinking it was going to be easy. I have mentioned ego in multiple chapters throughout this book because I know firsthand what ego looks like and how it can harm your business.

I went to Tucson, with my ego, to build a team down there. I interviewed agents in Tucson all day, yet I did not find one agent to join us. Nobody wanted to be a part of what we had. I came back to Phoenix with my tail between my legs.

I took time to reflect on what I needed. There was a key piece missing in my business. I did not have outstanding leadership beside me to assist me in expanding into other markets. Without it, I was able to build to Level Five in Phoenix, but in order to duplicate this model and expand into other markets, I needed help. I needed to find the right person for the position.

Next, I would need to share my vision with them. It is critical that they, too, believed in the vision. No matter how great an agent may be, if they do not see the vision I have for the business, it would never work.

In order to get to Level Five, you have likely mastered the art of attracting buyer's agents. Maybe you have even successfully attracted and retained outstanding support staff, but do not confuse this with the ability to attract outstanding leadership. Attracting great leadership is incredibly difficult. Those who have hired and retained a talented Director of Sales and Director of Operations understand this to be true.

The leadership team is motivated differently than buyer's agents. They are compensated differently, too. They want to be compensated with opportunity—opportunities to make more money and grow into what they want. They need resources for both.

Hiring and retaining leadership team is new territory for most Level Five agents. Before getting overwhelmed, take a moment to create a crystal clear vision for your expansion, your empire—it is yours after all.

Creating a Vision

Understand that it's going to take time, and it is worth the effort.

If you are at Level Five now, I want you to spend the next two weeks ensuring you have a vision. Secondly, you must communicate this vision to everyone on your team from the Leadership at the Top to the part-time staff at the bottom. It is crucial that everyone understands the vision and is a part of making the vision a reality.

Building a Roadmap

After you have your vision, make a roadmap to get there. You and your team will need to commit to the plan.

A roadmap says, "here is where I am today, this is where I want to end up. Now, this is how to get from Point A to Point B."

Sounds simple enough, right? But this will take time.

The great news is that you have a lot of support now compared to years ago when you were at Level One, Level Two, or Level Three. Empower your staff to be an active part in creating and improving the roadmap.

Once you have the Vision and Roadmap, you are ready to recruit great leadership. Then and only then will you be ready to build expansion teams.

Week 8 Day 5 WORKSHEET
Level 5

Are you functioning as the CEO of your company? Yes or No. *Circle one.*

If not, identify five things that need to change? *Perhaps you need to still get things off your plate. Perhaps you need to hire someone. Or maybe you are the one getting in your own way.*

How do you keep growing my empire? Because If you are doing $50 Million or more in production, you've created an empire.

Do I want to be a Mega Agent or a Mega Team? *Circle one.*

Can you trust your leadership team? Yes or No. *Circle one.*

If not, who do you need to consider getting rid of? Write their names here.

Now, write down everyone on your team that you can genuinely rely on.

As the CEO, your job is to drive business. Who can you meet in the next quarter who would drive a mass amount of business to your organization? Perhaps a referral partner, new construction builder or developer, a mortgage broker, or relocation company.

Next, examine your P&L Statement. You do not need to do this alone. Ideally, do this with your processor, accountant, and/or bookkeeper.

Ask them…

What's working and what's not?

How's your overhead?

How's your payroll?

What does your marketing budget look like? How much are you spending and on what? Are the marketing efforts working?

Where is most of your business coming from?

Ask your team, should we step on the gas and spend more there? What is not working?

Perhaps you have too many people on your team. Or maybe not enough? Can you get rid of somebody to potentially save $4,000-$5,000 a month?

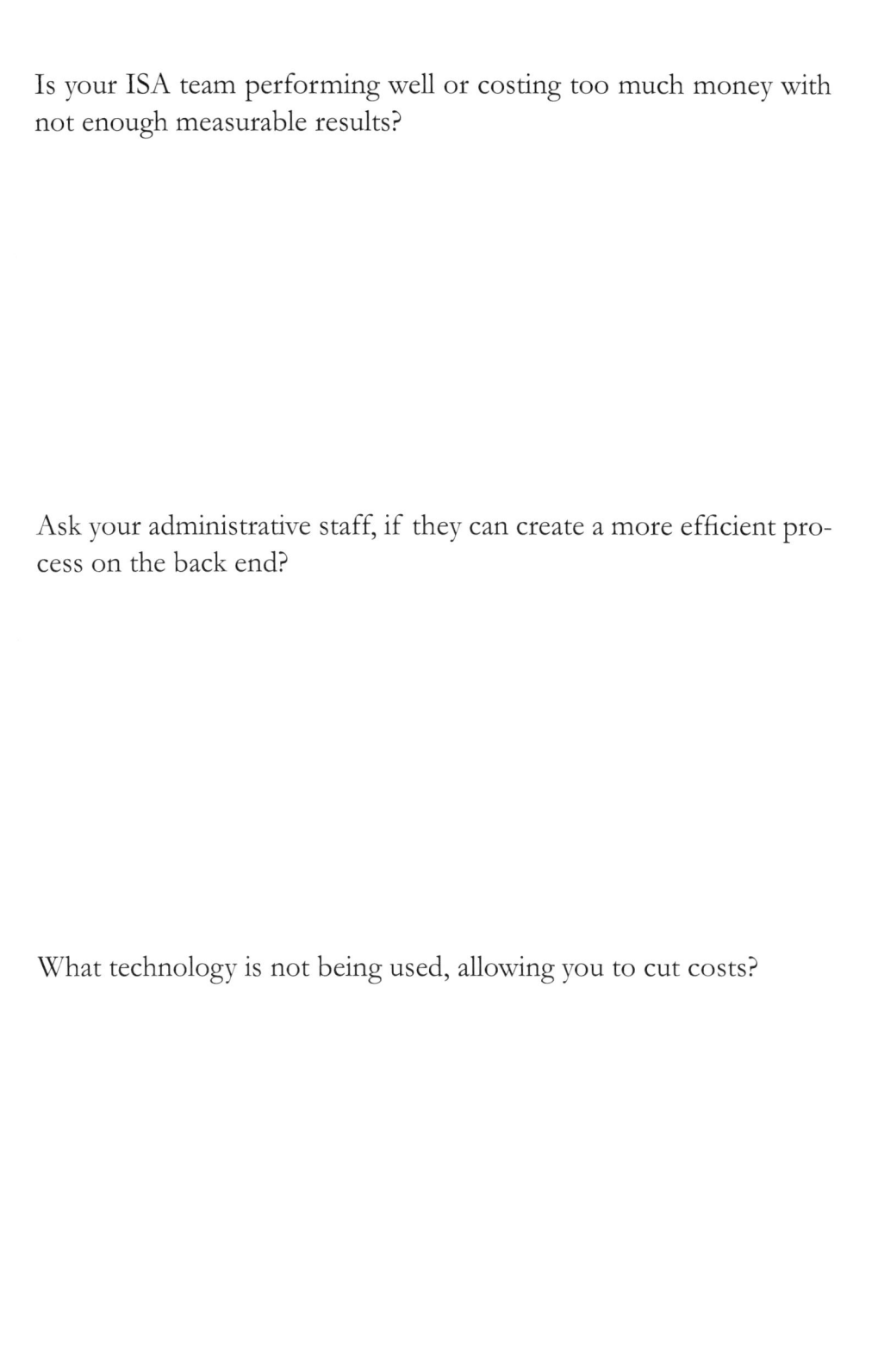

Is your ISA team performing well or costing too much money with not enough measurable results?

Ask your administrative staff, if they can create a more efficient process on the back end?

What technology is not being used, allowing you to cut costs?

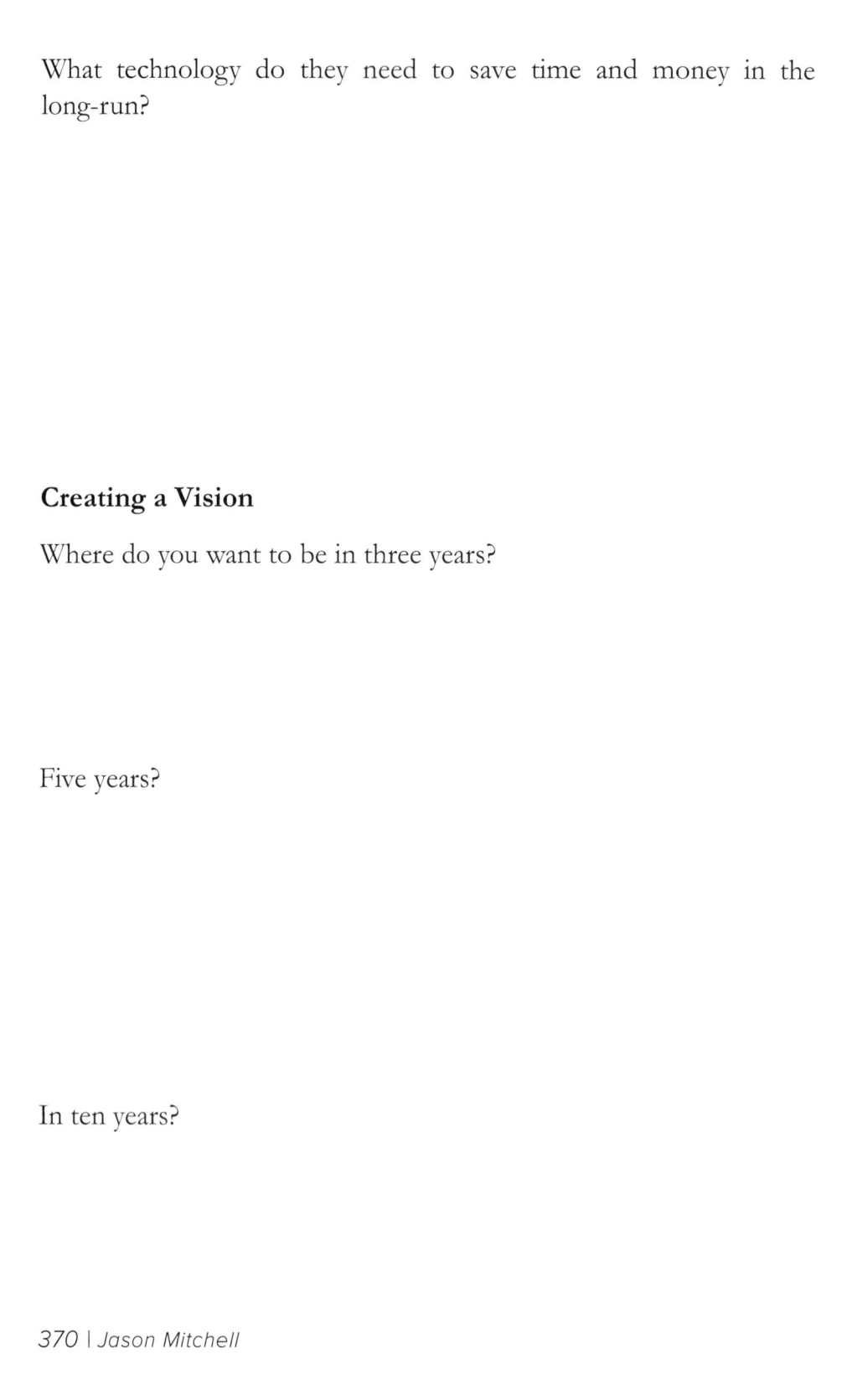

What technology do they need to save time and money in the long-run?

Creating a Vision

Where do you want to be in three years?

Five years?

In ten years?

What is your ultimate goal?

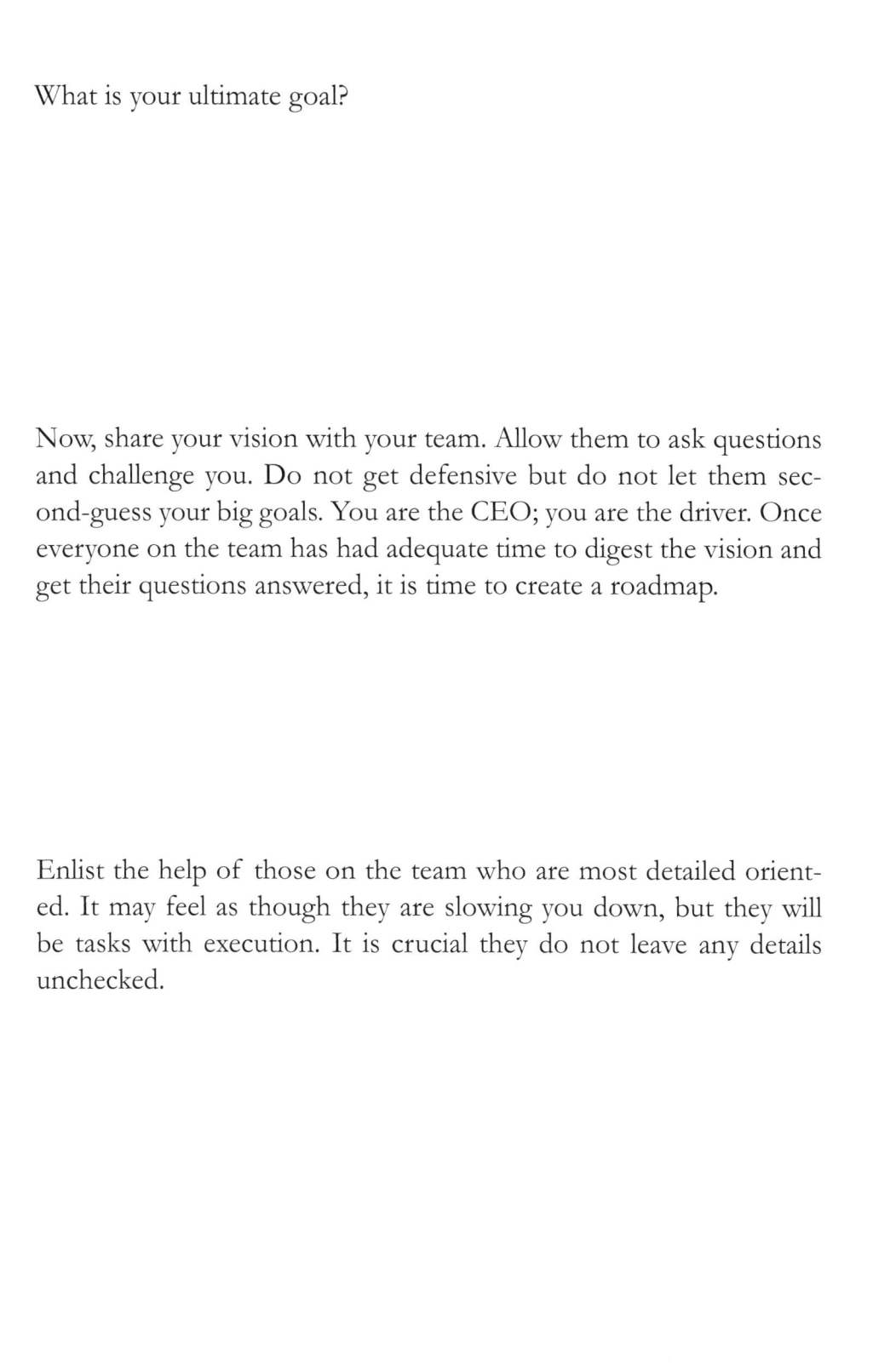

Now, share your vision with your team. Allow them to ask questions and challenge you. Do not get defensive but do not let them second-guess your big goals. You are the CEO; you are the driver. Once everyone on the team has had adequate time to digest the vision and get their questions answered, it is time to create a roadmap.

Enlist the help of those on the team who are most detailed oriented. It may feel as though they are slowing you down, but they will be tasks with execution. It is crucial they do not leave any details unchecked.

Creating a Roadmap

Where is the business now?

Where do we want the business to be in one year, three years, five years, and ten years?

How do we get there?

Revisit this roadmap each quarter. Your Director of Operations should revisit it each month to ensure everyone, and everything is on track. Empower them to adjust things accordingly.

Week 8 Conclusion

Working in sales is never an easy thing to do. You have to rely on the actions and behaviors of others, which are not always logical, reasonable, or even predictable.

This guidebook has provided you with the steps you need to get started with increasing your sales. It is now up to you to do the work. If you skipped workbooks, revisit them and complete them.

We covered many important topics such as how to make connections with your clients, how to set up your own sales plan without being too pushy, and how to listen to your clients. We reviewed how to find your clients the right solution. We even went over how to tell your clients "no" when you know that a solution isn't the right one for them. We learned how to avoid some of those clients who are not the best for you because, after all, they waste a lot of your time with no intention of paying you or actually making a purchase in the first place. When you bring all of these parts together, you are sure to get increased sales in no time.

When you are ready to see your sales increase even more, revisit this guidebook and learn the steps that you need to take to make your success a reality.

ABOUT THE AUTHOR

Jason Mitchell is a real estate powerhouse who founded Jason Mitchell Real Estate in 2006. The Jason Mitchell Group (JMG) has achieved over $5 Billion in sales volume. In 2016, 2017, and 2018, Jason was ranked the #1 Producing Agent in the state of Arizona. He has also been named Arizona's Most Influential Millennial. In 2019, Jason was awarded the National Homeownership award by RIS Media, and was named Real Estate Agent of the Decade in 2020. In 2021, Jason was named the most influential real estate professional by RISMedia.

Jason has been recognized by Forbes and WSJ as one of the nation's #1 Real Estate Professionals in the country and selected as a member of the FORBES Real Estate Council. He has been featured in GQ, The Wall Street Journal, FORBES Realtor Magazine and seen on ABC, NBC, BRAVO, CNBC, HGTV, The American Dream TV, and FOX News.

In 2020, Jason launched his real estate coaching program, Macrolisting. Jason serves as a national real estate consultant and speaker for numerous organizations for real estate professionals throughout the U.S.A.

thejasonmitchellgroup.com | 40dayblueprint.com

Macrolisting.com - Take Your Real Estate Career To The Next Level

Stay Connected

Instagram - @jasonmitchellgroup

Facebook - The Jason Mitchell Group

LinkedIn - Jason Mitchell Real Estate

Twitter - @JMG_realestate

Made in the USA
Columbia, SC
31 July 2021